KB054817

# 주한미군지위협정(SOFA)

# 서명 및 발효 22

_____

# 주한미군지위협정(SOFA)

# 서명 및 발효 22

# | 머리말

미국은 오래전부터 우리나라 외교에 있어서 가장 긴밀하고 실질적인 우호·협력관계를 맺어온 나라다. 6·25전쟁 정전 협정이 체결된 후 북한의 재침을 막기 위한 대책으로서 1953년 11월 한미 상호방위조약이 체결되었다. 이는 미군이 한국에 주둔하는 법적 근거였고, 그렇게 주둔하게 된 미군의 시설, 구역, 사업, 용역, 출입국, 통관과 관세, 재판권 등 포괄적인 법적 지위를 규정하는 것이 바로 주한미군지위협정(SOFA)이다. 그러나 이와 관련한 협상은 계속된 난항을 겪으며 한미 상호방위조약이 체결로부터 10년이 훌쩍 넘은 1967년이 돼서야 정식 발효에 이를 수 있었다. 그럼에도 당시 미군 범죄에 대한 한국의 재판권은 심한 제약을 받았으며, 1980년대 후반 민주화 운동과 함께 미군 범죄 문제가 사회적 이슈로 떠오르자 협정을 개정해야 한다는 목소리가 커지게 되었다. 이에 1991년 2월 주한미군지위협정 1차 개정이 진행되었고, 이후에도 여러 사건이 발생하며 2001년 4월 2차 개정이 진행되어 현재에 이르고 있다.

본 총서는 외교부에서 작성하여 최근 공개한 주한미군지위협정(SOFA) 관련 자료를 담고 있다. 1953년 한미 상호방위조약 체결 이후부터 1967년 발효가 이뤄지기까지의 자료와 더불어, 이후 한미 합동위원회를 비롯해 민·형사재판권, 시설, 노무, 교통 등 각 분과위원회의 회의록과 운영 자료, 한국인 고용인 문제와 관련한 자료, 기타 관련 분쟁 자료 등을 포함해 총 42권으로 구성되었다. 전체 분량은 약 2만 2천여 쪽에 이른다.

2024년 3월
한국학술정보(주)

## | 일러두기

· 본 총서에 실린 자료는 2022년 4월과 2023년 4월에 각각 공개한 외교문서 4,827권, 76만 여 쪽 가운데 일부를 발췌한 것이다.

· 각 권의 제목과 순서는 공개된 원본을 최대한 반영하였으나, 주제에 따라 일부는 적절히 변경하였다.

· 원본 자료는 A4 판형에 맞게 축소하거나 원본 비율을 유지한 채 A4 페이지 안에 삽입 하였다. 또한 현재 시점에선 공개되지 않아 '공란'이란 표기만 있는 페이지 역시 그대로 실었다.

· 외교부가 공개한 문서 각 권의 첫 페이지에는 '정리 보존 문서 목록'이란 이름으로 기록물 종류, 일자, 명칭, 간단한 내용 등의 정보가 수록되어 있으며, 이를 기준으로 0001번부터 번호가 매겨져 있다. 이는 삭제하지 않고 총서에 그대로 수록하였다.

· 보고서 내용에 관한 더 자세한 정보가 필요하다면, 외교부가 온라인상에 제공하는 『대한 민국 외교사료요약집』 1991년과 1992년 자료를 참조할 수 있다.

# | 차례

## 정/리/보/존/문/서/목/록

| 기록물종류 | 문서-일반공문서철 | 등록번호 | 10983 9624 | 등록일자 | 2006-07-27 |
|---|---|---|---|---|---|
| 분류번호 | 741.12 | 국가코드 | US | 주제 | |
| 문서철명 | 한.미국 간의 상호방위조약 제4조에 의한 시설과 구역 및 한국에서의 미국군대의 지위에 관한 협정 (SOFA) 전59권. 1966.7.9 서울에서 서명 : 1967.2.9 발효 (조약 232호) *원본 | | | | |
| 생산과 | 미주과/조약과 | 생산년도 | 1952 - 1967 | 보존기간 | 영구 |
| 담당과(그룹) | 조약 | 조약 | | 서가번호 | --- |
| 참조분류 | | | | | |
| 권차명 | V.53 민사청구권 관계자료, 1964-66 | | | | |

| 내용목차 | |
|---|---|
| | **★ 일지 :** |
| | 1953.8.7 이승만 대통령-Dulles 미국 국무장관 공동성명 - 상호방위조약 발효 후 군대지위협정 교섭 약속 |
| | 1954.12.2 정부, 주한 UN군의 관세업무협정 체결 제의 |
| | 1955.1월, 5월 미국, 제의 거절 |
| | 1955.4.28 정부, 군대지위협정 제의 (한국측 초안 제시) |
| | 1957.9.10 Hurter 미국 국무차관 방한 시 각서 수교 (한국측 제의 수락 요구) |
| | 1957.11.13, 26 정부, 개별 협정의 단계적 체결 제의 |
| | 1958.9.18 Dawling 주한미국대사, 형사재판관할권 협정 제외 조건으로 행정협정 체결 의사 전달 |
| | 1960.3.10 정부, 토지, 시설협정의 우선적 체결 강력 요구 |
| | 1961.4.10 장면 국무총리-McConaughy 주한미국대사 공동성명으로 교섭 개시 합의 |
| | 1961.4.15, 4.25 제1, 2차 한.미국 교섭회의 (서울) |
| | 1962.3.12 정부, 교섭 재개 촉구 공한 송부 |
| | 1962.5.14 Burger 주한미국대사, 최규하 장관 면담 시 형사재판관할권 문제 제기 않는 조건으로 교섭 재개 통고 |
| | 1962.9.6 한.미국 간 공동성명 발표 (9월 중 교섭 재개 합의) |
| | 1962.9.20~ 1965.6.7 제1-81차 실무 교섭회의 (서울) |
| | 1966.7.8 제82차 실무 교섭회의 (서울) |
| | 1966.7.9 서명 |
| | 1967.2.9 발효 (조약 232호) |

## 마/이/크/로/필/름/사/항

| 촬영연도 | ★롤 번호 | 화일 번호 | 후레임 번호 | 보관함 번호 |
|---|---|---|---|---|
| 2006-11-24 | I-06-0072 | 06 | 1-346 | |

0001

한·미국 간의 상호방위조약 제4조에 의한 시설과 구역 및 한국에서의 미국군대의 지위에 관한 협정(SOFA)
전59권. 1966.7.9 서울에서 서명 : 1967.2.9 발효(조약 232호) (V.53 민사청구권 관계자료, 1964-66)

7

# 법　무　부

법무법 810 12794( 4 - 4072 )　　　　　1964. 9. 14.

수신　　외무부장관

제목　　한·미 행정협정에 관한 자료 추송

　　　　한·미 행정협정 체결에 수반한 국가배상금 지급에

관한 참고자료를 별첨과 같이 추송합니다

유첨　한·미 행정협정에 관한 자료 1부 끝

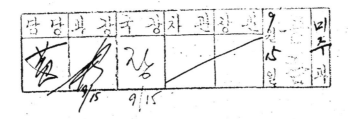

법무부장관　민　　　　복

3

19752

0002

# 國家賠償金申請事件處理現況

自1963年5月1日 ─ 至1964年8月31日現

總接受件數    560件
　處理件數    513件
未處理件數    47件

## 處理事件의 處理內容
1. 認定    358件
2. 棄却    117件
3. 取下    38件

## 認定事件의 內容
1. 死亡    182件    인정액 21,386,558원
2. 傷害    121件    8,218,714원
3. 車輛    31件    707,133원70전
4. 家屋    10件    678,213원
5. 其他    14件    386,874원68전
合計    358件    31,683,533원38전

※ 內訳別添

한·미국 간의 상호방위조약 제4조에 의한 시설과 구역 및 한국에서의 미국군대의 지위에 관한 협정(SOFA)
전59권. 1966.7.9 서울에서 서명 : 1967.2.9 발효(조약 232호) (V.53 민사청구권 관계자료, 1964-66)

9

死 之 事 件

認定 件數         182 件

認定 金額     21,384,558원

最高 認定額      650,000원

最低 認定額       10,000원

平均        117,497원

공  란

공      란

공 란

공       란

주한미군지위협정(SOFA) 서명 및 발효 22

# 공        란

공       란

공         란

공　　　　란

損害事件

認定件數　121 件
認定金額　8.718.714 천


最高認定額　343.000 원
最低 "　2000 "
平均　72.0ff "

한·미국 간의 상호방위조약 제4조에 의한 시설과 구역 및 한국에서의 미국군대의 지위에 관한 협정(SOFA)
전59권. 1966.7.9 서울에서 서명 : 1967.2.9 발효(조약 232호) (V.53 민사청구권 관계자료, 1964-66)

19

공      란

공          란

공　　　란

# 공         란

공               란

공　　　　란

車輛事故事件

認定事件        31件
認定金額        707,173천.전

最高認定額      76,890 원
最低    "        5,000 "
平均    "       22,812 "

공          란

공          란

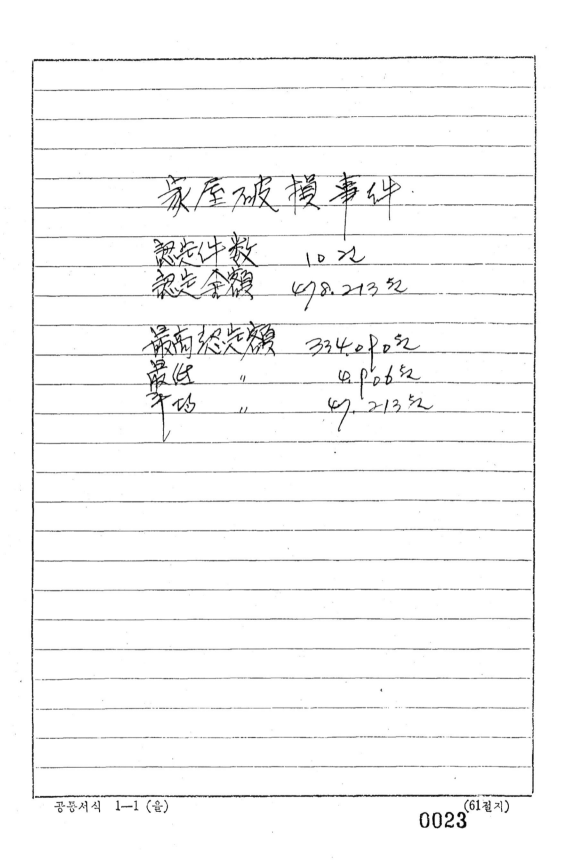

家屋破損事件

認定件数　　10건
認定金額　　478.213弗

最高認定額　　334.070弗
最低　　〃　　4.106弗
平均　　〃　　47.213弗

한·미국 간의 상호방위조약 제4조에 의한 시설과 구역 및 한국에서의 미국군대의 지위에 관한 협정(SOFA)
전59권. 1966.7.9 서울에서 서명 : 1967.2.9 발효(조약 232호) (V.53 민사청구권 관계자료, 1964-66)

29

공    란

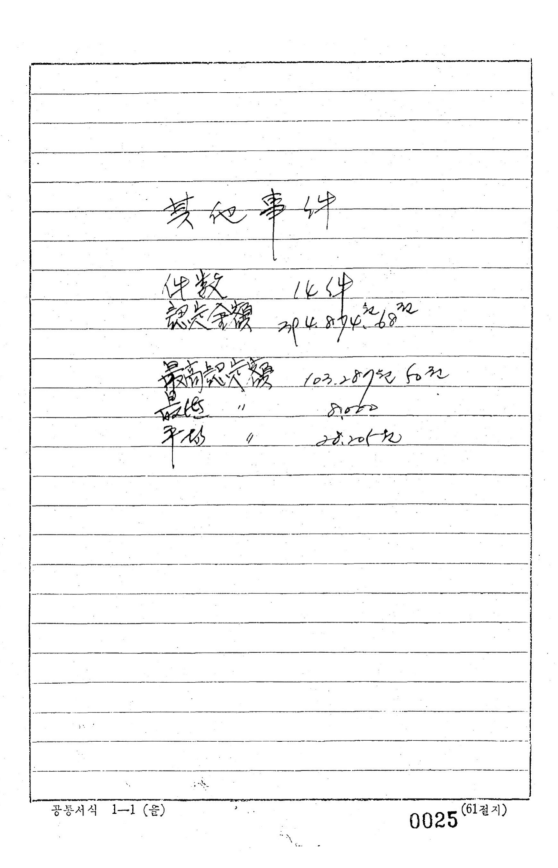

其他事件

件數　　　16件
認定金額　　304,874원 68전

最高認定額　103,287원 50전
最低　　"　　8,000
平均　　"　　28,204원

공          란

1. General.

Payment of the claims of citizens and residents of Korea is authorized by an act of the United States Congress called the "Foreign Claims Act." This law provides for the payment of maritorious claims by the inhabitants of countries in which United States troops are stationed, based on death, personal injury, or property demage caused by noncombat activities of U.S. armed forces. This law is implemented in detail by regulations of the Army, Navy and Air Force.

2. U.S. liability.

Under the foreign claims program United States liability is established when injury, death, or property damage is caused (partially or wholly) by the careless or wrongful act of a member or U.S. civilian employee of the United States Forces Korea, or by other noncombat activities of those forces. Liability also is assumed if the damages are caused by Korean civilian employees while acting within the scope of their employment. As would be expected, the United States cannot assume responsibility for damages caused by members of the Korean Army or employees of the Korean Government, even though these persons may be engaged with U.S. forces at the time in the joint mission of maintaining military readiness against a common enemy. Cognizance is taken, however, of the unique cooperation between the military forces of the Republic of Korea and of the United States by which Korean military persons are integrated into U.S. Army units, known as the Korean Augmentation to the United States Army (KATUSA). Liability is assumed and compensation is paid

0027

for injuries and damages caused by these persons when acting within the scope of their assigned duties for U.S. Army units.

3. Investigation of claims.

An elaborate system is prescribed by U.S. Army directives for the investigation and reporting of detailed facts and circumstances involved in every incident in which a person suffers injury, death, or property damage as the result of military activities. Hundreds of investigating officers and commanders of Army units and installations are responsible for investigating the incidents and accidents in which members of the USFK are involved. Detailed reports of the investigations are forwarded to higher authority for approval, and a copy of each report is forwarded to the Claims Service. In some instances additional investigation and inquiry may be required in order to fairly evaluate a claim. This further investigation is more effectively handled by personnel specially trained in the law and procedures pertaining to the payment of claims. Consequently, the investigation at this point is normally conducted by the claims service which processes the claims against the United States.

4. The Claims Service in Korea.

a. The Department of Defense has designated the Army to settle claims arising in Korea which are caused by the activities of members and employees of the United States Forces Korea. This is accomplished through the U.S. Armed Forces Claims Service, Korea, and Claims Commissions attached to that organization, located on the Yongsan Military Reservation. The establishment of Claims Commissions are required by the "Foreign Claims Act," and their primary duty is to consider and settle claims submitted by the inhabitants

0028

of the country involved. A commissioner must be a commissioned officer and normally is a judge advocate officer of the military service concerned. One-member commissions are empowered to adjudge and pay claims for not more than $1000 (129,500 Won) and three-member commissions may pay claims for not more than $15,000 (1,942,500 Won). Claims in excess of the latter amount are transmitted to the Department of the Army for approval by the Congress before payment may be made. Commissions of any of the military services may consider and pay claims caused by the activities and members of the other services.

      b. The U.S. Armed Forces Claims Service is manned by fourteen American persons and thirteen citizens of Korea. Seven of the Korean employees are specially trained claims investigators and classified among the highest paid Korean employees of the Eighth Army. Each of the three commissioned officers (including the Chief) is appointed as a one-member commission, and together they constitute a three-member commission. In addition to the office of the Chief and the Claims Commissions, the Claims Service is organized as follows:

| Administrative Branch | Investigation Branch | Claims Branch | Payment Branch |
|---|---|---|---|
| 5 U.S. | 1 U.S. | 3 U.S. | 2 U.S |
| KN | 5KN | 1 KN | 2 KN |

      c. The functions of the four branches are somewhat self-evident.
Briefly:

      (1) The Administration Branch maintains all records of claims, reports of investigation, and related files. When a claim initially is received in the Claims Service it is channeled to the Administration Branch for recording and

0029

indexing. A claim number is assigned by which the claim may be readily identified at all future times, and a portfolio prepared in which all documents are filed which pertain to the claim.

(2) The Investigation Branch is comprised of five (5) Korean national employees, all classified as senior investigators, and one commissioned officer as supervisor. Upon receiving a claims portfolio from the Administration Branch, the file is assigned to an investigator for translation of documents which are submitted in Korean and for development of the essential evidence required for complete adjudication of the claim. As a general principle the securing of evidence in support of a claim is the responsibility of the claimant. A large part of our investigators' duties, however, is to assist the claimant in securing the evidence and in many instances to secure the evidence for the claimant. When the Investigation Branch considers investigation is complete, the portfolio is transferred to the Claims Branch for further processing.

The Investigation Branch also interviews all claimants who visit the Claims Service, assists them in preparing their claims on bilingual forms provided, and advises of the nature of evidence and formal documents (such as family registers, certificates of land ownership) that are required to support their claims. It may be noted at this point that whether a claimant desires to employ an attorney to represent him in connection with his claim is a matter solely within the discretion of the claimant. The Claims Service offers all the advice and assistance that is needed to file and establish the claim.

(3) The Claims Branch examines the claims portfolio to

0030

determine whether evidence is sufficient to support final adjudication of the claim. A resume of the claim is prepared for the benefit of the Chief and the claims commissions, including a recommendation as to the amount of compensation that should be awarded.

(4) Upon completion of the processing of a claim by the Claims Branch, the portfolio is transferred to the Chief of the Claims Service for examination and consideration. The Chief assigns claims not in excess of $1,000 (129,500 Won) to the one-member commissions for final adjudication. As President of the three-member commission, he convenes the commission for consideration and adjudication of claims in excess of $1,000 (129,500 Won). If the claim exceeds $15,000 (1,942,500 Won), he prepares a detailed memorandum and recommendation that is forwarded with the claim file to the Department of the Army for final action.

(5) When a commission adjudges an award in a claim, the portfolio is transferred to the Payment Branch. This Branch notifies the claimant of the amount of award and prepares a settlement agreement for the claimant to sign. Upon receipt of the signed settlement agreement arrangements are made for claimant to receive his compensation. Most claimants are paid on the Yongsan Military Reservation. In many instances, however, arrangements are made for claimants to be paid at a military post near their homes. This is particularly true when claimant lives a long distance from Seoul, as in the Taegu or Pusan area. In addition, when a claimant is too old or ill to travel a representative of the Claims Service takes the compensation to him at his home. This also is done in most small claims in order that claimant may realize the full

한·미국 간의 상호방위조약 제4조에 의한 시설과 구역 및 한국에서의 미국군대의 지위에 관한 협정(SOFA) 전59권. 1966.7.9 서울에서 서명 : 1967.2.9 발효(조약 232호) (V.53 민사청구권 관계자료, 1964-66)

benefit of his award.

5. General criteria used in computing damages.

    a. Property damage. Allowable compensation normally represents the cost of repairs to or restoration of the property damaged to its state of condition immediately prior to the time of damage. The claimant may establish these costs by receipts for amounts expanded for repair, or by estimates of the cost of repair by reputable contractors or other repairman. Compensation for lost or completely destroyed property is computed at the actual value of the property at time of loss or destruction. Value of growing crops and trees are similarly computed.

    b. Compensation for personal injury and death. These computations usually are not as amenable to mathematical calculations as are cots of repair or destruction of vehicles, buildings, or other property. To obtain, however, as much consistency as may be possible standard elements are utilized in order to have a sound basis on which awards may be computed for death and in various types of personal injury. The Claims Commission is charged with the responsibility of evaluating each case in the light of these standard elements in order to arrive at fair awards. The Chief of the Claims Service supervises the activities of the Claims Commissions for the purpose of assuring that awards to claiments are fair and nondiscriminatory.

        (1) <u>Personal Injury</u>. Standard compensable items are:

            (a) Medical and hospital expenses, including immediate first aid treatment and ambulance service.

            (b) Reasonable costs of Chinese medicines which are prescribed by a doctor as treatment for the injury, or resulting illness, on which claim is based.

            (c) Loss of income for the period during which ⱥⱥⱥ claimant is absent from work or occupation.

0032

(d) Pain and suffering of the injured party.

(e) Permanent disability. A "Table of Disability Grades" is used. This table is patterned after the one provided in the Korean Labor Standard Act of 1953. The table includes four disability grades not appearing in the Korean table, and the number of days of compensation for each disability grade has been increased in recognition of the increased cost of living in Korea since 1953. If the injured party is not a wage or income earner (such as a child or housewife), emphasis is placed on the nature (rather them grade) of disability and age and pain and suffering of the injured party in order to arrive at comparable awards.

(f) Disfigurement. Scars and other disfigurements of a female are considered more serious than those suffered by a male. In addition, age, social status and occupation of both the male and female are taken into account.

(g) Cost of artificial limbs, and their repair and replacement for life expectancy of the injured party.

(h) Miscellaneous expenses attributable to the injuries sustained.

(2) Death. Standard compensable items are:

(a) Medical and hospital expenses incident to and preceding death.

(b) Funeral expenses. These include preparation of body for burial, purchase and preparation of grave site, reasonable amounts for traditional ceremonial expenses (including food and drink).

(c) Death award. Our Korean claimants frequently refer to this element as a "solatium"or "consolation award." The amount of this award varies from case to case, being affected by the age, income and social status of the deceased, as well as his family relationship (that is, whether the father, mother, minor daughter, first son, or other). Additional amounts are computed in this award for a surviving widow and for each surviving child under age of seventeen years. Our experience indicates that average death awards range from $772.20 (100,000Won) for young children to approximately $2702.70 (350,000 Won) for adults.

(d) Miscellaneous expanses attributable to the death on which claim is based.

6. Hospitalisation of claimants.

As a general rule United States law authorizes admission

0033

한·미국 간의 상호방위조약 제4조에 의한 시설과 구역 및 한국에서의 미국군대의 지위에 관한 협정(SOFA)
전59권. 1966.7.9 서울에서 서명 : 1967.2.9 발효(조약 232호) (V.53 민사청구권 관계자료, 1964-66)
39

to and treatment in U.S. hospitals only for U.S. persons (and some of their dependents) who are employed by the Government. Not all U.S. employees are eligible for this medical service. Exceptions may be made in emergency and unusual cases for a small number of other persons, in which event the individual is charged $37.00 (4792 Won) for each day of hospitalization and $7.00 (907 Won) for each outpatient treatment. Nevertheless special arrangements have been approved for the claims program in Korea which operates under the "Foreign Claims Act," whereunder any Korean citizen who is injured by the activities of United States Forces Korea may be admitted and treated (including all necessary surgery) in U.S. hospitals in Korea without any charge whatsoever for the medical services. In the past few years hundreds of Korean citizens have been treated under this program in Army medical facilities and furnished free hospitalization for weeks and months in our major hospitals. Several of the patients have received this hospitalization and medical service for more than one year in the 121st U.S. Hospital located near Inchon.

7. Statistics

The number of claims received by Claims Commissions and amounts of compensation paid since the Claims Service Began its operations on 1 June 1959 are shown below:

|                | 1959 (7 mos) | 1960       | 1961       | 1962       | 1963 (6 mos) |
|----------------|--------------|------------|------------|------------|--------------|
| Nr. Received:  | 517          | 2,125      | 1,163      | 979        | 378          |
| Amount Paid:   | 282,688.28   | 727,696.22 | 361,801.26 | 187,633.75 | 877,032.16   |

Total claims received since 1 June 1959:   5,162

Total compensation paid since 1 June 1959: $1,636,851.67 (12,639,775 Won)

0034

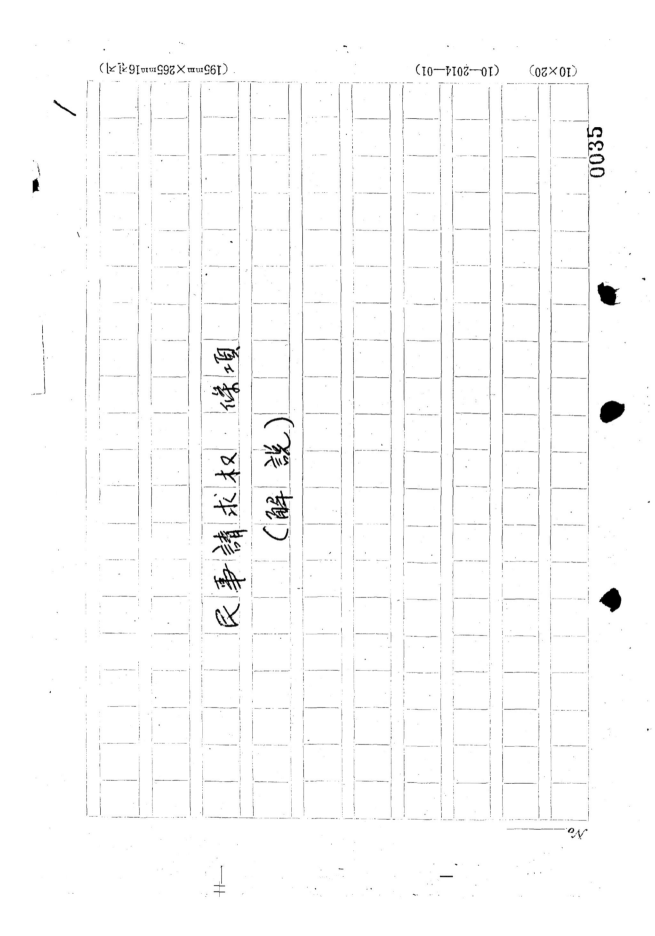

民事請求权 關x項

(解 説)

0035

N₂ —

한·미국 간의 상호방위조약 제4조에 의한 시설과 구역 및 한국에서의 미국군대의 지위에 관한 협정(SOFA)
전59권. 1966.7.9 서울에서 서명 : 1967.2.9 발효(조약 232호) (V.53 민사청구권 관계자료, 1964-66)　41

2.

## I 槪要

民事裁判
民事訴訟法 條項으로 成立的으로
事件이 성합으로 이루어 있는 바
事件Ⅰ項이 民事事件 3 類型이
問題[5]ㅎ 되지 이 관련
本 報告서에서 그 調整에서
構成되며 (四)項이 나는

이 事件을 다음과 ・ 公務 ・ 非公務人

3

莫論한 모든 故意 또는 過失로 因한 違法行爲로 일어나는 他人에 對한 諸般 損害, 或은 駐韓美軍當局이 法的으로 責任이 있는 行爲 또는 事件으로 發生하는 諸般損害를 賠償하는데 關한 節次를 各國의 協定例에 따라 規定한 것이다.

本條에서 特記할만한 点은 駐韓美軍의 構成員 或은 雇用員은 原則的으로 韓國의 民事裁判으로부터 免除되지 않는

(195mm×265mm16절지) (10—2014—01) (10×20)

No.

0037

Meyer

（10×20）　（10-2014-01）　（195mm×265mm16절지）

兩國이 利害를 서로 관계되는 것이며 따라서 兩國의 適應을 增加하고 이것이 不可避한 事項으로 一般國民은 賠償을 받지 못하는 事例가 있으나 公正과 正義의 見地에서 兩國이 事項의 權利를 解...

民事請求權 事項에 있어 우리나라의 金的으로 決定하기 때문에 美軍이 賠償...

北大西洋條約機構 諸國의

日 僱傭員,

美·濠 僱傭員의 三種의 違規

其他의 僱傭員은 美·新分이

美國의 關係法律에 다라

되여 있는 것이다.

制度에 屬하는,

諸復의 特徵은 請求事件이

加害者 公務執行 등

加害者의 相互 關係, 或은

版車業 基準으로 分類하며

諸車物의 所有 所有形態에

請求權이 解決될 수 있는 規則

處理하고, 또는 公務執行中의 行爲로

이나는 請求에 대하여는 損害賠償金을

推進될 國家와 請求國이 相互 抛棄한다는 一式

立法措置가 ── 制度를 한 Formula ── 을 두 國家가 아니라 그런 것이다.

損害賠償金을 「雙方」이 이 制度로 하고도 處理하는 Concept에

事務處理가 ── 關聯에는, 他國軍隊가 따르는 것이

한·미국 간의 상호방위조약 제4조에 의한 시설과 구역 및 한국에서의 미국군대의 지위에 관한 협정(SOFA)
전59권. 1966.7.9 서울에서 서명 : 1967.2.9 발효(조약 232호) (V.53 민사청구권 관계자료, 1964-66)

47

（195mm×265mm16절지）

勞動者에게 善良한 民國의

手段이 事許諾을 報償的으로 保障되이

取한 것이다.

使하는 使補에 償請의

類足 되

Ethiopia에 補償의

民事請求 物償은 되는 것이라고

償請求를 決定 의 解決된

다는 法律에 이 制度는 觀한 軍募

이 韓國에서 適用하고 있는것과 同一한

것이로서, 請求問題이 一面 加害

한·미국 간의 상호방위조약 제4조에 의한 시설과 구역 및 한국에서의 미국군대의 지위에 관한 협정(SOFA)
전59권. 1966.7.9 서울에서 서명 : 1967.2.9 발효(조약 232호) (V.53 민사청구권 관계자료, 1964-66)

49

(10×20)　(10-2014-01)　(195mm×265mm 16절지)

政府財産에 '政府財産'이라

함은 政府財産이

合衆國이 事項으로 服務하는 中에

事項中에 服務하는 中에

第 1, 2, 3, 4 項의

5項의 親屬으로

私的 輪廓을

金體的이 具體的으로

其體的 事務를 處理하는 데

補償하는데 있어서

리지는 못하는 것이라。

(195㎜×265㎜ 16절지). (10-2014-01) (10×20)
0045

3 項은 ─ 第1項 및 第2項의 規定에
設 서의 規定에 依한 關係國과
項은 ─ 諮問을 거쳐 當事國 間의
協調 또는 關係 當事國의 …
第3項은 ─ 第3項에 規定된 …
解決 …
第9項은 ─ 第7項 및 第8項의 …
關係國이 非公認 … 이 구성員 …
수 없다. 規定되어 있는 解決方法, 解
에 …國

한·미국 간의 상호방위조약 제4조에 의한 시설과 구역 및 한국에서의 미국군대의 지위에 관한 협정(SOFA)
전59권. 1966.7.9 서울에서 서명 : 1967.2.9 발효(조약 232호) (V.53 민사청구권 관계자료, 1964-66)

(10-2014-01)

(195mm×265mm 16절지)

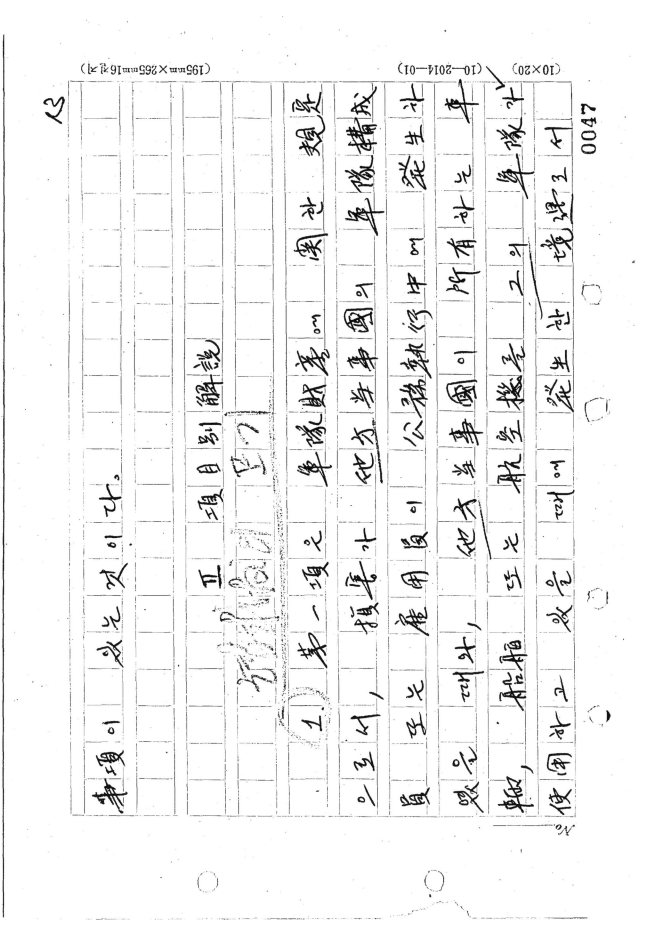

事項이 있는 것이다.

Ⅱ項目의 解說

Ⅱ項目으로 본？

1. 車, 船, 航空機, 其他 軍隊財產으로 軍隊構成

이로써, 構置 또는 使方 또는 美國이 所有하는 車

員이나 軍用員이 公務執行中에 發生하는

한다 또는 美國이 取得하는 그의 軍隊가

船, 航空機, 또는 使用하는 公路 그의 運送 3 서

員은 國(美)하는

(10×20)　　(10-2014-01)　　(195mm×265mm 16절지)

한·미국 간의 상호방위조약 제4조에 의한 시설과 구역 및 한국에서의 미국군대의 지위에 관한 협정(SOFA)
전59권. 1966.7.9 서울에서 서명 : 1967.2.9 발효(조약 232호) (V.53 민사청구권 관계자료, 1964-66)

韓國人　　　仲裁人，　選擧　賠償人으로　　決定

仲裁人으로　　賠償　春任과　賠償金額을

이를　賠償　賠償人，

決定된　있으며，仲裁人의

當事國은　約束　되게

決定과

當事國이　決定과　賠償金額이

1,400-　外　이　辨濟를

3,審査할　賠償　仲裁國은　　賦

이　22兩國을　　，　때

賠償國은　軍隊의

金額으로　決定　賠償金額은　賠償

주하게 된다

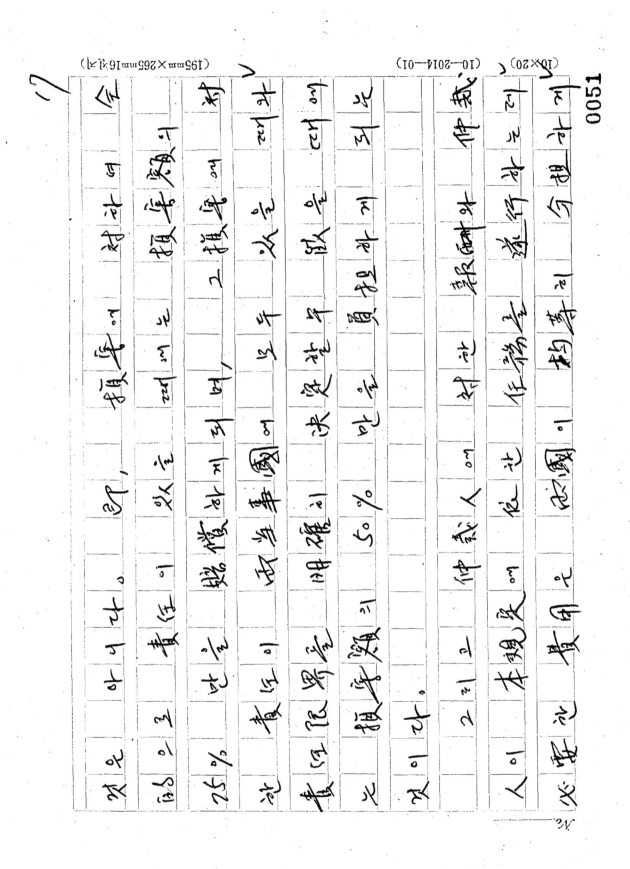

0052

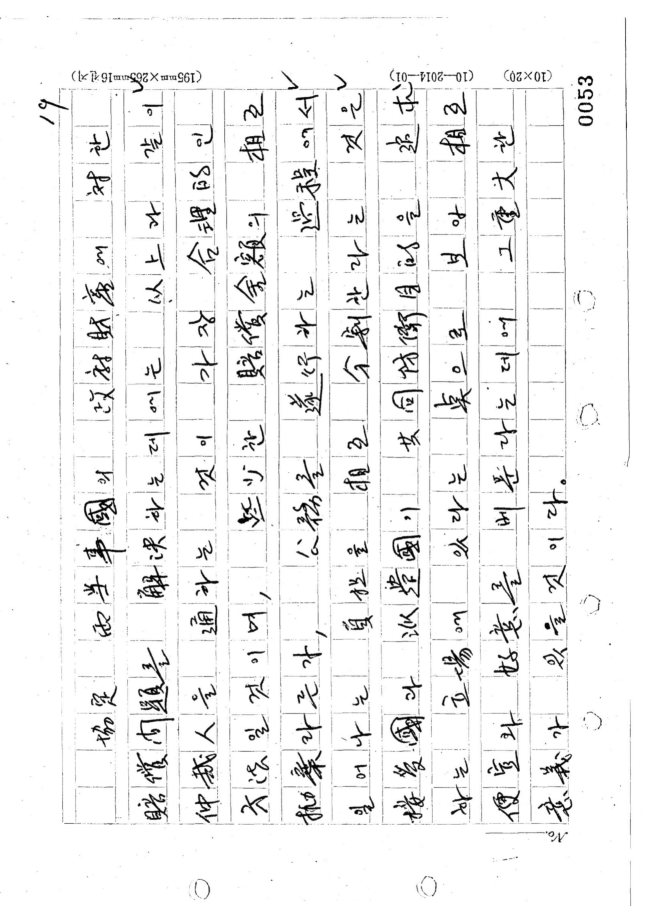

(195mm×265mm 16절지)　　　　(10-2014-01)　(10×20)

(10×20)　(10-2014-01)　(195mm×265mm 16절지)

21

政府는 權限으로 構成된

政府의 調로서 行使한

行使하기 불할 것이

政府와 行政府을 行政府의

한 事項에 있어 政府的으로

行政府는 美國의 行政 協定本規程은

行政府의 損害의 責任을 負担할 것이

行政府는 協定에서 負担하기로

本國에는 一部 事項에 責任이 있는

한·미국 간의 상호방위조약 제4조에 의한 시설과 구역 및 한국에서의 미국군대의 지위에 관한 협정(SOFA)
전59권. 1966.7.9 서울에서 서명 : 1967.2.9 발효(조약 232호) (V.53 민사청구권 관계자료, 1964-66)

構成된이 心器關係中에 및 償은 諸求권을
하시나 死亡하는 救邊에 해로 請求처리를
해業하이도 親足가였다。
이러한 親足은 우리와 例協
探取한 諸求나 이이나, 차
지우되다 親足되이 있는 것이, 다
補償에로 차서의 4項 아기는
5. 第 1, 2, 3 및 例에
要로는 當事國 해로(個) 發生하는 諸求에

22

(10-2012-01)    (195mm×265)(16절지)    (10X20)

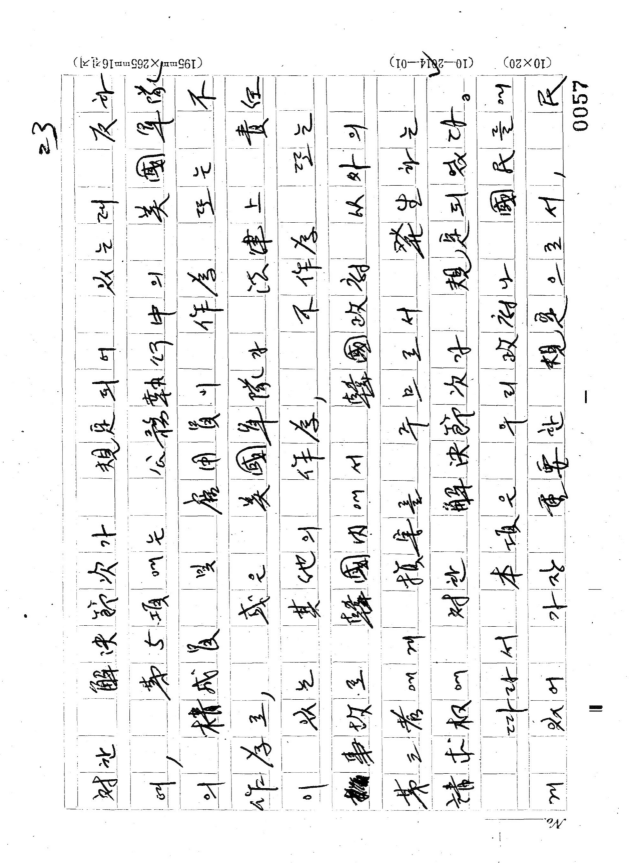

한·미국 간의 상호방위조약 제4조에 의한 시설과 구역 및 한국에서의 미국군대의 지위에 관한 협정(SOFA)
전59권. 1966.7.9 서울에서 서명 : 1967.2.9 발효(조약 232호) (V.53 민사청구권 관계자료, 1964-66)

(195mm×265mm16절지)　　　　(10-2014-01)　　(19×20)

0058

No.

25

(1)

(2)

한·미국 간의 상호방위조약 제4조에 의한 시설과 구역 및 한국에서의 미국군대의 지위에 관한 협정(SOFA)
전59권. 1966.7.9 서울에서 서명 : 1967.2.9 발효(조약 232호) (V.53 민사청구권 관계자료, 1964-66)

(195mm×265mm16절지)　(10-2014-01)　(10×20)

0900

(6)

28

(7) ...規則이 適用되는 被用者의 ...

(8) 美軍의 構成員 및 ...
協定의 ...에 服하기 ...에 服하기 ...

(9) ...의 被用者의 雇傭은 ...
美國이 ... 그 被用者가 ...
美國의 ... 에서 ...
國 政府에 ... 請求한다。

30

는 한편, 다른 한편으로는 加害者側인 美軍当局은 韓國의 裁判에 直接 服하지 않도록 하기 爲하여, 韓國政府가 中間에 介入하지 않을수 없는 不可避한 事情에서 必要하게 된것이라 할수 있다.

國際法上 國家平等의 原則에 歸結되는 한 主权國家는 다른 主权國家의 裁判管轄权으로부터 免除된다는 原則에 따라 韓國은 美國의 國家機関인 駐韓美軍当局에 對하여 裁判管轄权을 行使할수는

(195mm×255mm16절지) (10-2014-01) (10×20) No.

0064

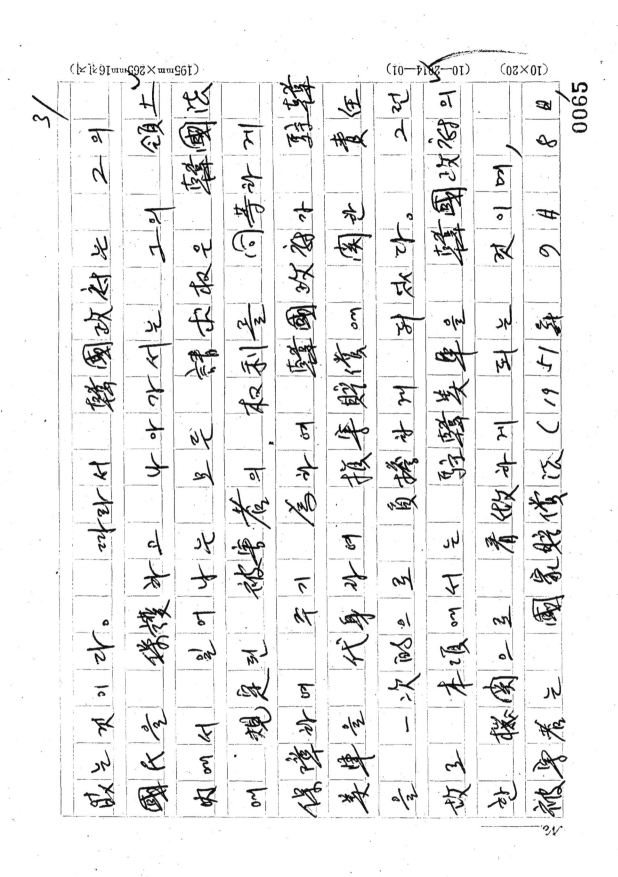

한·미국 간의 상호방위조약 제4조에 의한 시설과 구역 및 한국에서의 미국군대의 지위에 관한 협정(SOFA)
전59권. 1966.7.9 서울에서 서명 : 1967.2.9 발효(조약 232호) (V.53 민사청구권 관계자료, 1964-66)

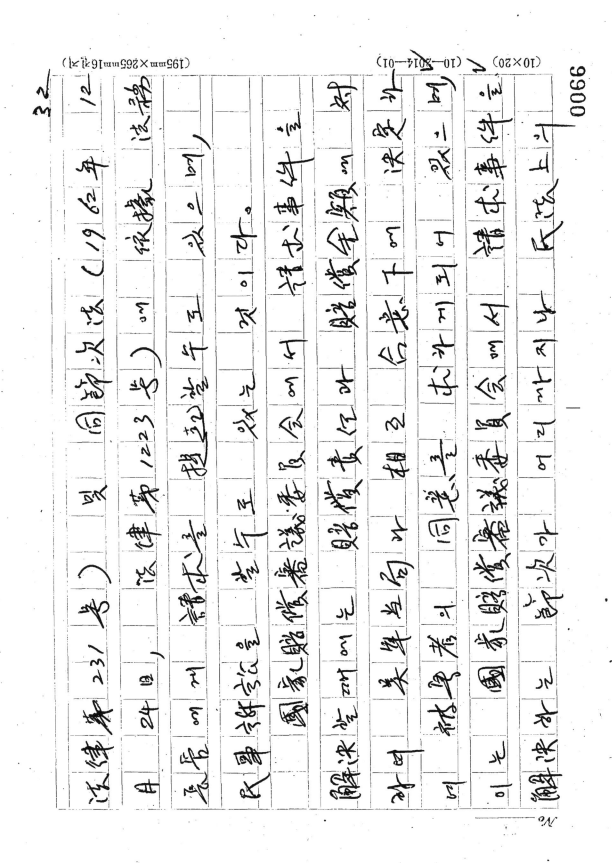

(195mm×265mm 16절지)  (10-2014-01)  (10×20)

33

한·미국 간의 상호방위조약 제4조에 의한 시설과 구역 및 한국에서의 미국군대의 지위에 관한 협정(SOFA)
전59권. 1966.7.9 서울에서 서명 : 1967.2.9 발효(조약 232호) (V.53 민사청구권 관계자료, 1964-66)

韓國政府와 美國政府 間의 協定이 締結된 후 美國政府가 美貨로 支拂하는 率은 25% ~ 가% 으로 이 率이 適用되는 物品은 있어서도

한·미국 간의 상호방위조약 제4조에 의한 시설과 구역 및 한국에서의 미국군대의 지위에 관한 협정(SOFA)
전55권. 1966.7.9 서울에서 서명 : 1967.2.9 발효(조약 232호) (V.53 민사청구권 관계자료, 1964-66)

36

0070

다 故로 各 擔保權을 賦與함에 있어 各國의
國際에서 發로하는 어느 程度 範
圍내에서 그 法律이 정을 것이나,
그 結果 政府가 政策을
그들의 取民을 適用할 程度의 로서
있는 適用國에 對한 注意할 費
用은 이를 負擔할 수 없다.
저으로도 解釋될 수 있다 本項에서 範圍의
이 範圍의 財産이 範圍의
다

(10×20)　(10-2014-01)　　　(195mm×265mm신국지)　　　0072

6. ...

(10×20)　　(10-2014-01)　　(195mm×265mm16절지)

(2)

(3)

한·미국 간의 상호방위조약 제4조에 의한 시설과 구역 및 한국에서의 미국군대의 지위에 관한 협정(SOFA)
전59권. 1966.7.9 서울에서 서명 : 1967.2.9 발효(조약 232호) (V.53 민사청구권 관계자료, 1964-66)

81

0076

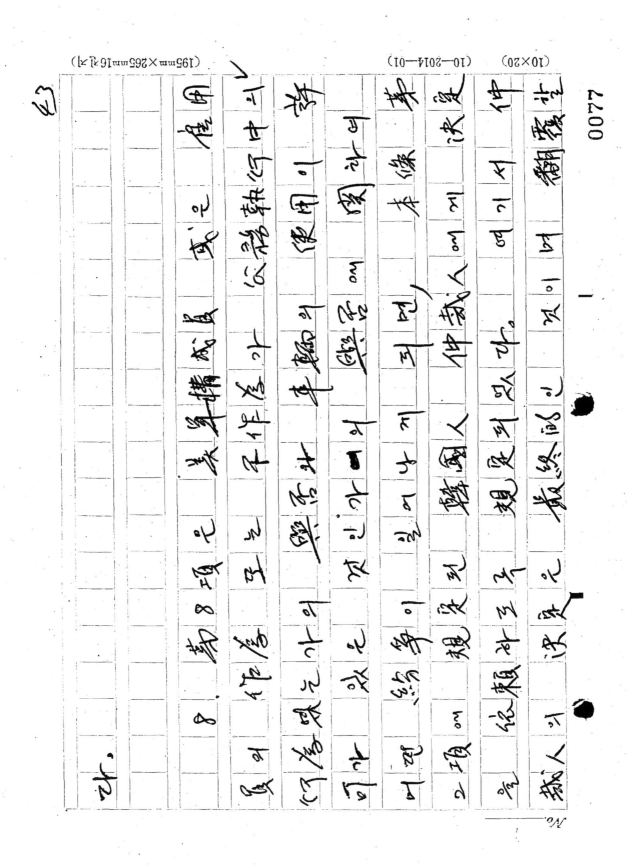

한·미국 간의 상호방위조약 제4조에 의한 시설과 구역 및 한국에서의 미국군대의 지위에 관한 협정(SOFA)
전65권. 1966.7.9 서울에서 서명 : 1967.2.9 발효(조약 232호) (V.53 민사청구권 관계자료, 1964-66)

83

44

수 없는 것이다.

美軍의 行爲가 公的인 것이냐 或은 그렇지 않은 것이냐에 따라 上述한 諸規定과 같이 請求의 解決方法이 相異하며, 때에 따라서는 請求權을 抛棄하지 않을 수 없는 境遇가 있는 것이므로 重要한 規定이라 할 수 있다.

1963年에 發效한 獨逸補充協定 第41條 11項에 依하면 于先 派遣國軍當局이 公務與否에 關한 證明書를 發行케 하고,

0078

한·미국 간의 상호방위조약 제4조에 의한 시설과 구역 및 한국에서의 미국군대의 지위에 관한 협정(SOFA)
전59권. 1966.7.9 서울에서 서명 : 1967.2.9 발효(조약 232호) (V.53 민사청구권 관계자료, 1964-66)

46

日本政府当局을 代表하는 防衛施設庁長官은 美軍当局과 協議하여 公務與否의 問題를 決定하지 못할때에 限하여 仲裁人을 通하여 決定하게 되어있다.

우리나라의 境遇에 있어서도 請求权條項을 為한 美軍構成員 및 雇用員의 公務遂行與否에 関한 決定節次를 具体的으로 마련하여야 될것이며, 紛争이 発生하였을 때에는 이 條項에 依하여 最終的인 決定을 내리게 됨을 意味하는 것

(195mm×265mm16절지) (10—2014—01) (10×20) No.

0080

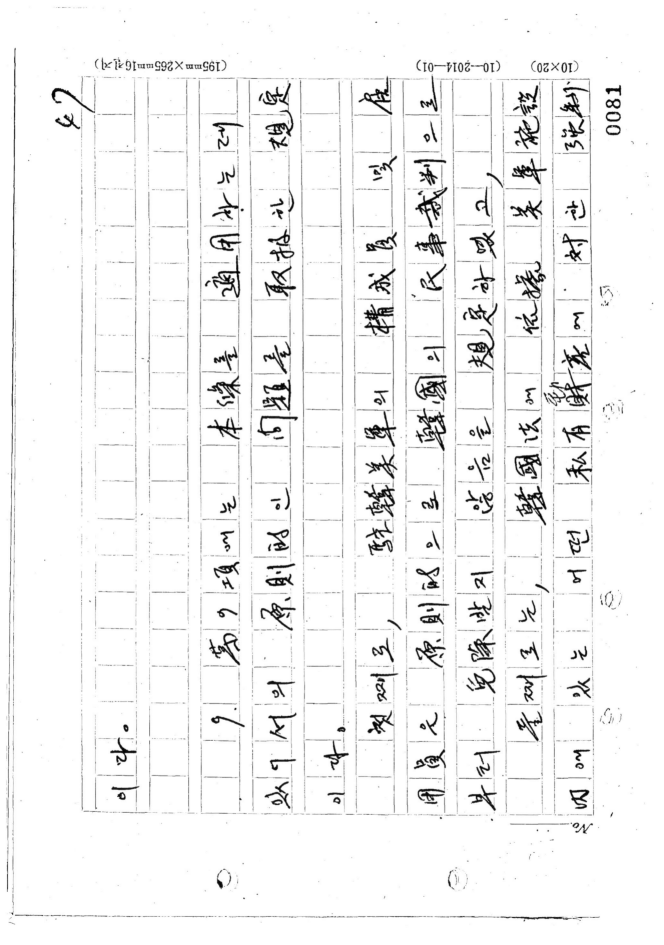

(10×20) (10--2014-01) (195㎜×265㎜16절지)
0081
1800

(10×20)　(10-2014-01)　〔195mm×265mm16절지〕

(10×20)　(10-2014-01)　(195mm×265mm16절지)

(10-2014-01)

(10×20)

0084

... KATUSA 構成 ...

51

13. 第13項은 本協定 發效前에 發生한 請求权에 対한 處理責任을 規定한 것이다. 本協定이 發效하기 前에 發生한 모든 請求는 美國当局에서 責任을 지게된 것이며, 이는 美國의 対外訴請法에 따라 解決하게 됨을 意味한다.

14. 마지막으로 本條에 対한 合議事錄으로 發効時期에 関한 例外事項이 規定되었다. 即, 本條 第5, 6, 7,

(10×20) (10—2014—01) (195mm×265mm16절지)

0085

| 협 조 전 | 응신기일 |
|---|---|

| 분류기호 외방조 ?// | 제 목  자료 송부 |
|---|---|

수신  구 미 국장          발신일자  1966.2.22      (협조제의)

<br/>

(발신명의) 방고 국장   이 문 용

---

(제1의견)

귀국의 요청에 기하여 한·미, 한·월간의 군사 실무자

약정 사본을 구각 2부 씩 송부하오니 참고하시기 바랍니다.

특히 한미약정서의 제3. 4항을 참고 바랍니다.

빈 첨 : 한미, 한월간 군사 실무자 약정 각 1부    끝.

---

(제2의견)

첩부물에서 분리되면 보통군서로 재분류

---

MILITARY WORKING ARRANGEMENT

BETWEEN

COMROKFV AND COMUSMACV

Group - 4
Downgraded at 3 year intervals;
Declassified after 12 years.
DOD Dir 5200.10

0087

한·미국 간의 상호방위조약 제4조에 의한 시설과 구역 및 한국에서의 미국군대의 지위에 관한 협정(SOFA)
전59권. 1966.7.9 서울에서 서명 : 1967.2.9 발효(조약 232호) (V.53 민사청구권 관계자료, 1964-66)

MILITARY WORKING ARRANGEMENT

BETWEEN

COMROKFV AND COMUSMACV


1. In response to a request from the Republic of Vietnam, the Government of the Republic of Korea will provide to the Republic of Vietnam the military augmentation forces consisting essentially of combat and combat support units and administrative headquarters listed below to the Republic of Vietnam to restore freedom and security in the area and to contribute to international peace by repelling communist-inspired insurgency and aggression.

    a. Headquarters ROKFV and Headquarters Units.

    b. One Army Infantry Division (-).

    c. One Marine Corps Regiment.

    d. One Field Support Command.

2. In order thoroughly to observe the purport of the request for augmentation forces made by the Government of the Republic of Vietnam to the Government of the Republic of Korea, these units will execute necessary operational missions in support of the National Pacification Program, and ROK units or personnel already in Vietnam will continue their respective missions in accordance with the existing arrangements.

3. Command of the Republic of Korea Armed Forces in Vietnam will be vested in the Commander of Republic of Korea Forces Vietnam (COMROKFV) designated by the Government of the Republic of Korea.  Command of ROK Armed Forces already in Vietnam previously vested in the ROKMAG-V Commander will be integrated into a single command upon the arrival of the COMROKFV in Vietnam.

- 1 -

0088

4. In order to maintain a close coordination between
ROKFV, RVNAF, and USMACV, and to insure that an appropriate
system of control is arranged for each element of the ROKFV,
the existing International Military Assistance Policy Council
(IMAPC) will continue its function for the ROK Augmentation.
The Council will consist of the Chief of the Joint General
Staff, RVNAF (Chairman), COMROKFV, and COMUSMACV plus working
level representatives of each of these agencies.  The basic
function of the Council is to establish policy concerning
missions, control, and operational areas of ROKFV elements.
The decisions made by the Council should be mutually agreeable
to the representatives of the respective governments.  Policy
matters involving the interests of the Military Forces of the
Republic of Korea, the Republic of Vietnam and the United
States will be referred as necessary to the International
Military Assistance Policy Council.

5. Viet Cong and suspects captured by ROK Armed Forces
in Vietnam will be treated in accordance with the provisions
of Geneva Convention of 1949 while in ROK custody and they
will be turned over to designated RVN interrogation center or
installations as soon as possible.

6. ROKFV and USMACV will mutually provide or exchange
intelligence directly or indirectly required in the execution
of their respective missions and USMACV will provide assistance
and support of intelligence activities of ROKFV elements.

7. USMACV will provide maps and aerial photographs in
addition to other intelligence material required by ROKFV
elements.

8. COMROKFV will undertake to provide for the indoctrination of his troops prior to their arrival in the Republic of
Vietnam and their continued indoctrination during the period
of their employment there.  The indoctrination will relate to

- 2 -

0089

the history, customs, and traditions of the Republic of
Vietnam with a view to insuring the best possible relationship between his command, the Vietnamese people, and the
Government of the Republic of Vietnam. To this end, COMUSMACV
will furnish COMROKFV with such indoctrination materials as he
has within his resources. It is further understood that
COMROKFV will consult with the appropriate RVNAF authorities
in regard to this program.

9. Logistical Suppot. USMACV will support ROKFV under
the same logistic criteria applied to similar US units. The
detailed logistical support plan and levels of accompanying
supplies and equipment will be the subject of a separate
arrangement.

a. USMACV will provide support of items contained in
Tables of Allowance, Equipment and Supplies which are not
obtainable through RVNAF channels, in accordance with the
mutually agreeable authorization documents and prescribed
allowances. ROKFV will submit to USMACV T_ables of Organization and Equipment, Tables of Allowance, and such other data as
may be required by USMACV to plan for and provide the support
required for each element of ROKFV for the effective accomplish-
ment of assigned mission, and USMACV agrees to make amendments
of TOE and TA recommended by ROKFV when it is required to
execute its assigned missions.

b. Title to ROK equipement (vessels included) and
supplies brought into Vietnam by ROKFV will be retained by
ROKFV. Equipment and supplies of ROKFV elements lost during
combat operations or through unavoidable causes, and/or become
unserviceable beyond repair through combat or fair, wear and
tear, and unavoidable causes will be replaced in kind and the
title transferred to ROKFV. Title to eqiupment other than

- 3 -

0090

that replaced in kind which is provided through the RVN
Military Assistance Program or US sources will be retained by
the source providing the equipment. Evacuation of equipment
whose title is not with ROKFV from the Republic of Vietnam will
require prior approval of COMUSMACV.

     c. USMACV will furnish subsistence items to the ROKFV
on the same basis not to exceed the value of like rations
issued to US troops. Special items peculiar to the indigenous
desires of the Koreans will not be provided by US sources,
however, transportation of these items from Korean ports to
the Republic of Vietnam will be provided by the US. Specific
details will be contained in the logistical and financial
annexes.

     d. USMACV agrees to render necessary coordination and
to support standards of troop billeting, health, and welfare
similar to that provided to US combat forces operating under
similar conditions.

     e. USMACV will provide emergency medical support and the
support beyond the capability of ROKFV on the same basis and
procedures as are provided to US personnel including treatment,
evacuation through US medical channels.

     f. USMACV will provide required in-country movement of
ROKFV personnel in the same manner and under the same conditions
and system of priorities as applied to US personnel.

     g. Out-of-country Transportation. USMACV will provide the
utilization of US transportation for ROKFV personnel and ROK
personnel traveling in connection with ROKFV activities, and for
the movement of equipment and goods under the same conditions and
system of priority applied to US units and military personnel.

- 4 -

한·미국 간의 상호방위조약 제4조에 의한 시설과 구역 및 한국에서의 미국군대의 지위에 관한 협정(SOFA)
전59권. 1966.7.9 서울에서 서명 : 1967.2.9 발효(조약 232호) (V.53 민사청구권 관계자료, 1964-66)

Such transportation includes authorized travel, such as rotation of ROKFV personnel, recall to Republic of Korea, return of remains of deceased personnel, movement of inspection teams in connection with ROKFV, and emergency evacuation and/or withdrawal of ROKFV. Other requirements will be considered on a case by case basis. The ROKFV will utilize its own transportation when available.

h. ROKFV will perform maintenance through fourth echelon. Equipment maintenance support beyond ROKFV and RVNAF capability will be provided by USMACV in accordance with mutually agreeable documentation and support levels. TOE and TA equipment which becomes unserviceable beyond repair either through combat or fair, wear and tear and/or other sufficient causes will be replaced.

i. USMACV agreed to provide unit and recreational facilities on the same basis as provided by USMACV to similar US units.

j. USMACV will support ROKFV Headquarters in Saigon, not to exceed 230 personnel (70 officers and 160 enlisted personnel) on condition that USMACV provides services support, such as communication, transportation, security, and local civilian employees essential to the support of the Saigon Headquarters. The real estate to include office building, billets, and mess facilities for this Headquarters will be provided by RVNAF, and USMACV will equip and maintain these facilities and provide office supplies, equipment, and other services described for ROK personnel in this arrangement. ROKFV will use IMAO building for office facilities temporarily until RVNAF provides other facilities.

10. Personnel Services. USMACV will provide ROKFV the following support normally extended to US personnel on the same basis, condition, and standards as US. ROKFV personnel who are

- 5 -

0092

authorized to utilize the US facilities herein are subject to
the same rules, regulations, and conditions as are applied to
US personnel.

a. Participation in US recreational programs.

b. Use of US military religious facilities.

c. Use of US exchange facilities. In locations where
125 or more ROK personnel are concentrated, ROKFV may establish
and operate exchange facilities except where a branch exchange
is readily available. The items to be sold in this facility
will be supplied by the US military service responsible for
exchange operation in Vietnam. USMACV agrees that the US
exchange service procure and supply items of peculiar indigenous
desire of Korean troops from Korea, not to exceed ten line items.

d. Use of US mess, billeting, and club facilities.
In locations where 125 or more ROK personnel are concentrated,
ROKFV may establish and operate mess and club facilities. In
locations where 125 or more ROK personnel are concentrated,
ROKFV may establish and operate mess and club facilities.
Consumable items for the operation of these facilities will be
supplied by US sources on a reimbursable basis.

e. Use of established US bus, sedan, taxi and aircraft
services.

f. Use of US postal facilities: Use of closed pouch
system for all personal mail (first through fourth class) and
official mail without US postage affixed between designated
US aerial mail terminals/APO facilities and Seoul, Korea.

g. Mortuary service. ROKFV will establish and operate
graves registration collecting point at the Division for the
disposition of the remains of the deceased in accordance with
appropriate custom. Mortuary supplies will be provided by
USMACV depending on the availability of these supplies in
Vietnam. Remains to be evacuated and subsequently interred in
Korea will be processed through US Channels.

한·미국 간의 상호방위조약 제4조에 의한 시설과 구역 및 한국에서의 미국군대의 지위에 관한 협정(SOFA)
전59권. 1966.7.9 서울에서 서명 : 1967.2.9 발효(조약 232호) (V.53 민사청구권 관계자료, 1964-66)  99

h. USMACV agrees to assign necessary ROKFV liaison officers to US military installations located between the Republic of Korea and Vietnam to assist and coordinate medical evacuation of ROK troops through US medical evacuation channels and other liaison matters in connection with ROKFV activities, and also agrees to provide support equivalent to US personnel in like assignments.

i. Republic of Korea Armed Forces will provide an identification card, with picture and English translation, to each individual. This document will be honored for access to US installations and services listed above.

j. Korean correspondents acknowledged by ROKFV will be granted the same treatment USMACV extends to US correspondents in the Republic of Vietnam.

11. Communication support for ROKFV will be the subject of a separate arrangement.

12. Financial arrangements between COMROKFV and COMUSMACV will be the subject of a separate arrangement.

13. COMUSMACV is responsible for the security of ROK combat forces in each ROK assisgned area of responsibility until such time as the ROK units, in their particular areas, have completed their deployment.

14. USMACV will provide ROKFV local national employees required to accomplish its assigned missions. The details of the procedures are as set forth in the aforementioned financial arrangement.

15. COMROKFV and COMUSMACV waive claims against each other for property damage, personal injury, and death caused by members or employees of the Armed Forces of each country in the Republic of Vietnam. Indemnity claims for property damage, personal injury and death inflicted on the Republic of Vietnam Government or its population by elements of ROKFV arising from

- 7 -

0094

both combat and non-combat activities will be subject to a separate arrangement.

16. COMROKFV and COMUSMACV each agree to cooperate fully in making necessary witnesses and other assistance, such as interpreters, available for the courts-martial and administrative proceedings of the other forces.

17. COMROKFV and COMUSMACV each agree to take the security measures necessary to prevent the disclosure or compromise of classified articles, services, or information received under this arrangement.

18. It is noted that the Republic of Korea has obtained from the Government of Vietnam an understanding that rights, privileges, and exemptions accorded US military personnel under the provisions of the Pentalateral Agreement of 1950 are also accorded Korean armed services personnel.

19. Arrangements.

a. Upon signature by duly authorized officers, this working arrangement is in effect and constitutes a general military arrangement agreed to by both parties. This arrangement is subject to confirmation by appropriate representatives of the Governments of the Republic of Korea and the United States. Either party, upon ninety (90) days notice to the other, may request renegotiation of all or any part of this arrangement.

b. The Military Working Arrangement co-signed by the representatives of ROK and USMACV on 5 September 1964 concerning the ROKMASH remains effective unless otherwise noted in this arrangement.

c. The Military Working Arrangement co-signed by the representatives of ROK and USMACV on 8 February 1965 concerning the ROKMAG-V remains effective unless otherwise noted in this arrangement.

- 8 -

한·미국 간의 상호방위조약 제4조에 의한 시설과 구역 및 한국에서의 미국군대의 지위에 관한 협정(SOFA) 전59권. 1966.7.9 서울에서 서명 : 1967.2.9 발효(조약 232호) (V.53 민사청구권 관계자료, 1964-66) 101

This arrangement is signed on <u>6 September</u> 1965

---------------------------                    ---------------------------
Major General LEE, SAE HO                      W. B. ROSSON
ROK Armed Forces Representative                Maj Gen, USA
                                               Chief of Staff

- 9 -

0096

MILITARY WORKING ARRANGEMENT

BETWEEN

ROKFV AND RVNAF

0097

MILITARY WORKING ARRANGEMENT

BETWEEN

ROKFV AND RVNAF

1. In response to a request from the Republic of Vietnam,
the Government of the Republic of Korea will provide to the
Republic of Vietnamt the military augmentation forces consisting
essentially of combat units listed below to the Republic of
Vitenam to restore freedom and security in the area and to
contribute to international peace by repelling communist-
inspired insurgency and aggression.

    a. Headquarters Republic of Korea Forces Vietnam
(ROKFV).

    b. One Combat Division (reinforced) consisting of two
Army Infantry Regiments (reinforced), one Marine Corps Regiment
(reinforced), and one Field Support Command.

2. In order thoroughly to observe the purport of the
request for augmentation forces made by the Government of the
Republic of Vietnam to the Government of the Republic of Korea,
these units will execute necessary operational missions in
support of National Pacification Program, and ROK units or
personnel already in Vietnam will continue their respective
missions in accordance with the existing arrangements.

3. Command of the Republic of Korea Armed Forces in Vietnam
will be vested in the Commander of Republic of Korea Forces
Vietnam (COMROKFV) designated by the Government of the Republic
of Korea.

4. Command of ROK Armed Forces already in Vietnam
previously vested in the ROKMAG-V Commander will be integrated
into a single comand upon the arrival of the CMROKFV in
Vietnam.

- 1 -

0098

5. The rights, privileges, duties and immunities or ROKFV personnel in Vietnam are as set forth in the previous exchange of notes between the Ambassador of the Republic of Korea to Vietnam and the Minister of Foreign Affairs of the Republic of Vietnam on 31 October 1964, however, when further agreement is negotiated between two governments, then, new agreement will apply.

6. When ROK combat units in Vietnam are allocated a Tactical Area of Responsibility (TAOR), the operational Commanders of ROK Armed Forces within the TAOR will exercise equivalent authorities as granted to unit commanders of all the allied countries by the Government of the Republic of Vietnam.

7. Viet Cong and suspects captured by ROK Armed Forces in Vietnam will be treated in accordance with the provisions of the Geneva Convention of 1949 while in ROK custody, and they will be turned over to designated RVN interrogation center or installation as soon as possible.

8. ROKFV and RVNAF will mutually provide or exchange intelligence directly or indirectly required in the execution of their respective missions and RVNAF will provide assistance and support of intelligence activities of ROKFV elements.

9. RVNAF will provide maps and aerial photographs in addition to other intelligence collecting material required by ROKFV elements.

10. A Liaison Teams of the RVNAF will be set up at the ROKFV Headquarters. Necessary RVNAF liaison teams will be assigned at each necessary echelon of ROKFV. These liaison teams will have the responsibility of assisting ROK unit commanders in dealing with Vietnamese administrative officials, Vietnamese military commanders, and people living in the TAOR or area of activities.

- 2 -

0069

11. a. To the extent required for military purpose, ROKFV may set up, operate and maintain,

(1) Wire telecommunication facilities within accommodations,

(2) Radio stations for fixed services within Vietnam subject to prior consultation with RVNAF authorities,

(3) Other radio receiving facilities, and

(4) Temporary telecommunication facilities of any kind for training exercises and in case of emergency subject to prior consultation with Vietnamese regional military commanders.

b. Within its capability, RVNAF will install and operate necessary communication network between ROKFV elements, RVNAF units, and administrative agencies concerned upon the request made by the ROK unit commanders.

12. Logistical Support.

Supply and services support from U.S. Military Assistance Program will be provided ROKFV by RVNAF. Equipment and supplies compatible to RVNAF will be supported on the same basis as RVNAF as follows:

a. Supply Support.

(1) Class I - Rice as same basis as furnished to RVNAF personnel.

(2) Class II & IV - Establishment of safety level, operating level, and prescribed load list of ROKFV elements and continued replenishment.

b. Maintenance support.

(1) Maintenance support of equipment above fourth echelon.

(2) Maintenance support of ROK Navy vessels in Vietnam within VN Navy capability.

- 3 -                          0100

c. Accommodations.

(1) RVNAF will provide land area, as jointly agreed upon for ROKFV element Base Camp.

(2) Units of the ROK combat infantry division will bring in tentage to meet sleeping, dining and service requirements.

(3) Construction for the ROK Combat Infantry Division Base Camp will be provided by RVNAF on the same basis as Vietnamese combat unit.

(4) RVNAF will provide land area and facilities to accommodate ROKFV Headquarters in Saigon.

d. Medical Support.

ROKFV personnel will be primarily evacuated to ROK medical channels, however, when the situation calls for urgency or existing facilities are incapable, ROKFV personnel will be evacuated to U.S. medical facilities for further treatment.

13. Title to eqiupment (vessels included) and supplies brought into Vietnam by ROKFV will be retained by ROKFV. Equipment and supplied of ROKFV elements lost during the combat operations or through unavoidable causes, and or become unserviceable beyond repair through combat or fair, wear and tear, and unavoidable causes will be replaced in kind by U.S. Military Assistance Program provided to the Government of Vietnam and the title transferred to ROKFV. Title to equipment, other than that replaced in kind, which is provided through the Republic of Vietnam Military Assistance Program or U.S. sources, will be retained by the source providing the equipment.

14. Transportation. In-country transportation will be provided through coordination between Vietnam Area Logistic Command (Transportation Zone Office), USMACV and ROKFV representatives.

15. Within its capability, RVNAF will provide ROKFV inter-preters as required.

0101

16. The COMROKFV will furnish RVNAF a roster of all ROKFV personnel to include name, rank, service number and unit. ROKFV will inform RVNAF on subsequent changes of personnel.

17. COMROKFV agrees to coordinate prior to the entry into the Republic of Vietnam by personnel of the Republic of Korea in connection with ROKFV activities.

18. RVNAF and ROKFV authorities will take all necessary measures mutually agreed upon to prevent the disclosure or compromise of classified documents, services or information which either exchanges with or furnishes the other in furtherance of this military working arrangement.

19. Indemnification for property damage, personnel injury and death inflicted on the Government or individual population of the Republic of Vietnam by members of ROKFV will be subject to separate negotiations between authorities of the two Governments.

20. Military Working Arrangements co-signed by the representatives of ROK and RVN on 5 September 1964 and 7 February 1965 remain effective unless otherwise noted in this arrangement.

This arrangement is mutually agreeable and co-signed on 5 September 1965.


./s/                                    /s/

---

Major General LEE SAE HO        Major General TRAN-NGOC TAM
ROK Armed Forces Representative RVNAF Representative

1. United States Forces, Korea civilian component includes 84 third state nationals.

2. a. All incoming and outgoing APO air mail goes via Kimpo International Airport.

   b. All incoming and outgoing APO surface mail goes via Inchon.

   c. Other important APO post offices in Korea are located at:

   > Seoul
   > Taegu
   > Pusan
   > Uijongbu
   > Tongduchon (7th Division)
   > Munsanni (2d Division)
   > Osan (Air Force)

3. USFK Claims Service Operations in Korea:

| | Number Considered | Number Paid | Amount (US $) | Number Disallowed |
|---|---|---|---|---|
| 1965 | 1,123 | 770 | $167,884.86 | 353 |
| 1966 (1Jan-30June) | 626 | 410 | 78,148.77 | 216 |

0103

AR 25-20 Investigating and Processing of Claims
(1 Nov 1959)

AR 25-25 Claims Arising from Activities of Military
or Civilian Personnel or Incident to Non-
Combat Activities(Title 10, U.S. Code, Sec2733:
1 Nov 1959)

AR 25-30 Claims Arising from Negligence of Military
Personnel or Civilian Employees under The
Federal Tort Claims Act (Title 28, U.S. Code,
Sec 2671-2680: 1 Nov 1959)

AR 25-35 Claims Incident to Use of Government Vehicles
and Other Property of The United States Not Cognizable
under Other Law (Act of 9 Oct 1962, 76 Stat. 767)

AR 25-50 (NAVEXOS P-1444, AFR 113-13)

Claims under Article VIII of The Agreement
Regarding The Status of Forces of Parties to the
North Atlantic Treaty (20 April 1955)

AR 25-60 Maritime Claims (Title 10, U.S. Code, 4801-
4806: L April 1958)

AR 25-90 Claims Arising in Foreign Countries (10 U.S.
Code, 2734: 26 April 1957)

AR 25-105 Claims in Favor of the United States for
Damage to or Loss or Destruction of Army Property
(20 June 1958)

AR 25-110 Claims in Favor of the United States for the
Reasonable Value of Medical Care Furnished
by the Army (8 Jan 1963)

0104

Army Regulations⎱
No. 25-35          ⎰

HEADQUARTERS,
DEPARTMENT OF THE ARMY
Washington 25, D.C., *13 May 1963*

CLAIMS

# CLAIMS INCIDENT TO USE OF GOVERNMENT VEHICLES AND OTHER PROPERTY OF THE UNITED STATES NOT COGNIZABLE UNDER OTHER LAW

## (Act of 9 October 1962, 76 Stat. 767)

**1. Statutory authority.** The statutory authority for these regulations is contained in the act of 9 October 1962 (76 Stat. 767), commonly known as the "Non-Scope of Employment Claims Act of 1962."

**2. Definitions.** The definitions of terms set forth in paragraph 4, AR 25-20, are applicable to these regulations unless otherwise defined herein:

*a. Civilian official or employee.* Includes civilian officials or employees of the Department of the Army, or of the Army, paid from appropriated funds at the time the incident resulting in the claim occurred.

*b. Government installation.* A United States Government facility having fixed or relatively fixed boundaries owned or controlled by the Government.

*c. Vehicle.* Includes every description of carriage or other artificial contrivance used, or capable of being used, as a means of transportation on land (1 U.S.C. 4).

**3. Scope.** These regulations prescribe the substantive bases and special procedural requirements for the settlement of claims against the United States not cognizable under any other provision of law, determined to be meritorious in an amount not more than $1,000, for damage to, or loss of, property, or personal injury or death caused by a member of the Army or a civilian official or employee of the Department of the Army, or of the Army, incident to the use of a vehicle of the United States at any place, or any other property of the United States on a Government installation.

**4. Claims payable.** *a. General.* A claim for personal injury, death, or damage to or loss of property, real or personal, which arose on and after 9 October 1962 is payable under these regulations when—

  (1) Caused by a member of the Army, or a civilian official or employee of the Department of the Army, or the Army.

    (*a*) Incident to the use of a vehicle of the United States at any place.

    (*b*) Incident to the use of any other property of the United States on a Government installation.

  (2) The claim is not cognizable under any other provision of law and regulations.

  (3) The claim has been determined to be meritorious in an amount not in excess of $1,000, and the approving authority has obtained a settlement agreement in full satisfaction of the claim prior to approval of the claim for payment.

*b. Personal injury or death.* A claim for personal injury or death is allowable only for the cost of reasonable medical, hospital, and burial expenses actually incurred, not otherwise furnished or paid by the United States.

0105

**5. Claims not payable.** A claim is not allowable under these regulations which—

*a.* Is cognizable under any other provision of law administered by the military departments or regulations of the Department of the Army.

*b.* Results wholly or partly from the negligent or wrongful act of the claimant, his agent, or his employee. The doctrine of comparative negligence is not applicable.

*c.* Is for medical, hospital, and burial expenses furnished or paid by the United States.

*d.* Is for any element of damage pertaining to personal injuries or death other than provided in paragraph 4*b.* All other items of damage, for example, compensation for loss of earnings and services, diminution of earning capacity, anticipated medical expenses, physical disfigurement, and pain and suffering, are not payable.

*e.* Is legally recoverable by the claimant under an indemnifying law or indemnity contract. If the claim is legally recoverable in part, that part recoverable by the claimant is not payable.

*f.* Is a subrogated claim.

*g.* Examples—

(1) The claimant has collision insurance covering his automobile with a deductible amount of $100. While the claimant is sitting in his vehicle which he parked properly in the street in front of his residence, the vehicle is struck from the rear by an Army truck operated by a civilian employee of the Department of the Army who had misappropriated the Government vehicle. The claimant sustains personal injuries requiring his hospitalization for 6 weeks during which he actually incurs medical and hospital expenses in the amount of $1,200. He has no medical or hospitalization insurance. The damage to his vehicle totals $300. The claimant's insurance carrier reimburses him in the amount of $200 for the damage to his vehicle and becomes subrogated in that amount under the terms of the policy. The claimant files a claim in the amount of $1,500, alleging $300 for property damage to his automobile and $1,200 for medical and hospital expenses. The claim is allowable in the total amount of $1,000, consisting of $100, the deductible amount for property damage under the terms of his collision insurance coverage, and $900 of the medical and hospital expenses he actually incurred. The amount claimed for medical and hospital expenses and for property damage merely constitute separable interests in a single claim which may not be allowed in an amount in excess of $1,000 under these regulations. The claimant's insurer is not a proper party claimant and no payment is allowable for the insurer's subrogated interest.

(2) Claimant has medical and hospitalization insurance under which he would be entitled to reimbursement up to the amount of $500 for the reasonable cost of medical and hospital expenses incurred by him for personal injuries. While visiting at an Army installation the claimant is wounded as the result of the negligent discharge of a Government issue caliber .45 pistol by an enlisted man who had stolen the weapon. The injury required that he be hospitalized at a civilian hospital for 1 month. During this period the claimant actually incurs medical and hospital expenses in the amount of $750. The claimant may be paid $250, the amount allowable for reasonable medical and hospital expenses actually incurred after deduction of the amount of $500 legally recoverable by him under his insurance policy.

**6. When claim must be presented.** A claim may be settled under these regulations only if the incident which gave rise to the claim occurred on or after 9 October 1962, and the claim is presented in writing within 2 years after it accrues.

**7. Procedures.** So far as not inconsistent with these regulations the procedures for the investigation and processing of claims contained in AR 25-20 will be followed.

**8. Settlement agreement.** No claim is payable under these regulations unless a settlement agreement has been obtained from the claimant accepting the amount determined to be meritorious in full satisfaction of any claim against the United States arising out of the incident. See figure 7, AR 25-20.

**9. Settlement authority.** *a. Approval authority.* Subject to the provisions of paragraph 8

2

herein, each of the following is delegated authority under these regulations to—

(1) *Approve claims for payment in an amount not to exceed $1,000.*

(a) The Chief, U.S. Army Claims Service, Office of The Judge Advocate General, and all officers of The Judge Advocate General's Corps assigned to that service, subject to such limitations as the Chief, U.S. Army Claims Service, may prescribe;

(b) The commanding general of an army or comparable command, including the Military District of Washington, within the United States, its territories, possessions, and the Commonwealth of Puerto Rico, or his staff judge advocate;

(c) Any commanding officer authorized to exercise general courts-martial jurisdiction or his staff judge advocate;

(d) Any officer of The Judge Advocate General's Corps assigned to a maneuver claims service when designated by the commander concerned, subject to such limitations as the designating commander may prescribe;

(e) Any officer of The Judge Advocate General's Corps assigned to a disaster claims field office when designated by a commander listed in (b) or (c) above. The authority of such a designee to approve claims is limited to the monetary limits of the designating commander and such other limitation as that officer may impose;

[JAG]

By Order of the Secretary of the Army:

(f) The district and division engineer, Corps of Engineers; and the Chief of Engineers or the Chief, Legal Division, Office of the Chief of Engineers;

(g) A chief of a command claims service when established as prescribed in paragraph 14, AR 25-90.

(2) *Approve claims for payment in an amount not to exceed $500.* Any commanding officer not authorized to exercise general courts-martial jurisdiction, but having a judge advocate assigned to his staff, or his judge advocate.

b. *Authority to disapprove claims.* The authority to disapprove claims under these regulations is delegated only to—

(1) The Judge Advocate General of the Army; and

(2) The Chief, U.S. Army Claims Service, Office of The Judge Advocate General, and all officers of The Judge Advocate General's Corps assigned to that service, subject to such limitations as the Chief, U.S. Army Claims Service, may prescribe.

**10. Claims over $1,000.** A claim presented in an amount over $1,000 which the claimant declines to settle for an amount determined to be meritorious not in excess of $1,000 under these regulations will be forwarded with the related file and a seven paragraph memorandum of opinion (see par. 8, app. I, AR 25-20) to the Chief, U.S. Army Claims Service, Office of The Judge Advocate General, Fort Holabird, Baltimore 19, Md.

EARLE G. WHEELER,
*General, United States Army,*
*Chief of Staff.*

Official:
J. C. LAMBERT,
*Major General, United States Army,*
*The Adjutant General.*

Distribution:
*Active Army, NG, and USAR:* To be distributed in accordance with DA Form 12-9 requirements for DA Regulations, Inspections and Investigations—B.

TAGO 1387A

3

U.S. GOVERNMENT PRINTING OFFICE:1963

0107

한·미국 간의 상호방위조약 제4조에 의한 시설과 구역 및 한국에서의 미국군대의 지위에 관한 협정(SOFA) 전59권. 1966.7.9 서울에서 서명 : 1967.2.9 발효(조약 232호) (V.53 민사청구권 관계자료, 1964-66) 113

ARMY REGULATIONS⎫
No. 25-90　　　　⎭

DEPARTMENT OF THE ARMY
WASHINGTON 25, D. C., *26 April 1957*

# CLAIMS

## CLAIMS ARISING IN FOREIGN COUNTRIES

### (10 U. S. C. 2734)

## SECTION I

## GENERAL

**1. Statutory authority.** The statutory authorities for these regulations are contained in—

*a.* Title 10, United States Code, Section 2734, as amended (70 Stat. 703), as to claims arising after 9 August 1956, and the act of 2 January 1942 (55 Stat. 880), commonly referred to as the Foreign Claims Act, as amended by the act of 22 April 1943 (57 Stat. 66); act of 31 July 1945 (59 Stat. 511); act of 25 July 1947 (61 Stat. 449, 454; 31 U. S. C. 224d, 1952 ed.); National Security Act of 1947 (61 Stat. 501; 5 U. S. C. 181-1, 1952 ed.); and act of 28 July 1956 (70 Stat. 703), as to claims which arose before 10 August 1956;

*b.* The act of 31 July 1945 (59 Stat. 511), as to claims which arose before 25 July 1947 in the Philippines;

*c.* The act of 4 March 1923 (42 Stat. 1509), as amended (36 U. S. C. 121 and the act of 25 July 1956, 70 Stat. 40), as to claims arising out of

---

*These regulations supersede AR 25-90, 22 June 1951, including C 2, 29 September 1955.

0108

acts or omissions of personnel of the American Battle Monuments Commission.

**2. Purpose.** The purpose of these regulations is to promote and maintain friendly relations by the prompt settlement of meritorious claims.

**3. Definitions.** See AR 25-20. As used in these regulations, the following terms will have the meanings here indicated:

*a. Settle.* Consider, ascertain, adjust, determine, and dispose of a claim, whether by full or partial allowance or by disallowance.

*b. Military personnel.* Forces or individual members of the Army.

*c. Civilian employees.* Civilian employees of the Army, prisoners of war and interned enemy aliens engaged in labor for pay, volunteer workers and others serving as employees of the Army without compensation; and, after 28 July 1956, civilian employees of the Department of Defense who are not employees of the Department of the Army, Navy, or Air Force.

*d. Noncombat activities.* Authorized activities which have little parallel in civilian pursuits or which historically have been considered as furnishing a proper basis for the payment of claims, such as maneuvers, special field exercises, practice firing of heavy guns or other weapons, practice bombings, operation of aircraft, use of barrage balloons, escape of animals, use of instrumentalities having latent mechanical defects, movement of combat or other vehicles designed especially for military use, and use and occupancy of real estate.

**4. Scope.** These regulations prescribe the substantive basis for the settlement of claims against the United States by inhabitants of a foreign country for death or personal injury, or damage to or loss or destruction of public or private property, arising outside the United States, its Territories, and possessions, caused by military personnel or civilian employees, including claims arising before 10 August 1956 under the act of 2 January 1942 (55 Stat. 880), as amended (31 U. S. C. 224d, 1952 ed., and the act of 28 July 1956, 70 Stat. 703), and not settled under AR 25-90, 22 June 1951.

**5. Claims payable.** *a. General.* Unless otherwise prescribed, claims for death, personal injury, or damage to property, real or personal, may be settled under these regulations.

*b. Death.* Only one claim arises. The amount allowed will, to the extent found practicable, be apportioned among the beneficiaries as prescribed by the law or custom of the place where the incident resulting in the death occurred.

*c. Property.* Included in the property for damage to which claims may be settled under these regulations are real property used and occupied under lease, express or implied, or otherwise, and personal property loaned, rented, or otherwise bailed to the Government under an agreement, express or implied, unless the owner has expressly assumed the risk of damage or loss. Claims enforceable under a lease or other contract may be settled under these regulations, or under contractual procedures, as deemed in the best interest of the Government. Claims for rent, as such, may not be settled under these regulations (see AR 25-405), but allowance may be made for the use or occupancy of property arising out of trespass or other tort, even though claimed as rent.

0109

**6. Claims not payable.** No claim will be settled under these regulations if it—

*a.* Results from combat activities; *or*

*b.* Any portion of it falls under any workmen's compensation law or regulation, whether Federal Employees Compensation Act of 7 September 1916 (39 Stat. 742), as amended (5 U. S. C. 751), Longshoremen's and Harborworkers Compensation Act (44 Stat. 1424; 33 U. S. C. 901), or local law or custom;

*c.* Is waived or assumed by a foreign country under treaty or agreement (see par. 7, AR 25–20), or is one for the settlement of which a foreign country is responsible under Article VIII of the Agreement Regarding the Status of Forces of Parties to the North Atlantic Treaty, Article XVIII of the Japanese Administrative Agreement, or other similar treaty or agreement;

*d.* Is purely contractual in character;

*e.* Arises from private domestic obligations;

*f.* Is based solely on compassionate grounds;

*g.* Is a bastardy claim;

*h.* Is for patent infringement; or

*i.* Arose before 29 July 1956 outside a foreign country, its territories, possessions, or territorial waters.

**7. Claims under other laws and regulations.** *a. AR 25–25 and AR 25–80.* Claims will be settled under these regulations, if applicable, although they might otherwise be settled under AR 25–25 and AR 25–80.

*b. AR 25–100.* Claims which may be settled under AR 25–100 will not be settled under these regulations.

*c. AR 25–60.* Claims which may be settled under AR 25–60 may be settled under these regulations only when specifically authorized by The Judge Advocate General in each case. Authority may be requested by letter containing a summary of the facts, without forwarding the claim file.

**8. Claims under treaties and agreements.** When a foreign government is responsible for dealing with claims against the United States under Article VIII of the Agreement Regarding the Status of Forces of Parties to the North Atlantic Treaty (extracted in app. I, AR 25–50), Article XVIII of the Japanese Administrative Agreement, or other similar treaty or agreement:

*a.* The investigation by United States authorities will generally be limited to obtaining all relevant evidence from American sources.

*b.* The United States Sending State Office for claims in NATO countries and the comparable office or officer assigned claims responsibility by the United States under the Japanese Administrative Agreement or similar treaty or agreement, where the Army has been assigned claims responsibility, will send to the Chief, Claims Division, Office of The Judge Advocate General, a copy of each voucher evidencing reimbursement with a copy of the bill submitted by the foreign government, and a letter report of the number and total amount claimed of claims disapproved by the foreign government.

**9. When claim must be presented.** A claim may not be considered under these regulations unless presented within 1 year after

0110

the incident from which it arose, or filed within that year with a foreign government under Article VIII of the Agreement Regarding the Status of Forces of Parties to the North Atlantic Treaty, Article XVIII of the Japanese Administrative Agreement, or other similar treaty or agreement. A claim arising in the Philippine Islands on or before 25 July 1947 could, however, have been presented on or before 25 July 1948, if good cause was shown for the delay in excess of 1 year. If examination of a claim discloses that it was not seasonably presented, the claimant may be advised to that effect without further action being required. A claim otherwise within these regulations but not presented within one year will not be settled under AR 25–25.

**10. Claimants.** *a. General.* See paragraph 5c, AR 25–20. Each claimant, and, as to a claim based on death, the decedent, must have been an inhabitant of a foreign country at the time of the incident and not otherwise barred from allowance of a claim. As used in these regulations, an inhabitant of a foreign country is one who dwells or resides in the country; neither citizenship nor domicile is required. A corporation or other business association doing business in a foreign country is not necessarily excluded as a claimant because organized under United States law. As to claims arising before 29 July 1956, the claimant must have been an inhabitant of the foreign country in which the incident which gave rise to the claim occurred; a transient was not a proper claimant; and an inhabitant of any part or subdivision of a foreign country is considered to have been an inhabitant of the foreign country as to any claim arising in that country or any part of it.

*b. Claimants excluded.* The following are excluded as claimants:

(1) A national or an ally, or a corporation controlled by a national or an ally, of a country at war or engaged in armed conflict with the United States, or of any country allied with such enemy country, unless the foreign claims commission considering the claim or the local military commander shall determine that the claimant was at the time of the incident, and is, friendly to the United States.

(2) Members and civilian employees of the Armed Forces of the United States and their dependents who are inhabitants of the United States and in a foreign country primarily because of their sponsor's or their own military orders.

*c. Insurers and other subrogees.* An insurer or other subrogee (par. 5i, AR 25–20) may not present a claim in his own name under these regulations. A claim for the entire amount of damage or injury suffered will be presented by, and settlement made solely with, the insured, without regard to the insurance; not with the insurer or with both the insured and the insurer. This leaves undisturbed, as between the parties, the rights of the insured and of the insurer or another who has become subrogated to the rights of the owners of the property lost, damaged, or destroyed, or of the person who is injured or whose death results. This permits the Government to settle with a single claimant and no inquiry into, nor determination of, the relative rights of the parties will be made.

0111

**11. Form of claim.** A claim may be presented orally, but must be reduced to writing before final action is taken by the appropriate approving authority. Any report or complaint to United States authorities of the incident and damage, with request for compensation, although not itemized, is a claim. Any written claim, although not on the prescribed form, will be considered, and may serve as the basis of payment if allowed, if it states substantially the material facts with such definiteness as to give reasonable notice of the time, place, and nature of the incident out of which the claim arose and an estimate or statement of the amount claimed for death, injury, property damage, loss, or destruction. A claim must be stated and, if allowed, paid in the currency either of the country in which the incident occurred or that of which the claimant was or is an inhabitant.

**12. Causation.** *a.* A claim may be allowed under these regulations when the act or omission causing the injury or death, or damage to or loss or destruction of property, except for so-called "other noncombat activities" (par. 3*d*), was negligent, wrongful, or otherwise involved fault and was caused by—

    (1) Military personnel;

    (2) Civilian employees who are citizens of the United States;

    (3) Civilian employees who are not citizens of the United States and were hired in one country for employment in another;

    (4) Civilian employees who are not citizens of the United States, other than those in (3) above, acting within the scope of their employment; or

    (5) Officers or employees of the American Battle Monuments Commission acting within the scope of their employment, as to claims arising on or after 25 July 1956, which will be paid from appropriations for the purposes of the American Battle Monuments Commission.

*b.* Local law or custom pertaining to contributory or comparative negligence, and to joint tort-feasors, will be applied so far as practicable to determine liability.

*c.* Scope of employment will be determined by United States law.

**13. Determination of compensation.** See paragraphs 10 and 11, AR 25-20. Local law and custom relating to elements and quantum of damages will generally be applied in settling claims under these regulations, but neither court costs, including attorney's fees, bail or the like, punitive damages nor interest is allowable.

**14. Command claims service.** The commanding general of each major oversea command or other command which include areas outside the United States, its Territories, and possessions, reporting direct to the Department of the Army will establish under his judge advocate a command claims service for the prompt investigation of incidents occurring within his command, and the processing and settlement of claims in favor of or against the United States. He will designate in orders as the chief of the claims service an officer of his command, preferably a judge advocate, who has had claims experience. Required military and civilian personnel will be detailed to the claims service and necessary branch offices will be established. Direct correspondence within the command claims service, and between officers

0112

of the command claims service and other personnel within the command, is authorized. Claims under these regulations and AR 25–25 will be referred to foreign claims commissions for settlement. The command claims service or any of its offices may furnish administrative services to, and establish and maintain, on a consolidated basis, necessary records of one or more foreign claims commissions.

Section II

FOREIGN CLAIMS COMMISSIONS

**15. General.** All claims under these regulations and AR 25–25 arising outside the United States, its Territories, and possessions, shall be settled by foreign claims commissions. One or more foreign claims commissions may be appointed for each major oversea command to permit prompt settlement of claims within reasonable proximity to the places where the incidents giving rise to the claims occur. A commander reporting direct to the Department of the Army who does not have authority to appoint foreign claims commissions will report to the Chief, Claims Division, Office of The Judge Advocate General, Fort Holabird, Baltimore 19, Maryland, the necessity, if any, in his command for any such commission, its recommended composition, number and location, and the names, grades and qualifications of officers recommended for appointment.

**16. Appointment.** The commander of each major oversea command; the Chief, Claims Division, Office of The Judge Advocate General; and any other officer designated by the Secretary of the Army, are authorized to appoint foreign claims commissions. One copy of each appointing order will be sent immediately to the Chief, Claims Division, Office of The Judge Advocate General, Fort Holabird, Baltimore 19, Maryland.

**17. Qualifications of members.** Each member of a foreign claims commission must be a commissioned officer of the Army with legal training or business or other experience enabling him to analyze evidence, determine facts, and apply laws.

**18. Composition.** Commissions will be composed of one or three members. At least one member of every commission, except one authorized to pay only small claims (sec. III, AR 25–20), will have had legal training and experience. The senior officer of a commission of three members shall be its president; two members present in the command shall constitute a quorum; any action concurred in by two members shall be the action of the commission.

**19. Monetary jurisdiction.** Unless specifically limited in the appointing orders, a commission of one member shall have authority to settle claims not over $500. A commission of three members has authority to settle claims not over $15,000, including claims over $15,000 determined by the Secretary of the Army or his designee to be meritorious in an amount not over $15,000, but any allowance for over $5,000 shall be subject to the approval of the major oversea commander or other appointing officer, or his staff judge advocate, or, when the commission was otherwise appointed, the Chief, Claims

Division, Office of The Judge Advocate General, or, if the claim arose from an act or omission of personnel of the American Battle Monuments Commission, the Secretary of the American Battle Monuments Commission. The officer whose approval is required as to allowances over $5,000 may—

*a.* Approve the allowance in whole or in any specific lesser amount over $5,000, which approval authorizes payment of the amount so approved; or

*b.* Disapprove the allowance in any amount over $5,000 and return the claim file, with necessary comment and recommendation, to the commission for its consideration and action.

**20. Procedure.** A foreign claims commission, upon receipt of a claim and allied documents,. will consider the claim for settlement. It may, if necessary, conduct a further investigation or refer the claim to appropriate authority for the purpose. It may confer with the claimant to resolve or determine facts and, if deemed in the best interest of the Government and permitted by the exigency of the situation, conduct a hearing and take testimony.

**21. Action.** *a. Form.* A foreign claims commission will accomplish its action on DA Form 1978 (Action of Foreign Claims Commission), which will be requisitioned through normal publications supply channels. This action will constitute findings of all necessary facts, and no other form is required for the commission's determination of a claim, but the claim file will contain a statement signed by the commission with calculations or reasoning when the amount allowed differs from the amount claimed, a statement of the applicable local law when the action depends on peculiar local law, and the reason when the claim is disallowed. The action will be in triplicate (each copy signed), but only an original is needed for a disallowance.

*b. Effect.* The action of a foreign claims commission upon claims under these regulations is, by statute, final and conclusive.

*c. Reconsideration.* A foreign claims commission may reconsider an action at any time prior to payment. When the commission is composed of different personnel than at the time of the original action, this may be done only upon presentation of new and material evidence, or to correct manifest mistakes of facts such as errors in calculation, or for fraud or collusion. *Ms. Comp. Gen. B–34728, 3 June 1943.*

**22. Claims over $15,000.** A claim over $15,000 under these regulations will be considered by a foreign claims commission, which will forward the claim and supporting papers as prescribed in paragraph 15*d*, AR 25–20, with its findings of fact and opinion (original only) as to the action to be taken by the Secretary of the Army.

**23. Cross servicing of claims.** Any claim, whether arising from activities of the Army, Navy, Air Force, Marine Corps, or, when operating as a service in the Navy, Coast Guard, may upon request by the service concerned, and shall when the Army has been assigned sole responsibility for its settlement in a foreign country, be settled by a foreign claims commission appointed by the Secretary of the Army or his designee. A claim arising from Army activities in an area

0114

8

where another service has been assigned responsibility for its settlement will be sent for settlement to that service.

[AG 153 (15 Apr 57) JAGD]

By Order of *Wilber M. Brucker*, Secretary of the Army :

MAXWELL D. TAYLOR,
*General, United States Army,*
*Chief of Staff.*

Official :
HERBERT M. JONES,
*Major General, United States Army,*
*The Adjutant General.*

Distribution :
*Active Army:* B.
    To be distributed on a need-to-know basis to all units and headquarters down to and including separate battalions (administrative) and to units and headquarters of comparable size and responsibility.
*NG:* State AG.
*USAR:* None.

0115

## CLAIMS

### CLAIMS ARISING IN FOREIGN COUNTRIES
### (10 U.S.C. 2734)

CHANGES ⎫
⎬
No. 4 ⎭

HEADQUARTERS,
DEPARTMENT OF THE ARMY
WASHINGTON 25, D.C., *4 May 1962*

AR 25-90, 26 April 1957, is changed as follows:

**1. Statutory authority.** The statutory authorities for these regulations are contained in—

*a.* Title 10, United States Code, section 2734 * * * as to claims which arose before 10 August 1956; **title 10, United States Code, section 2736;**

\* \* \* \* \* \* \*

**6. Claims not payable.** No claim will be settled under these regulations if it—

*a.* Results from combat activities; or

*b.* (As superseded by C 2, 28 Apr 58) Falls under any workmen's compensation law or regulation, whether Federal Employees Compensation Act of 7 September 1916 (39 Stat. 742), as amended (5 U.S.C. 751), Longshoremen's and Harborworkers Compensation Act (44 Stat. 1424; 33 U.S.C. 901), or local law or custom, except when specifically authorized by The Judge Advocate General, or his designee, in each case;

\* \* \* \* \* \* \*

**19.** (As changed by C 1, 20 Dec 57) **Monetary jurisdiction.** Unless specifically limited in the appointing orders, a commission of one member shall have authority to settle claims not over $1,000. A commission of * * * over $5,000 may—

\* \* \* \* \* \* \*

**23.** (Superseded) **Cross servicing of claims.** Claims arising in foreign countries under the Foreign Claims Act of January 2, 1942 (55 Stat. 880), as amended (31 U.S.C. 224d), and the Act of July 3, 1943, chapter 189 (57 Stat. 372), as amended (31 U.S.C. 223b), and sections 2733 and 2734 of Title 10, United States Code, as amended, will be settled without regard to the service of the tortfeasor. Any claim, whether arising from activities of the Army, Navy, Air Force, Marine Corps, or the Coast Guard, when operating as a service in the Navy, may, upon request by the service concerned, and shall, when the Army has been assigned responsibility for claims in a particular country, be settled under AR 25-25 or these regulations by a foreign

---

*These changes supersede C 3, 29 September 1958.

0116

claims commission appointed by the Secretary of the Army or his designee. A claim arising from Army activities in an area where another service has been assigned responsibility for claims will be sent to that service for settlement under its regulations. *DOD Directive 5515.3, 22 August 1958.*

**24.** (Added) **Advance payments.** Advance payments pursuant to title 10, United States Code, section 2736, on meritorious claims for compensation for personal injury or death, or property damage, resulting from incidents involving aircraft or missiles, which are otherwise payable under these regulations, are authorized as provided in section V, AR 25–20. However, no advance payment is authorized if the incident occurred in a foreign country in which the Agreement Regarding the Status of Forces of Parties to the North Atlantic Treaty or other similar treaty or agreement is in effect, and the injury, death, damage, or loss was caused by a member or employee of the Department of the Army acting within the scope of employment, or occurred incident to noncombat activities of the Department of the Army, for which the foreign country concerned has responsibility under the treaty or agreement for the settlement of such scope claims.

[AG 153 (12 Jan 62) JAGD]

By Order of the Secretary of the Army:

G. H. DECKER,
*General, United States Army,*
*Chief of Staff.*

Official:

J. C. LAMBERT,
*Major General, United States Army,*
*The Adjutant General.*

Distribution:
*Active Army:* To be distributed in accordance with DA Form 12–9 requirements for DA Regulations, Inspections and Investigations—B.
*NG:* State AG (3).
*USAR:* None.

0117

PPRC, Japan

ARMY REGULATIONS

No. 25-110

HEADQUARTERS,
DEPARTMENT OF THE ARMY
WASHINGTON 25, D.C., *8 January 1963*

## CLAIMS

### CLAIMS IN FAVOR OF THE UNITED STATES FOR THE REASONABLE VALUE OF MEDICAL CARE FURNISHED BY THE ARMY

### Section I. GENERAL

**1. Purpose.** *a.* These regulations are in implementation of the Act of September 25, 1962 (76 Stat. 593, 42 U.S.C. 2651-3). That act provides generally, that in any case in which the United States is authorized or required by law to furnish medical care to a person who has been injured or suffered a disease because of the wrongful or negligent act or omission of a third person, the United States shall have a right to recover from such third person the reasonable value of the medical care furnished. The act applies, for example, to instances in which medical care has been furnished to a member of the Army as a result of either an on or off duty injury, to a dependent, and to any other person who is authorized to receive medical care in Army medical facilities.

*b.* Pursuant to Executive Order 11060, 7 November 1962, the Bureau of the Budget has established rates representing the reasonable value of the medical care furnished or to be furnished (app. II). In each case in which medical care is furnished, a determination is required to be made whether it was for an injury or disease caused under circumstances entitling the United States to recover its costs from a third person. If such circumstances exist, a claim must be asserted for the reasonable value of the medical care. In addition, the individual who received the care may be required to assign to the United States his claim or cause of action against the third person to the extent of the reasonable value of the medical care furnished, to cooperate in the prosecution of claims and actions by the United States against

0113

the third person, and to notify appropriate authorities of a settlement with, or offer of settlement from the third person.

**2. Scope.** These regulations prescribe the procedures for the investigation, determination, assertion, compromise, and settlement of claims for the reasonable value of medical care furnished by the Army for an injury or disease caused by the wrongful or negligent act or omission of some third person.

**3. Definitions.** The definitions of terms set forth in paragraph 4, AR 25–20 are applicable to these regulations except that the following terms as used in these regulations will have the meanings here indicated:

*a. Claim.* The Government's right to recover the reasonable value of medical care.

*b. Medical care.* Includes hospitalization, outpatient treatment, dental care, nursing service, drugs, and other adjuncts such as prostheses and medical appliances furnished or to be furnished by the United States.

*c. Reasonable value of medical care.* The value of the medical care determined in accordance with rates prescribed by the Bureau of the Budget.

*d. Judge advocate.* The judge advocate or staff judge advocate of any command or the legal counsel of a command to which no such officer is assigned, if such counsel is a member of the bar of a Federal court or of the highest court of a state.

*e. Uniformed services.* The Army, the Navy, the Marine Corps, the Air Force, the Coast Guard, the Commissioned Corps of the Coast and Geodetic Survey and the Commissioned Corps of the Public Health Service.

*f. Injured party.* The person who received an injury or contracted a disease which resulted in the medical care. Such a person may be a member of the uniformed services, a dependent, or any other person who is eligible for medical care at Army medical treatment facilities (see sec. III and table I, AR 40–3).

*g. Defendant.* An individual, partnership, association, corporation, or governmental body, foreign or domestic, other than an instrumentality of the United States, against whom the United States has a claim under these regulations.

**4. Application.** *a. Cognizable claims.* Unless otherwise prescribed, cognizable claims comprise all claims for the reasonable value of medical care which has been furnished either by the Army or at the expense of the Army as a result of an injury or disease occurring after 31 December 1962 which was caused by the wrongful or negligent act or omission of some third person (other than or in addition to the United States) under circumstances creating a tort liability upon such person.

*b. Claims not cognizable.*

(1) Claims for not in excess of $50 unless a Government property damage claim is to be asserted under AR 25–105.

(2) Claims for medical care furnished by the Veterans Administration to an eligible veteran for a service connected disability under the provisions of chapter 17, title 38, United States Code.

(3) Claims against employers of seamen treated under the provisions of section 322 of the act of July 1, 1944 (58 Stat. 696), as amended (42 U.S.C. 249).

**5. Basic considerations.** The following basic considerations apply to the investigation, assertion, and processing of claims under these regulations:

*a.* Claims for medical care furnished to persons for which reimbursement is authorized from another uniformed service, or from another Federal department or agency will ordinarily be investigated, asserted, and processed by the uniformed service, department, or agency responsible for making the reimbursement.

*b.* The official responsible for the investigation, assertion, and processing of a claim for medical care may request appropriate assistance from another command of the uniformed services, or from another department or agency. This requested assistance may be to any extent found necessary by the requesting agency, including a complete investigation of the incident, the assertion and processing of the claim, or merely the taking of a statement of a witness. In such cases the requested assistance will be rendered in conformity with the regulations of the service, department, or agency to whom the request is made. Requests for assistance will be made only when the requesting service, department, or agency does not have a facility conveniently located for conducting the investigation or furnishing the assistance requested. Expenses resulting from any assistance given will not be reimbursed.

2

*c.* Claims against a foreign government or a political subdivision, agency, or instrumentality thereof, or against a member of the armed forces or an official or a civilian employee of such foreign government will not be asserted without prior approval of the Department of the Army. Investigation and report thereof, however, will be made as provided in these regulations, unless the provisions of applicable agreements, or regulations in implementation thereof, negate the requirement for such investigation and report.

*d.* The commander of a major oversea command, or of an oversea command designated as a major command for claims purposes, may establish procedures for the processing of claims under these regulations which arise in his command. Such procedures may, to the extent deemed necessary, modify the procedures prescribed herein.

*e.* In the assertion and processing of claims under these regulations due regard will be given to the interests of the injured party. A claim will not be asserted if it appears that collection will result in undue hardship upon the injured party, i.e., preclude or make impracticable his recovery of damages for other than medical care furnished at the expense of the United States. To the extent feasible, the collection effort on behalf of the injured party and on behalf of the Government will be coordinated. Although the judge advocate should not assert a claim on behalf of the injured party, the latter may, if he is eligible therefor, be given legal advice and assistance to the extent authorized by AR 608–50. Similarly, it is not desirable to permit the injured party or a person acting on his behalf to assert or collect a claim for medical care on behalf of the Government. There is no authority to pay attorney's fees for the collection of claims under these regulations.

*f.* Claims against members of the uniformed services or civilian employees of the United States which arise out of acts or omissions committed within the scope of their employment as such members or employees will be investigated and processed in conformity with these regulations, except that such claims will not be asserted without the approval of the Department of the Army (par. 12*f*).

*g.* Claims for medical care which are based upon an incident or circumstances which may give rise to a claim for damage to Army property should be consolidated with the claim for the property damage and processed in accordance with AR 25–105.

**6. Investigative responsibility.** *a.* The commanding general of an army or comparable area command is responsible for the investigation of all incidents which may give rise to claims under these regulations occurring in his area except those within the purview of *b* and *c* below. However, those cases in which the Army is entitled to receive reimbursement in accordance with paragraph 5*a*, will ordinarily be the investigative responsibility of another uniformed service, department, or agency of the United States.

*b.* The commanding officer of a separate company, battalion, battle group, or corresponding unit, or higher echelon, or installation, or activity is responsible for the investigation of incidents involving members of his command or their dependents which may give rise to a claim under these regulations and which occur while the member is assigned to his command.

*c.* State National Guard authorities are responsible for the investigation of incidents involving members of their respective organizations which may give rise to claims under these regulations who are injured while performing armory training under section 502 of title 32, United States Code, or full-time training duty under sections 503–505 of title 32, United States Code, except that in those cases in which the injured party is performing full-time training duty at a service school or with an organization of the active Army, the commander thereof will be responsible for the investigation.

*d.* In a foreign country where no appropriate commander is located the Army attaché is responsible for the required investigation (see sec. VI, AR 1–75).

*e.* Transfer of responsibility for investigation is authorized under the circumstances prescribed in paragraph 7*d*, AR 25–20, and paragraph 5*b* of these regulations.

## Section II. PROCEDURES

**7. Medical care furnished by other Federal medical facilities.** The commanding officer or officer in charge of a Federal medical facility other than an Army medical treatment facility, or of a facility operated by the Panama Canal Company, which gives medical care, the cost of which is reimbursable by the Army, will submit a report thereof to the commanding general of the army or comparable area command in which the medical facility is located. The commander who receives such a report will take the action prescribed in paragraph 10.

**8. Medical care furnished by civilian medical facilities.** When Army authorities are notified that a civilian medical facility has furnished medical care at the expense of the Army, the following action will be taken:

*a. Member of the Army in receipt of medical care.* The commander of the Army medical facility designated in acordance with paragraph 88, AR 40–3, to assume responsibility for the medical records of the member who received the care will take the action prescribed in paragraph 9a.

*b. Nonmilitary patients, except dependents in receipt of medical care.* When civilian medical care is furnished to nonmilitary patients (see par. 21, AR 40–3) under the provisions of section VIII, AR 40–3, the commanding general of the army or comparable area command in which the civilian medical care is obtained will take the action prescribed in paragraph 10. However, if the medical care is furnished to a patient in an Army medical treatment facility, the procedures set forth in paragraph 9 will be followed.

*c. Dependents in receipt of medical care.*

(1) The army or comparable area commander who receives a claim for reimbursement for charges paid by sponsors or patients for civilian medical care to authorized dependents under the provisions of AR 40–122 or AR 40–123, will take the action prescribed in paragraph 10.

(2) When dependents receive medical care outside the United States and Puerto Rico, and payment is made by the Army direct to the civilian source of care, the commander authorizing the payment will take the action prescribed in paragraph 10.

(3) When dependents receive medical care which is paid for in accordance with contractual arrangements under the Dependents Medical Care Program within the United States and Puerto Rico, statements of account together with other available information will be forwarded by The Adjutant General to the commanding general of the Army or comparable area where the treatment was rendered. That officer will take the action prescribed in paragraph 10.

**9. Medical care furnished by Army medical facilities.** *a. Initial report.* The facility furnishing medical care to a person who has been injured will advise the judge advocate thereof, or if there be no such officer assigned, the staff judge advocate of the officer exercising general court-martial jurisdiction over the facility. If only outpatient treatment is involved, a report will not be made unless the value of the medical care exceeds $50.

*b. Action by judge advocate.*

(1) The judge advocate will review the report and if it is incomplete endeavor to obtain the required supplementary information. Unless the provisions of (2) below are applicable, he will then take the action prescribed in paragraph 10 *b* or *c*.

(2) If the command of the officer responsible for making the investigation prescribed in paragraph 11 is not in the vicinity or if the patient is a member of the category of persons for whose medical care the Army is entitled to receive reimbursement from another uniformed service or from a department or agency of the United States, the judge advocate will—

(a) Advise the injured party of his obligations as set forth in paragraph 11b, and obtain a complete statement from him regarding the facts and circumstances surrounding the incident which resulted in the injury or disease; and

(b) Have the injured party execute a Power of Attorney and Assignment (SF 96–A) in triplicate, the injured party retaining one, and the other two

4

한·미국 간의 상호방위조약 제4조에 의한 시설과 구역 및 한국에서의 미국군대의 지위에 관한 협정(SOFA) 전59권. 1966.7.9 서울에서 서명 : 1967.2.9 발효(조약 232호) (V.53 민사청구권 관계자료, 1964-66) 127

to be attached to the report received from the medical treatment facility.

(c) Then take the action prescribed in paragraph 10.

**10. Action on reports of medical care.** *a.* A commander who receives a report, claim for reimbursement, statement of account, or other information indicating that a person has been furnished medical care at the expense of the Army in one of the circumstances described in paragraphs 7 and 8, will refer pertinent information concerning the case to his judge advocate. However, if such a commander does not have a judge advocate on his staff, he will obtain a statement from the injured party regarding the facts and circumstances surrounding the incident which resulted in the injury and subsequent medical care, and forward it together with a brief report of the matter to either the judge advocate providing legal service to his command or to the staff judge advocate of the commander exercising general court-martial jurisdiction over his command dependent upon which office is most accessible to him. Such a report may be made orally or in writing.

*b.* The judge advocate who receives the report or other information of the type described in *a* above, will review it. Unless the report of the other information furnished to him, clearly negates the existence of a claim under these regulations, he will refer the matter to a claims officer appointed by his commander for investigation or forward the report and any other available information:

(1) To the officer responsible for the investigation (par. 6 *b* or *c*), or

(2) To the commander of a subordinate command for investigation by a claims officer of that command or one subordinate thereto, or

(3) To another command of the Army, other uniformed service, or other department or agency of the United States if transfer of responsibility is authorized (par. 6*e*), or

(4) In case the injured party is a member of a category of persons for whose medical care the Army is entitled to receive reimbursement from another uniformed service or from a department or agency of the United States, to the appropriate authority of the uniformed service, department, or agency responsible for making reimbursement. To determine the addressee in such cases see AR 40-3, and appendix I of these regulations.

*c.* If the existence of the claim is negated, the judge advocate will so notify either the commander who referred the case to him, or the commander of the Army medical facility who made an initial report of the case as provided in paragraph 9.

*d.* In those cases in which a report of the type described in paragraph 9 is forwarded to another command, uniformed service, or other department or agency of the United States, the judge advocate should notify the commander of the appropriate Army medical facility in order that any further medical reports concerning that particular case may be sent directly to the same place.

*e.* The commander to whom such a matter is referred pursuant to the provisions of *b* above will refer it to his claims officer for investigation, or take appropriate action to transfer responsibility therefor (par. 6*e*).

**11. Investigations.** *a. Conduct.* Investigations under these regulations will be conducted in the manner prescribed herein and in AR 25-20. However, unnecessary investigation and duplication of investigative effort will be avoided. Thus a line-of-duty investigation should be fully utilized (see AR 600-140). If Army property has been damaged in the same incident in which the injuries were received, the investigation should satisfy the requirements of these regulations and of AR 25-105, and AR 735-11, as may be appropriate.

*b. Advice to injured party.*

(1) The claims officer should promptly contact the injured party and advise him that—

(a) Under 76 Stat. 593, 42 United States Code, §§ 2651-2653, the United States is entitled to recover from the person responsible for his injury the reasonable value of medical care furnished or to be furnished him in the future;

(b) He should seek the advice of legal counsel concerning any possible claim he may have for personal injury;

(c) He should not execute a release or settle any claim which he may have as a result of his injury without first notifying the claims officer or the judge advocate whose address is shown on SF 96–A;

(d) He should not furnish the person responsible for his injury or that person's insurance company with any information or signed statements which might prejudice his personal injury claim; and

(e) If he notifies his own insurance company relative to any injury or property damage he may have suffered, he should inform that company of the right of the United States to recover the reasonable value of the medical care furnished him.

(2) The claims officer should further advise the injured party that a person furnished medical care at the expense of the Army for an injury or disease caused by the negligent or wrongful acts or omissions of another *is required by these regulations:*

(a) To assign in writing to the United States his claim or cause of action against the third person to the extent of the reasonable value of the medical care furnished or to be furnished, or any portion thereof;

(b) Subject to the provisions of Article 31, UCMJ, to furnish such information as may be requested concerning the circumstances giving rise to the injury or disease for which the medical care is being given and concerning any action instituted or to be instituted by or against a third person;

(c) To notify the department or agency concerned of a settlement with, or an offer of settlement from a third person; and

(d) To cooperate in the prosecution of all claims and actions by the United States against such third person.

(3) After giving the injured party the foregoing instructions the claims officer should obtain a complete statement from the injured party regarding the facts and circumstances surrounding the incident which resulted in the injury or disease, and have the injured party execute a Power of Attorney and Assignment (SF 96–A) in triplicate. One copy should be retained by the injured party, and the other copies attached as exhibits to the report of the claims officer. The claims officer should enter in the appropriate space on the reverse side of SF 96–A the address of the judge advocate of the command, or if the command does not have such an officer, the judge advocate of the commander to whom the report will be forwarded (g below).

(4) In appropriate cases the claims officer should give the foregoing advice and instructions to either the next of kin, or the personal representative of the injured party, or the executor or administrator of his estate. Records as to medical history, diagnosis, findings, or treatment may be withheld by the Army pending compliance with the provisions of this paragraph (11b) by the injured party or someone acting for him.

c. *Notice to defendant.* The claims officer will unless the defendant falls within the categories enumerated in paragraph 5c or f complete and mail to the defendant a letter in the form shown in figure 1, in duplicate together with a copy of the executed Power of Attorney and Assignment (SF 96–A). A copy of the letter will accompany the report of investigation. Before sending such a letter, the claims officer may consult with the appropriate judge advocate.

TO:

Pursuant to 76 Stat. 593, 42 United States Code, §§ 2651–2653, the United States of America is entitled to recover the reasonable value of hospital, medical, surgical, or dental care and treatment (including prostheses and medical appliances) furnished or to be furnished to _____ in connection with injuries

(Name of injured party)

sustained on _____ at _____, if investigation should establish that your wrongful

(Date)

or negligent acts or omissions were the proximate cause of the mentioned injuries.

You should immediately send a copy of this notice to your insurance company.

Inquiries concerning this matter should be addressed to: (enter here the address of the judge advocate of the command, or if the command does not have one, of the judge advocate of the commander to whom the report will be forwarded (par. 11g)).

*Figure 1*

6

*d. Notice of legal proceedings.* If the claims officer receives information that legal proceedings arising out of the incident which he is investigating have been commenced, he will telephonically advise the judge advocate of his command, or if the command does not have such an officer, the judge advocate of the commander to whom the report will be forwarded (*g* below).

*e. Report.* The claims officer will prepare a report of his investigation as provided in AR 25-20 and will include all pertinent information required by DA Form 1208 (Report of Claims Officer), complete in specific detail as to the location, time, circumstances, and personnel involved in the incident, the nature and extent of any damage to Government property, and identification and statements of all material witnesses. In addition the report will contain—

(1) Identification of each defendant by name, address, and occupation.

(2) In case a defendant is a member of a uniformed service or an employee of the United States, findings whether such defendant was acting within or without the scope of his employment at the time of the incident.

(3) Findings and recommendations as to the liability or nonliability of each defendant and the basis or reasons therefor.

(4) Available information as to the financial responsibility of the defendant, including the nature and extent of any insurance coverage and the name and address of the insurance carrier.

(5) A statement as to whether a voluntary offer of payment or compromise has been made by the defendant or his insurer, and whether such offer is deemed fair and reasonable under the circumstances. Include also the original of the offer if in writing, or a statement of the terms of the offer, if verbal, and any check or money order voluntarily submitted as payment or as a compromise offer.

(6) A statement indicating whether the injured party, his next of kin, or the executor or administrator of his estate has received any payments from a defendant or his insurance company or signed any releases.

(7) Information with respect to any legal proceedings which have been instituted as a result of the incident which he is investigating. This information should include the names and addresses of the parties to the proceedings and of their attorneys, and the name and address of the court.

(8) Appropriate exhibits in support of the findings and recommendations. These should include:

(a) Statements of the reasonable value of the medical care furnished. These should be obtained from the medical treatment facilities which rendered the medical care. If the medical care has not been concluded, the report should indicate the prognosis and the names and addresses of the medical facilities rendering the medical care. In addition the claims officer should make suitable arrangements to insure that the statements are obtained when the medical care is concluded.

(b) The initial and any subsequent reports of medical care from medical treatment facilities.

(c) In cases of damage to Army property itemized repair bills or estimates (see par 5b(4), AR 25-105).

(d) A copy of the executed Power of Attorney and Assignment (SF 96-A).

(e) Copies of any releases given to a defendant or his insurance company by the injured party, his next of kin, or the executor or administrator of his estate.

(f) Copies of any pertinent correspondence with a defendant including—a copy of the letter sent to him by the claims officer (fig. 1), copies of letters addressed by the injured party, his next of kin, or the executor or administrator of his estate to a defendant or the latter's insurance company, or letters received from those sources by the claims officer, the injured party, his next of kin, or the executor or administrator of his estate.

*f. Disposition of report.* The claims officer will forward his report when it is completed to the commander who appointed him. He will not delay its submission pending completion of the medical care or receipt of statements of medical expenses from distant medical facilities. He will make no demand on a defendant.

*g. Action by commander.* If he has a judge advocate, the commander will refer the report to such officer for action as indicated in paragraph 12. If he has no judge advocate, he will review the file and, after taking any corrective action deemed necessary to assure completeness of the file, will either approve the recommendation of the claims officer or make new or additional recommendations of his own, provided the basis for such action is shown. He will then forward the report through claims channels to a higher command which has a judge advocate.

**12. Determination and assertion of claims.** The judge advocate who receives the claims officer's report will review the file and, after taking any corrective action deemed necessary to assure completeness of the file, will make a written determination as to the liability or nonliability of the defendant, and his basis or reasons for such determination. He will attach his determination to the report. He will take further action as indicated below:

*a.* If he determines that the defendant is liable, he will, unless the defendant falls within one of the categories enumerated in paragraph 5 *c* or *f*, promptly notify the defendant of the right of the United States to recover the reasonable value of the medical care furnished the injured party. He may use SF 96 (Notice of Claim) for this purpose.

*b.* If the judge advocate determines that the defendant is not liable, he will dispose of the file as provided in paragraph 14.

*c.* If it appears that a defendant or insurer has presented or filed a claim against the Government arising from the same incident which gave rise to the claim under these regulations, the claims in favor of and against the Government will be processed together and action under this regulation will be taken by the authority authorized to pay the claim against the Government under AR 25-20 and associated regulations. Disposition of the claim in favor of the Government will be consistent with action upon the claim against the Government.

*d.* He will establish liaison with the injured party or persons acting on his behalf to insure that:

(1) If the medical care has not been concluded, arrangements are made to obtain periodic reports from the injured party regarding his convalescence.

(2) The United States has an opportunity to join or intervene in any action or proceeding brought by or against the injured party, or persons acting on his behalf including his insurance company, for damages arising out of the incident which resulted in the claim (par. 18).

(3) Action by the United States to collect the claim on behalf of the Government will not result in undue hardship upon the injured party or operate to deny to the injured party recovery of damages for other than medical care.

(4) The injured party is aware of the right of the United States to recover the reasonable value of the medical care provided, and of his obligations to the United States with respect to this right.

*e.* He will determine the amount of the claim to be asserted against the defendant—

(1) If the medical care has been concluded the judge advocate should insure that the file contains complete statements of the cost of the medical care provided the injured party. If all or a portion of the medical care was furnished by an Army medical facility he may request the commander thereof to prepare a consolidated statement showing the total cost of the medical care provided. However, if a portion of the medical care was provided in a facility other than the one to which the request for the statement is made, he should furnish the commander who is asked to prepare the statement with copies of the reports of medical care contained in the claim file in order that none may be overlooked in the preparation of the consolidated statement.

(2) If the medical care has not been concluded, and it appears that it will continue over a long period of time, the judge advocate should attempt to obtain an estimate of the reasonable value of the medical care to be furnished, and use this estimate to determine the amount of the claim. It is desirable that a claim be

8

0125

한·미국 간의 상호방위조약 제4조에 의한 시설과 구역 및 한국에서의 미국군대의 지위에 관한 협정(SOFA)
전59권. 1966.7.9 서울에서 서명 : 1967.2.9 발효(조약 232호) (V.53 민사청구권 관계자료, 1964-66) 131

asserted at the earliest possible time, therefore action should not be deferred indefinitely pending conclusion of the medical care.

(3) If a reasonably accurate estimate of the value of the medical care cannot be obtained, the judge advocate may if he deems it impracticable to retain the file, forward it through claims channels to the judge advocate of the Army or comparable area command with a request that further action on the claim be taken by that officer.

(4) A claim file may also be transmitted to another command for assertion and processing in an appropriate case (par. 5b). Such a case might arise if the injured party is transferred to another medical facility for further treatment, or accompanies a sponsor on a change of station.

f. If the defendant falls within the categories enumerated in paragraph 5 c or f, he will make no demand for payment upon such defendant but will forward the claim file together with his recommendations regarding assertion of the claim through claims channels to The Judge Advocate General, Department of the Army, Washington 25, D.C., ATTN: Chief, Litigation Division.

g. If he determines that the defendant is liable but that for the convenience of the Government or because it will result in undue hardship upon the injured party (par. 5e) the claim of the United States should not be asserted, the judge advocate will—

(1) If the claim is in excess of $2,500, or if he does not have authority to waive the claim or does not believe that the claim should be waived, prepare a seven paragraph memorandum of opinion (see par. 8, app. I, AR 25-20) and forward it together with the claim through claims channels to The Judge Advocate General, Department of the Army, Washington 25, D.C., ATTN: Chief, Litigation Division.

(2) If the claim is not in excess of $2,500 he may, subject to the provisions of paragraph 13b, waive the claim in whole or in part and if necessary execute a release on behalf of the United States. He will then dispose of the file as prescribed in paragraph 14.

h. If he determines that the defendant is liable and that a claim should be asserted against him at this time, cause a written demand to be made upon such defendant for payment in full of the amount determined to be due. A copy of the demand and any response thereto will be attached to the claim file.

i. If payment in full is received, the judge advocate will accept payment, deposit it with the nearest disbursing officer, execute a release on behalf of the United States, and dispose of the file as prescribed in paragraph 14.

j. If the defendant admits liability and offers to discharge his indebtedness by means of installment payments, the judge advocate will accept such payments and deposit them with the nearest disbursing officer. He will retain the file until full payment has been made or until it becomes apparent that the defendant is not going to make full payment. In the latter case the judge advocate will take the action prescribed in k below. If it is impracticable for the judge advocate to retain the file pending the collection of the claim by means of installment payments, he may forward it through claims channels to the judge advocate of the Army or comparable area command with a request that collection be effected by that officer.

k. If the defendant fails to comply with the demand for payment within a reasonable time or if he makes an offer of compromise which the judge advocate does not have authority to accept (par. 13) or which he does not deem acceptable, the judge advocate will prepare a seven paragraph memorandum of opinion (see par. 8, app. I, AR 25-20) and forward the claim file through claims channels (par. 15) to The Judge Advocate General, Department of the Army, Washington 25, D.C., ATTN: Chief, Litigation Division.

l. If the defendant makes an offer of compromise which the judge advocate has authority to accept, and which in his opinion should be accepted, the judge advocate will take the action prescribed in i above. If he does not deem the offer acceptable he will take the action prescribed in k above.

13. Settlement and waiver of claims. a. Authority. The judge advocate who asserts a claim under these regulations, or the judge advocate to whom such a claim has been forwarded as provided in these regulations, or the chief of a United

0126

States Army Claims Service, or a designee of The Judge Advocate General may, subject to the restrictions in *b* below:

(1) Accept the full amount of a claim and execute a release therefor,

(2) Compromise or settle and execute a release of any such claim, not in excess of $2,500, or

(3) Waive and in this connection release any claim, not in excess of $2,500, in whole or in part for the convenience of the Government or for one of the reasons set forth in paragraph 5*e*.

*b. Restrictions.* The authority granted in *a* above will not be exercised in any case in which—

(1) A claim has been asserted against the Government which is based upon the same incident which gave rise to a claim under these regulations, pending final action on that claim.

(2) The claim has been referred to the Department of Justice.

(3) A suit by a defendant has been instituted against the United States or the injured party and the suit arises out of the occurrence which gave rise to the claim.

(4) The claim is in excess of $2,500. Such claims may be compromised, waived, and released only with the prior approval of the Department of Justice.

## Section III. ADMINISTRATIVE MATTERS

**14. Disposition of claims files.** If the claim has been compromised or settled and payment has been received, or if a determination of nonliability has been made, the claim file will be forwarded to the judge advocate of the army or comparable area command, if it is not already at that headquarters. The file will be placed in the records of the army, or comparable area command and will be disposed of in accordance with chapter 4, AR 345-210. Retained records will satisfy the requirements of paragraph 22, AR 25-20.

**15. Review of claims files.** The judge advocate of an army or comparable area command will review all claims files received from the judge advocate of a subordinate command unless final

action has been taken thereon pursuant to the provisions of paragraphs 12*b*, *g*(2), *i*, and *l*, and will enter his own determinations and recommendations therein. In appropriate cases he may take further action to compromise, settle, or waive a claim, subject to the provisions of paragraph 13.

**16. Releases.** In those cases in which a judge advocate is authorized to execute a release (pars. 12 and 13) care should be taken that the release extends only to the claim of the United States and does not purport to release any claim the injured party may have for his other damages. An acceptable form for such a release is shown in figure 2.

GENERAL RELEASE
(AR 25-110)

----------------------
(Date)

The United States Army, in consideration of the payment of $_____, does hereby release and forever discharge
------------------------------------------ from all claims and demands for and by reason of the reasonable value of
(Name of defendant)
medical care furnished by the Army to ---------------------------------------- resulting from an injury or disease
(Name of injured party)
to such person arising out of an accident or incident occurring on or about _____ at _____.
(Date)          (Location)
Witnessed by:                                                          UNITED STATES ARMY
------------------------------------.                         By ----------------------------
(Name, grade, and title)
------------------------------------.

*Figure 2*

**17. Receipts.** The commanding officer appointing a claims officer, his superior commander, the judge advocate of any command, or any officer designated by them for that purpose, may on request, execute and deliver to any defendant making payment in full or a payment as an offer of compromise settlement subject to the approval of the proper authority, a receipt. An acceptable form for such a receipt is shown in figure 3.

RECEIPT FOR PAYMENT FOR REASONABLE VALUE OF MEDICAL CARE
(AR 25-110)

-------------------
(Date)

Acknowledgment is hereby made of the receipt by the United States of America of a (check, money order) in the amount of $_____ payable to the order of the Treasurer of the United States by _____

(Name of defendant)

_____ as (full, payment, an offer of compromise settlement subject to the approval by proper authority) under the provisions of AR 25-110, of the amount due the United States by reason of medical care furnished to

_____ resulting from an injury or disease to such person arising out of an

(Name of injured party)

accident or incident occurring on or about _____ at _____.

(Date) (Location)

-------------------
(Name, grade, and title)

*Figure 3*

**18. Litigation.** In order to collect a claim for medical care the Department of Justice may intervene or join in any action, or bring suit in an appropriate court. To protect the rights of the United States there must be reported to the Department of Justice the commencement of legal proceedings by the injured party, his guardian, personal representative, estate, dependents, or survivors, against the third person who is liable for the injury or disease, or the commencement of legal proceedings by a third party against the injured party or his estate if it appears that the United States has an interest therein. Commencement of legal proceedings will be reported in accordance with paragraph 7, AR 27-5, followed by a litigation report. If necessary, the judge advocate may communicate directly with the local United States Attorney with regard to such proceedings.

**19. Administrative claims report.** Pending changes to AR 25-21 and DA Form 3 (Administrative Claims Report) commands to which a judge advocate is assigned will report in section D of DA Form 3, the following information concerning claims under these regulations:

*a.* Number and total amount of claims asserted.

*b.* Number and total amount of claims collected in full.

*c.* Number and total amount of claims waived.

*d.* In the case of compromise settlements, the number and total amount originally claimed and the total amount for which settled.

0128

# APPENDIX I

## ADDRESSEES OF REPORTS OF MEDICAL CARE

Reports of medical care furnished by Army medical facilities or at the expense of the Army in civilian medical facilities to persons for whose medical care the Army is entitled to receive reimbursement from another uniformed service or from a department, or agency of the United States (par. 10b(4) should be forwarded to the appropriate addressee shown below:

| Service, department, or agency responsible for reimbursement | Addressee |
|---|---|
| U.S. Air Force | Base Staff Judge Advocate of the Air Force base nearest the place where the medical care was provided. |
| U.S. Navy | Commander of the Naval District wherein the incident occurred ATTN: District Legal Officer if in the United States; if outside the United States, The Judge Advocate General, U.S. Navy, Washington 25, D.C. |
| U.S. Coast Guard | Public Health Division, Office of The General Counsel, Department of Health, Education and Welfare, Washington 25, D.C. |
| Department of Labor | Subrogation Branch, Office of The Solicitor, Bureau of Employees Compensation, Department of Labor, Washington 25, D.C. |
| Veterans Administration | Director of Veterans Hospital responsible for providing medical care to the injured party if known, otherwise to the Director of the nearest Veterans Hospital. |

## APPENDIX II

## BUREAU OF THE BUDGET RATES

ESTABLISHMENT AND DETERMINATION OF CERTAIN RATES FOR USE IN CONNEC-
TION WITH RECOVERY FROM TORTIOUSLY LIABLE THIRD PERSONS OF COST
OF HOSPITAL AND MEDICAL CARE AND TREATMENT FURNISHED BY THE
UNITED STATES

By virtue of the authority vested in the President by section 2(a) of the Act of September 25, 1962 (Public Law 87–693; 76 Stat. 593) and delegated to the Director of the Bureau of the Budget by section 1 of Executive Order No. 11060 of November 7, 1962 (27 F.R. 10925), the following rates are established for use in connection with the recovery, as authorized by such Act, from tortiously liable third persons of the cost of hospital and medical care and treatment furnished by the United States (Part 43 of Chapter I of Title 28 of the Code of Federal Regulations), and have been determined to represent the reasonable value of hospital, medical, surgical or dental care and treatment (including prostheses and medical appliances) furnished or to be furnished:

(a) For such care and treatment furnished by the United States in Federal hospitals, with the exception of Freedmen's Hospital, Washington, D.C., and Canal Zone Government Hospitals—

| | Effective July 1, 1962 to June 30, 1963 | Effective July 1, 1963 and thereafter |
|---|---|---|
| *Hospital care—per inpatient day* | | |
| Federal general and tuberculosis hospitals | $36.00 | $37.00 |
| Federal mental hospitals | 14.25 | 14.75 |
| *Outpatient Medical and Dental Treatment* | | |
| Per facility visit | 7.00 | 8.00 |

(b) For such care and treatment furnished at Government expense in a facility not operated by the United States, the rates shall be the amounts expended by the United States for such care and treatment;

(c) For such care and treatment at Freedmen's Hospital, Washington, D.C., the rates shall be those charged full-pay private patients by the hospital at the time the care and treatment is furnished by the United States; and

(d) For such care and treatment at Canal Zone Government Hospitals, the rates shall be those established, and in effect at the time the care and treatment is furnished, by the Canal Zone Government for such care and treatment furnished to beneficiaries of other United States Government agencies.

| December 6, 1962 | /s/ Daird S. Bell |
|---|---|
| | Director, Bureau of the Budget |

[AG 153 (2 Jan 63) JAG]

By Order of the Secretary of the Army:

EARLE G. WHEELER,
*General, United States Army,*
*Chief of Staff.*

Official:
J. C. LAMBERT,
*Major General, United States Army,*
*The Adjutant General.*

Distribution:
*Active Army, NG, and USAR:* To be distributed in accordance with DA Form 12–9 requirements for DA Regulations, Inspections and Investigations—B.

EX GRATIA:

Out of grace; as a matter of grace, favor, or
indulgence; gratuitous. A term applied to anything
accorded as a favor; as distinguished from that which
may be demanded ex debito, as a matter of right.

EXDEBITO JUSTITIAE:

From or as a debt of justice; in accordance with
the requirement of justice; of right; as a matter of
irght. The opposite of ex gratia.

0131

# 손해배상 청구에 관한 독일 보충협정 개요

## ( 보충협정 41조 )

1. 손해배상은 "나토"협정 8조와 하기보충조항의 규정에 의하여 처리한다.

2. 아래 경우에는 손해배상을 하지 않는다 :

   가. 군인 및 군속이 정상적인 통행목적으로 사용시에 일어나는 공공도로, 고량, 수로 및 기타 공공교통 시설에 대한 손해.

   나. 점령비, 위임 혹은 지원비로 건설 혹은 구입한 재산 으로서 군인 및 군속이 사용하는 중에 일어난 손해.

3. 가. 독일연방이 소유하는 재산으로서 군인 및 군속이 배타적으로 사용중에 있는 재산의 손해에 대하여는 청구를 포기한다. 이는 수개의 파견국 군대 혹은 독일군대와 파견국 군대가 공동으로 사용할때에도 동일하다.

   단, 상기의 포기는 고의 또는 중대한 과실로 일어난 손해와 독일연방 철도 혹은 독일연방우편에 대한 손해에는 적용하지 않는다.

   나. "나토"협정 8조 2항의 (ⅱ)(공무중 ..1,400 이하의 정부재산 손해청구 포기)의 규정은 독일연방 철도, 독일연방 우편 및 연방도로의 손해에는 적용하지 않는다.

4. 독일연방은 협정발효전에 일어난 주정부( Land )가 소유하는 재산의 손해에 대한 파견국의 배상책임을 해제한다.

5. 독일연방의 군인 및 군속의 공무수행 혹은 선박, 차량 및 항공기의 운행으로 일어나는 독일연방내에 있으며 군인 및 군속이 사용하는 파견국의 정부재산에 대한

0132

손해는 그 청구를 포기한다.

단, 고의 혹은 중대한 과실로 일어나는 손해는 포기
하지 않는다.

6. "나토" 협정 8조 5항 (공무중 제3자에 대한 손해)
과 본조항의 규정은 파견국의 군인 및 군속 상호간의
손해 혹은 파견국 당국이 법적으로 책임이 있는
파견국 군인 및 군속에 대한 손해에는 적용하지 않는다

7. 보충협정 72조 2항의 비독일 비상업기관은 별도의 합의가
없는한 소속국의 군대의 일부로 간주하여 손해배상청구의
해결은 "나토" 협정 8조와 본조항에 의한다.

8. 군인 및 군속의 손해배상 책임은 독일의 제반 규정의
적용을 받지 않는다는 이유로 면제되지 않으며 독일
군대에게도 규정 적용이 면제되어 있는 사항에 대하여
는 그 사항에 대한 독일군대의 손해배상 책임과 동일한
범위내에서 책임을 부담한다.

9. 가. 공무진행중 제3자에 손해를 가하거나 혹은 법적으로
제3자에 대한 손해의 책임이 있는 경우로서, 동
제3자가 파견국측에도 손해를 가하여 그 배상책임이
있을 때에는, 제3자의 손해배상청구에 대하여 파견
국의 손해배상 청구를 상쇄한다.

나. 독일연방은 행정적인 합의사항에 의거 또한 파견국의
요청에 의하여, 독일 연토내에 거주하는 사람이 그
파견국에 가한 손해에 대한 배상청구를 한다.
단, 이는 계약상의 손해배상 청구에는 적용되지 않으
며, 독일연방이 손해배상 청구를 함에 있어
행정에 필요한 일반적인 비용보다 초과하여 경비
지출을 하는 경우에는 파견국이 그 초과 경비를
보상한다.

10. 1955년 5월 5일 이전에 군인 혹은 군속이 배타적으로
사용하기 시작하여 현행협정이 발효한 후에 반환한
독일연방 및 각주의 소유를 제외한 기타 시설 혹은
동산의 손해에 대한 배상은 독일연방과 파견국이 균등
하게 분담한다.

0133

한·미국 간의 상호방위조약 제4조에 의한 시설과 구역 및 한국에서의 미국군대의 지위에 관한 협정(SOFA)
전59권. 1966.7.9 서울에서 서명 : 1967.2.9 발효(조약 232호) (V.53 민사청구권 관계자료, 1964-66) 139

11. 가. 관기 파견국측이 조사후 손해책임을 정할수 없을
　　　경우를 제외하고는, 파견국은 "나토"협정8조8항
　　　에서 취급된 문제에 관한 증명서를 제공하여야
　　　하며 ; 파견국은 만일 독일당국 혹은 독일법정이
　　　손해배상청구에 대한 조사를 진행하고 있는 동안에
　　　상기 증명서에 포함된 내용과 상이한 결론으로
　　　도달될 사정이 있다고 고려할때에는, 독일 당국의
　　　요청에 의거하여, 동 증명서를 재검토한다.
　　나. 만약 양측의 고위관계 당국간에 토의로서 그이상
　　　해결될수 없는 의견의 차이가 있을 때에는
　　　"나토"협정8조8항의 절차에 따라 해결한다.
　　다. 독일당국이나 혹은 법정은 상기 증명서 혹은 중재
　　　인의 결정과 일치되게 결정을 내려야 한다.
12. 가. "나토"협정 8조와 본조의 규정은 협정 발효후
　　　그원인이 발생하였거나 혹은 발생한 것으로 생각되는
　　　손해에 적용하여야 한다.
　　나. 협정발효전에 발생하였거나 혹은 발생된 것으로
　　　보이는 손해에 대하여는 협정 발효전까지 적용하던
　　　규정에 의거 취급되어야 한다.
13. 손해배상 청구의 해결을 위한 파견국당국과 독일당국간의
　　절차를 조정하기 위하여 행정적인 협정을 체결하여야
　　한다.

### 합의 의사록

1. 보충협정 41조는 계약 혹은 준계약관계에서 일어나는
　　손해에 관한 배상청구에는 적용하지 않는다.
2. 가. (i) 독일연방 철도와 우편에 속하는 재산을 제외
　　　하고는 공공도로나 기타 독일연방의 재산이 기동
　　　연습이나 기타의 훈련때문에 손해를 입은 경우로서
　　　보충협정 41조에 의거 배상을 지불할 성질의 사건인
　　　때에 파견국 군대는 배상금을 지불하는 대신 그들

0134

자신이 그손해에 대한 원상 회복을 시킬수 있다.

(ii) 파견국 군대가 공공도로에 대한 손괴를 스스로 보수하려 할때에는 권위있는 독일당국과 협의하여야 하며, 만약 독일당국이 상당히 기술적인 건설이라든가 혹은 교통정리상의 이유로 반대할때에는 그들자신이 보수작업을 하여서는 안된다.

이상의 경우 혹은 (i)항에서 지적한 기타 손해의 경우, 파견국 군대가 보수를 한다는 일반적인 양해가 사전에 성립되었을 때에는 개별적인 사건에 대하여 독일당국과의 접촉을 필요로 하지 않는다.

나. 상기 (가)항 이외의 경우, 파견국 군대가 직접 피해자와의 합의하에 손해에 대한 원상회복을 하는 것을 금지하지 않는다.

다. 상기 (가) 및 (나)항의 경우, 피해자는 그의 견해로 보아 손해가 충분히 혹은 적합히 원상회복이 되지 않았을 때에는 그의 합리적인 손해배상을 주장하는 것을 금지하지 않는다.

3. 손해배상업무가 신속히 처리될수 있도록 "나토"협정 8조와 보충협정 41조에 의한 손해배상청구를 할수있는 합리적인 기간을 설정하여야 한다. 이런 목적을 위하여 독일연방은 적합한 입법조치를 하여야 한다.

4. 보충협정 41조 3 (가)항에 의한 독일연방의 포기 (파견국이 사용중인 독일연방재산의 손해에 대한 배상청구 포기) 는 수선과 정비의 책임을 이행하지 못하는 데에서 일어나는 손해에는 적용되지 않는다.

상기 손해배상청구에 대한 해결규정이 다른 합의된 내용에 고합되어 있지 않는 사항에 대하여는 행정적인 합의사항으로 그 절차를 규정하여야 한다.

0135

5. 독일연방이 그주를 소유하는 법인의 재산으로서 파견국
   의 군인 혹은 군속에게 무료로 배타적인 사용을
   인정한 범위내에서는 독일연방은 보충협정 41조 3 (가)
   항에 의거 독일연방이 소유하는 재산에 대한 손해배상
   청구를 포기한것과 같은 방법으로 그재산에 대한 파견국
   의 손해배상책임을 면제시켜야 한다.

6. (가) 보충협정 41조 3 (가)항과 5항의 후단에 규정된 경우
   ( 고의 또는 중대한 과실로 인한 손해에 대하여는
   독일당국이 포기하지 않는다는 단서)에 관한 문제로
   견위있는 독일당국과 파견국 당국간에 고의 또는 중대한
   과실 여부에 관하여 의견의 차이가 있을 때에는, 양 측
   의 당국은 협상을 하여야 한다.
   (나) 상기 의견의 차이를 양측 고위당국이 더이상 토의
   를 계속 하여도 해결할수 없을 때에는 "나토"협정
   8조 2 (a)항에 의한 중재인이 결정한다.

7. 보충협정 41조 4항 주 ( Land )가 소유하는 재산으로서
   파견국 군대가 사용하는 재산에 대하여는 파견국 당국
   과 독일당국이 보충협정 발효일자로 그재산의 상태를
   합동으로 결정하여야 한다. 이와 같은 결정은 재산을
   반환할때에도 하여야 한다. 손해에 대한 배상청구는
   상기 재산상태에 대한 결정을 근거로 하여 해결하여야
   한다.

8. 미국적십자 및 Maryland 대학은 보충협정 41조 7항의
   목적을 위하여 군대의 일부로서/되거나 혹은 취급되지
   않으며, 손해배상청구에 대한 해결에 있어서는 독일
   관할건으로 부터 면제되지 않는다.

9. 보충협정 41조 13항의 행정적인 합의사항에는 "나토"
   협정 8조에 도합된 절차와 상이한 합의도 포함될수
   있다.

0136

1. General.

Payment of the claims of citizens and residents of Korea
is authorized by an act of the United States Congress called the
"Foreign Claims Act." This law provides for the payment
of maritorious claims by the inhabitants of countries in which
United States troops are stationed, based on death, personal
injury, or property demage caused by noncombat activities of
U.S. armed forces.  This law is implemented in detail by
regulations of the Army, Navy and Air Force.

2.  U.S. liability.

Under the foreign claims program United States liability is
established when injury, death, or property damage is caused
(partially or wholly) by the careless or wrongful act of a member
or U.S. civilian employee of the United States Forces Korea,
or by other noncombat activities of those forces.  Liability also
is assumed if the damages are caused by Korean civilian
employees while acting within the scope of their employment.
As would be expected, the United States cannot assume responsibility
for damages caused by members of the Korean Army or employees
of the Korean Government, even though these persons may be
engaged with U.S. forces at the time in the joint mission of
maintaining military readiness against a common enemy.  Cognizance
is taken, however, of the unique cooperation between the military
forces of the Republic of Korea and of the United States by
which Korean military persons are integrated into U.S. Army
units, known as the Korean Augmentation to the United States
Army (KATUSA).  Liability is assumed and compensation is paid

0137

for injuries and damages caused by these persons when
acting within the scope of their assigned duties for U.S.
Army units.

3. Investigation of claims.

An elaborate system is prescribed by U.S. Army directives
for the investigation and reporting of detailed facts and
circumstances involved in every incident in which a person
suffers injury, death, or property damage as the result of military
activities. Hundreds of investigating officers and
commanders of Army units and installations are responsible for
investigating the incidents and accidents in which members
of the USFK are involved. Detailed reports of the investigations
are forwarded to higher authority for approval, and a copy of
each report is forwarded to the Claims Service. In some instances
additional investigation and inquiry may be required in order
to fairly evaluate a claim. This further investigation is more
effectively handled by personnel specially trained in the law
and procedures pertaining to the payment of claims. Consequently,
the investigation at this point is normally conducted by the claims
service which processes the claims against the United States.

4. The Claims Service in Korea.

a. The Department of Defense has designated the Army to
settle claims arising in Korea which are caused by the
activities of members and employees of the United States
Forces Korea. This is accomplished through the U.S. Armed
Forces Claims Service, Korea, and Claims Commissions attached
to that organization, located on the Yongsan Military
Reservation. The establishment of Claims Commissions are
required by the "Foreign Claims Act," and their primary duty
is to consider and settle claims submitted by the inhabitants

0138

of the country involved. A commissioner must be a commissioned officer and normally is a judge advocate officer of the military service concerned. One-member commissions are empowered to adjudge and pay claims for not more than $1000 (129,500 Won) and three-member commissions may pay claims for not more than $15,000 (1,942,500 Won). Claims in excess of the latter amount are transmitted to the Department of the Army for approval by the Congress before payment may be made. Commissions of any of the military services may consider and pay claims caused by the activities and members of the other services.

b. The U.S. Armed Forces Claims Service is manned by fourteen American persons and thirteen citizens of Korea. Seven of the Korean employees are specially trained claims investigators and classified among the highest paid Korean employees of the Eighth Army. Each of the three commissioned officers (including the Chief) is appointed as a one-member commission, and together they constitute a three-member commission. In addition to the office of the Chief and the Claims Commissions, the Claims Service is organized as follows:

| Administrative Branch | Investigation Branch | Claims Branch | Payment Branch |
|---|---|---|---|
| 5 U.S. | 1 U.S. | 3 U.S. | 2 U.S |
| KN | 5KN | 1 KN | 2 KN |

c. The functions of the four branches are somewhat self-evident.

Briefly:

(1) The Administration Branch maintains all records of claims, reports of investigation, and related files. When a claim initially is received in the Claims Service it is channeled to the Administration Branch for recording and

0133

indexing. A claim number is assigned by which the claim may be readily identified at all future times, and a portfolio prepared in which all documents are filed which pertain to the claim.

(2) The Investigation Branch is comprised of five (5) Korean national employees, all classified as senior investigators, and one commissioned officer as supervisor. Upon receiving a claims portfolio from the Administration Branch, the file is assigned to an investigator for translation of documents which are submitted in Korean and for development of the essential evidence required for complete adjudication of the claim. As a general principle the securing of evidence in support of a claim is the responsibility of the claimant. A large part of our investigators' duties, however, is to assist the claimant in securing the evidence and in many instances to secure the evidence for the claimant. When the Investigation Branch considers investigation is complete, the portfolio is transferred to the Claims Branch for further processing.

The Investigation Branch also interviews all claimants who visit the Claims Service, assists them in preparing their claims on bilingual forms provided, and advises of the nature of evidence and formal documents (such as family registers, certificates of land ownership) that are required to support their claims. It may be noted at this point that whether a claimant desires to employ an attorney to represent him in connection with his claim is a matter solely within the discretion of the claimant. The Claims Service offers all the advice and assistance that is needed to file and establish the claim.

(3) The Claims Branch examines the claims portfolio to

determine whether evidence is sufficient to support final adjudication of the claim. A resume of the claim is prepared for the benefit of the Chief and the claims commissions, including a recommendation as to the amount of compensation that should be awarded.

(4) Upon completion of the processing of a claim by the Claims Branch, the portfolio is transferred to the Chief of the Claims Service for examination and consideration. The Chief assigns claims not in excess of $1,000 (129,500 Won) to the one-member commissions for final adjudication. As President of the three-member commission, he convenes the commission for consideration and adjudication of claims in excess of $1,000 (129,500 Won). If the claim exceeds $15,000 (1,942,500 Won), he prepares a detailed memorandum and recommendation that is forwarded with the claim file to the Department of the Army for final action.

(5) When a commission adjudges an award in a claim, the portfolio is transferred to the Payment Branch. This Branch notifies the claimant of the amount of award and prepares a settlement agreement for the claimant to sign. Upon receipt of the signed settlement agreement arrangements are made for claimant to receive his compensation. Most claimants are paid on the Yongsan Military Reservation. In many instances, however, arrangements are made for claimants to be paid at a military post near their homes. This is particularly true when claimant lives a long distance from Seoul, as in the Taegu or Pusan area. In addition, when a claimant is too old or ill to travel a representative of the Claims Service takes the compensation to him at his home. This also is done in most small claims in order that claimant may realize the full

0141

benefit of his award.

5. General criteria used in computing damages.

a. Property damage. Allowable compensation normally represents the cost of repairs to or restoration of the property damaged to its state of condition immediately prior to the time of damage. The claimant may establish these costs by receipts for amounts expanded for repair, or by estimates of the cost of repair by reputable contractors or other repairman. Compensation for lost or completely destroyed property is computed at the actual value of the property at time of loss or destruction. Value of growing crops and trees are similarly computed.

b. Compensation for personal injury and death. These computations usually are not as amenable to mathematical calculations as are cots of repair or destruction of vehicles, buildings, or other property. To obtain, however, as much consistency as may be possible standard elements are utilized in order to have a sound basis on which awards may be computed for death and in various types of personal injury. The Claims Commission is charged with the responsibility of evaluating each case in the light of these standard elements in order to arrive at fair awards. The Chief of the Claims Service supervises the activities of the Claims Commissions for the purpose of assuring that awards to claiments are fair and nondiscriminatory.

(1) Personal Injury. Standard compensable items are:

(a) Medical and hospital expenses, including immediate first aid treatment and ambulance service.

(b) Reasonable costs of Chinese medicines which are prescribed by a doctor as treatment for the injury, or resulting illness, on which claim is based.

(c) Loss of income for the period during which the claimant is absent from work or occupation.

0142

(d) Pain and suffering of the injured party.

(e) Permanent disability. A "Table of Disability Grades" is used. This table is patterned after the one provided in the Korean Labor Standard Act of 1953. The table includes four disability grades not appearing in the Korean table, and the number of days of compensation for each disability grade has been increased in recognition of the increased cost of living in Korea since 1953. If the injured party is not a wage or income earner (such as a child or housewife), emphasis is placed on the nature (rather them grade) of disability and age and pain and suffering of the injured party in order to arrive at comparable awards.

(f) Disfigurement. Scars and other disfigurements of a female are considered more serious than those suffered by a male. In addition, age, social status and occupation of both the male and female are taken into account.

(g) Cost of artificial limbs, and their repair and replacement for life expectancy of the injured party.

(h) Miscellaneous expenses attributable to the injuries sustained.

(2) <u>Death</u>. Standard compensable items are:

(a) Medical and hospital expenses incident to and preceding death.

(b) Funeral expenses. These include preparation of body for burial, purchase and preparation of grave site, reasonable amounts for traditional ceremonial expenses (including food and drink).

(c) Death award. Our Korean claimants frequently refer to this element as a "solatium"or "consolation award." The amount of this award varies from case to case, being affected by the age, income and social status of the deceased, as well as his family relationship (that is, whether the father, mother, minor daughter, first son, or other). Additional amounts are computed in this award for a surviving widow and for each surviving child under age of seventeen years. Our experience indicates that average death awards range from $772.20 (100,000Won) for young children to approximately $2702.70 (350,000 Won) for adults.

(d) Miscellaneous expanses attributable to the death on which claim is based.

6. Hospitalisation of claimants.

As a general rule United States law authorizes admission

( 0143

to and treatment in U.S. hospitals only for U.S. persons
(and some of their dependents) who are employed by the
Government. Not all U.S. employees are eligible for this
medical service. Exceptions may be made in emergency and
unusual cases for a small number of other persons, in which
event the individual is charged $37.00 (4792 Won) for each
day of hospitalization and $7.00 (907 Won) for each outpatient
treatment. Nevertheless special arrangements have been
approved for the claims program in Korea which operates
under the "Foreign Claims Act," whereunder any Korean citizen
who is injured by the activities of United States Forces Korea
may be admitted and treated (including all necessary surgery)
in U.S. hospitals in Korea without any charge whatsoever
for the medical services. In the past few years hundreds of
Korean citizens have been treated under this program in Army
medical facilities and furnished free hospitalization for
weeks and months in our major hospitals. Several of the patients
have received this hospitalization and medical service for more
than one year in the 121st U.S. Hospital located near Inchon.

7. Statistics

The number of claims received by Claims Commissions and
amounts of compensation paid since the Claims Service Began its
operations on 1 June 1959 are shown below:

|  | 1959 (7 mos) | 1960 | 1961 | 1962 | 1963 (6 mos) |
|---|---|---|---|---|---|
| Nr. Received: | 517 | 2,125 | 1,163 | 979 | 378 |
| Amount Paid: | 282,688.28 | 727,696.22 | 361,801.26 | 187,633.75 | 877,032.16 |

Total claims received since 1 June 1959:  5,162

Total compensation paid since 1 June 1959: $1,636,851.67 (12,639,775 Won)

0144

# 國家賠償金에 對한 関係法令

## 法 務 部

0145

# 國家賠償金에 對한 関係法令

(1) 國家賠償法

(2) 國家賠償金請求에 関한 節次法

(3) 同法施行令

(4) 同法施行規則

(5) 民法 ( 第 5 章 　 不法行爲 )

0146

# 國家賠償法

(1951.9.8)
(法律第 231 号)

第 1 條 國家 또는 公共团体의 損害賠
償의 責任에 關하여는 本法의 規定에
依한 外에 民法의 規定에 依한다.
但 民法以外의 다른 法律에 別段의
規定이 있을때에는 그 規定에 依한다

第 2 條 公務員이 그 職務를 行함에 當
하여 故意 또는 過失로 法令에 違反
하여 他人에게 損害를 加하였을 때에
는 公共团体는 그 損害를 賠償할 責
任이 있다

前項의 境遇에 公務員에게 故意 또는
重大한 過失이 있을때에는 國家 또는

~/~

C 0147

公共団体는 그 公務員에게 求償할 수

있다

第3條 道路·河川 其他 公共의 營造

物의 設置 또는 管理에 瑕疵가 있기

때문에 他人에게 損害가 發生하였을

때에는 國家 또는 公共団体는 그

損害를 賠償할 責任이 있다

前項의 境遇에 損害의 原因에 對하

여 責任을 질 者가 따로 있을 때

에는 國家 또는 公共団体는 그 者

에 對하여 求償할 수 있다

第4條 前2條의 規定에 依하여 國家

또는 公共団体가 損害를 賠償할 責

0143

任이 있는 境遇에 公務員의 選任

監督 또는 營造物의 設置·管理를

받은 者와 公務員의 俸給·給與 其

他의 費用 또는 公共의 營造物의

設置·管理의 費用을 負擔하는 者가

同一하지 아니한 境遇에는 其費用을

負擔하는 者도 損害를 賠償할 責任

이 있다.

前項의 境遇에 損害를 賠償한 者는

內務關係에서 그 損害를 賠償할 責

任이 있는 者에게 求償할수 있다

第5條 本法은 外國人이 被害者인 境

遇에는 相互의 保障이 있는 때에

~3~

0143

－4－

限하여 適用한다

附　　則

本法은　公布日로　부터　施行한다.

0150

# 國家賠償金 請求에 關한 節次法

(法律第1223號公布)

第1條 (適用) 國家에 對한 損害賠償金 (以下 賠償金이라 한다)의 請求節次는 다른 法律에 特別한 規定이 있는 境遇를 除外하고는 本法의 定하는 바에 依한다.

第2條 (賠償金 支給請求) 賠償金을 支給 받고자 하는 者는 法務部長官에게 賠償金 支給申請書를 提出하여 그의 決定을 받을수 있다.

第3條 (賠償金審議會) ① 前條의 決定에 關한 事項을 審議하게하기 爲하여 法務部에 賠償金審議會 (以下 審議會라

-5-

한다)를 둔다

② 審議會의 構成 運營 其他 必要한 事項은 閣令으로 定한다

第4條 (決定) ① 法務部長官은 前2條의 規定에 依한 申請이 있는 때에는 審議會의 審議를 거쳐 賠償金支給 또는 棄却의 決定을 하여야 한다

② 前項의 支給決定은 申請人의 同意가 있는 때에 그 効力을 發生한다

③ 法務部長官은 賠償金支給申請을 받은 날로부터 二月內에 前一項의 決定을 하여야 한다

第5條 (決定書의 送達) 法務部長官은

( 0152

前條第１項의 決定을 한때에는 그

決定이 있는 날로 부터 一週日內에

그 決定正本을 申請人에게 發送하여

야 한다

第 6 條 ( 申請人의 同意 ) ① 賠償金支給의

決定을 받은 申請人은 그 決定正本

을 받은 날로 부터 三週日內에 그

決定에 對한 同意書를 添付하여 法

務部長官에게 賠償金支給의 請求를

하여야 한다

② 賠償金支給의 決定을 받은 申請人

이 前項의 規定에 依한 請求를 하

지 아니한 때에는 그 決定에 同意

~7~

0153

하지 아니한 것으로 본다

第7條 (決定等의 效力) 第4條 第1項
의 規定에 依한 決定에 依한 決定
은 申請人이 同意한 때에는 民事訴
訟法의 規定에 依한 裁判上의 和解
가 成立된 것으로 보며 그 決定正本
은 執行力 있는 判決正本과 同一한
效力을 가진다

第8條 (施行令) 本法의 施行에 關하여
必要한 事項은 閣令으로 定한다

附 則

① (施行日) 本法은 1963年 1月 1日
부터 施行한다.

0154

# 國家賠償金 請求에 関한 節次法施行令

1963. 2. 5
閣令第 1157 号公布

1964. 4. 21
大統領令第 1773号改正

第 1 條 (目的) 이 令은 國家賠償金請求에 関한 節次法 (以下法이라 한다)의 施行에 関하여 必要한 事項을 規定함을 目的으로 한다.

第 2 條 (申請書의 記載事項) ① 法第 2 條의 規定에 依한 賠償金支給申請書에는 다음 各號의 事項을 記載하고 申請人이 記名 捺印하여야 한다.

1. 申請人의 姓名·年令·職業及 住所

2. 申請人의 趣旨 及 理由

~9~

0155

한·미국 간의 상호방위조약 제4조에 의한 시설과 구역 및 한국에서의 미국군대의 지위에 관한 협정(SOFA)
전59권. 1966.7.9 서울에서 서명 : 1967.2.9 발효(조약 232호) (V.53 민사청구권 관계자료, 1964-66)

3. 申請年月日

② 賠償金 支給申請書에는 証據書類가

있을 때에는 其 原本 또는 謄本을

添付하여야 한다

第3條 ( 決定書의 記載事項等 ) ① 法第4

條第1項의 規定에 依한 決定書에는

다음 各號의 事項을 記載하여야 한다

1. 申請人의 姓名 및 住所

2. 決定主文

3. 事實 및 理由

4. 決定年月日

② 法第5條의 決定正本에는 法務部長

官 또는 法務部長官이 指名하는 公

務員이 記名 捺印한다

㈂ 法 第4條의 合意가 있을 때에는
決定正本의 末尾에 民事訴訟法 第4
79條 第2項의 規定에 準한 文言을 記載하고
法務部長官 또는 法務部長官이 指名와는
公務員이 記名 捺印한 執行文을 지
체 없이 附與하여야 한다.

第4條(審議會의 構成등) ① 賠償金審議
會(以下審議會라 한다)는 委員長을
포함한 <u>委員7人으로</u> 構成한다

② 委員長은 <u>法務部次官이</u> 되고 委員
은 다음 各號에 依하여 法務部長官
이 任命 또는 委囑한다. 다만 關係

-11-

—12—

院、部、處、廳 (以下"關係部處"라 한다)의 委員은 그 關係部處의 事件에만 關與한다

1. 法務部職員 法官과 辯護士中에서 5人.

2. 關係部處의 職員中에서 1人.

③ 委員長은 委員會를 代表하고 會務를 統理한다

④ 委員長이 事故가 있을 때에는 委員長이 指定한 委員이 其職務를 代行한다

第5條 (審議會의 議事) ① 審議會의 會議는 委員長이 이를 召集하고 그 議長이 된다

( 0158

② 審議會의 會議는 在籍委員 過半數
의 出席으로 開議하고 出席委員 3
分의 2 이상의 贊成으로 議決한다

③ 議長은 表決權을 가지며 可否同數
인 때에는 決定權을 가진다

第 6 條 ( 事務職員 ) ① 審議會에 그 事務
를 担當하게하기 爲하여 幹事 1 人 及
書記 若干人을 둔다

② 幹事는 法務部 訟務課長이 되고 書
記는 法務部 所屬 公務員中에서 委員
長이 委囑한다

③ 幹事는 委員長의 命을 받아 審議
會의 事務를 處理하고 書記는 幹事

-13-

0159

를 補助한다

第7條 (手當) 審議會의 會議에 出席
한 法務部所屬 公務員이 아닌 委員
에 對하여는 豫算의 範圍안에서 手
當을 支給한다

第8條 (準用規定) 民事訴訟法 第2編
第3章의 規定은 法의 規定에 依한
申請의 審議에 關하여 이를 準用한
다 다만 民事訴訟法 第282條와
第283條의 規定을 準用하지 아니
한다

第9條 (施行細則) 이 令의 施行에
關하여 必要한 事項은 法務部令으로

0160

定한다

## 附　則

① （施行日） 이 令은 公布한 날로

부터 施行한다

② （經過措置） 이 令 施行當時의 委

員은 이 令에 依하여 任命 또는 委

囑된 것으로 본다

~15~

한·미국 간의 상호방위조약 제4조에 의한 시설과 구역 및 한국에서의 미국군대의 지위에 관한 협정(SOFA)
전59권. 1966.7.9 서울에서 서명 : 1967.2.9 발효(조약 232호) (V.53 민사청구권 관계자료, 1964-66)

# 國家賠償金請求에 關한 節次法施行規則

1963. 4. 27.
法務部令第 63호 公布

1964. 5.
法務部令第 79호 改正

第1條 (目的) 이 令은 國家賠償金請求에 關한 節次法 施行令 (以下 "施行令" 이라 한다) 第9條의 規定에 依하여 申請書의 書式 其他 施行令의 施行에 關하여 必要한 事項을 規定함을 目的으로 한다

第2條 (申請書의 書式) ① 國家賠償金請求에 關한 節次法 (以下 "法" 이라 한다) 第2條의 賠償金支給申請書는 別紙 第1號書式에 依하여 作式하여

-17-

0162

야 한다

② 賠償金支給申請書에는 申請人의 戸
籍謄本 또는 抄本을 添付하여야 한다.

第 3 條 ( 決定書의 書式 ) 施行令第 3 條
의 決定書는 別紙第 2 號書式에 依하
여 作成하여야 한다.

第 4 條 ( 記錄 및 簿冊等의 備置 ) 賠
償金審議會 ( 以下 "審議會" 라 한다 )
는 別紙第 3 號書式에 依한 賠償金支
給申請事件簿 및 別紙第 4 號書式에
依한 決定正本台帳을 備置하여야 한다

第 5 條 ( 審議報告 ) 審議會는 賠償金支
給에 關한 審議를 마쳤을 때에는

0163

別紙第5號書式에 依하여 그 結果를
法務部長官에게 報告하여야 한다

第6條 (通知) 法第5條의 規定에 依
하여 決定正本을 送達받을 때에는 別
紙第6號書式에 依한 通知書를 붙여
서 하여야 한다

第7條 (申請人의 同意 및 請求書)
法第6條 第1項의 同意書 및 賠償
金支給請求書는 別紙第7號書式에 依
하여 作成하여야 한다

第8條 (賠償金支給) 法務部長官은 法
第6條 第1項의 規定에 依한 賠償金請求를
받은 때에는 지체없이 賠償金을 支

—19—

給하여야 한다

第9條 (準用規定) 國家賠償金申請에

關한 送達에 關하여는 民事訴訟法

第1編第4章第3節 送達의 規定을

準用한다

　　　　　　附　則

이 令은 公布한 날로 부터 施行한다.

한·미국 간의 상호방위조약 제4조에 의한 시설과 구역 및 한국에서의 미국군대의 지위에 관한 협정(SOFA)
전59권. 1966.7.9 서울에서 서명 : 1967.2.9 발효(조약 232호) (V.53 민사청구권 관계자료, 1964-66) 171

第 1 號書式

# 국가배상금지급신청서

주　소

신청인　　　　　　　　　　직업　　년령　　세

신청취지

신청원안

입증방법

첨부서류　1.

　　　　　2.

년　　월　　일

신청인 ( 대리인 )

법무부장관　귀하

0166

第 2 號 書式

# 법 무 부

国賠審第     호

# 결 정 서

주 소

신청인             직 업       년 령    세

위의 사람이 신청한 国家賠償金 지급청구에 대하여 다
음과 같이 결정한다.

주 문

사실 및 이유의요지

                     년    월    일

              법무부장관   [인]

                  ~22~              ( 0197

한·미국 간의 상호방위조약 제4조에 의한 시설과 구역 및 한국에서의 미국군대의 지위에 관한 협정(SOFA)
전59권. 1966.7.9 서울에서 서명 : 1967.2.9 발효(조약 232호) (V.53 민사청구권 관계자료, 1964-66)

# 국가배상금지급신청사건부

| 사건번호 | | 년국배쇱 제 호 | | 담 |
|---|---|---|---|---|
| 접수월자 | | 년 월 일 | | 당 |
| 사 건 표 목 | | | | 신 청 인 |
| | | | | |
| 심 의 월 자 | | 년 월 일 제 회 | | |
| | | 년 월 일 제 회 | | |
| | | 년 월 일 제 회 | | |
| 심 의 결 과 | | | | |
| 결 정 월 자 | | 년 월 일 | | |
| 결 정 내 용 | | | | |
| 결 정 송 달 월 자 | | 년 월 일 | | |
| 등 본 및 배 상 금 청 구 월 자 | | 년 월 일 | | |
| 배 상 금 지 급 의 뢰 월 자 | | 년 월 일 | | |
| 배 상 금 지 급 월 자 | | 년 월 일 | | |
| 관 계 부 쳐 | | | | |
| 비 고 | | | | |

~23~

第4號書式

## 결정정본대장

| 사건번호 | 신청인의 성명 | 접수번호 | 접수연월일 | 결정번호 | 결정연월일 | 결정요지 | 비고 | 고 |
|---|---|---|---|---|---|---|---|---|
|  |  |  |  |  |  |  |  |  |
|  |  |  |  |  |  |  |  |  |
|  |  |  |  |  |  |  |  |  |
|  |  |  |  |  |  |  |  |  |
|  |  |  |  |  |  |  |  |  |
|  |  |  |  |  |  |  |  |  |
|  |  |  |  |  |  |  |  |  |
|  |  |  |  |  |  |  |  |  |
|  |  |  |  |  |  |  |  |  |

0169

한·미국 간의 상호방위조약 제4조에 의한 시설과 구역 및 한국에서의 미국군대의 지위에 관한 협정(SOFA)
전59권. 1966.7.9 서울에서 서명 : 1967.2.9 발효(조약 232호) (V.53 민사청구권 관계자료, 1964-66)  175

# 보 고 서

국배심제            호

     년    월    일

국가배상금심의회위원장

법무부장관  귀하

제    차 국가배상금 심의회 심의결과를 별첨
심의결정서와 같이 보고하나이다.

　　　유  첨  1, 심의결정서 1부
　　　　　　　2, 조   서
　　　　　　　3, 증거서류

(  0170

第 5 號 書式의 2

국 가 배 상 금 심 의 회

국배심제            호

# 심 의 결 정 서

로부터  신청한  국가배상금  지급청구에

대하여  다음과  같이  심의  결정한다

주  소

신청인                직업        년령        세

주  문

사실및
이  유

년    월    일

위 원 장                                ㉑

위 원

-26-

한·미국 간의 상호방위조약 제4조에 의한 시설과 구역 및 한국에서의 미국군대의 지위에 관한 협정(SOFA)
전59권. 1966.7.9 서울에서 서명 : 1967.2.9 발효(조약 232호) (V.53 민사청구권 관계자료, 1964-66)    177

# 법 무 부

법무송

수 신

제 목    국가배상금지급심의결과 통지서

1,    년   월   일자로 귀하가 신청한 국배심제    호 국가배상금 청구에 대하여 별첨 정본과 같이 결정하였기 이에 통지합니다.

2.   이 통지를 받은 날로부터 3주일 이내에 동의서를 첨부하여 배상금 지급을 청구 하시기 바랍니다.

유첨   결정서 정본 I부   끝.

## 법 무 부 장 관

-지-

0 0172

# 동의및청구서

국배심제            호

년    월    일


주  소

신청인        직업      연령      세


## 법무부장관  귀하


196  년    월    일자로 통지하신 국가배상금 지급결

정에 대하여 본인은 하등의 이의없이 동의하옵고 부본

및 인감증명을 첨부하여 다음과 같이 청구하나이다


일금            원정

신  청  인            ㊞


-28-


( 0173

# 民 法

## 第五章 不法行爲

第750條 ( 不法行爲의 內容 ) 故意 또는 過失로 因한 違法行爲로 他人에게 損害를 加한 者는 그 損害를 賠償할 責任이 있다

第751條 ( 財産以外의 損害의 賠償 )

① 他人의 身体 自由 또는 名譽를 害하거나 其他 精神上 苦痛을 加한 者는 財産以外의 損害에 對하여도 賠償할 責任이 있다

② 法院은 前項의 損害賠償을 定期金債務로 支給할 것을 命할 수 있고 그 履行을 確保하기 爲하여 相當한 担保의 提供을 命할 수 있다

~29~

0174

第752條 (生命侵害로 因한 慰藉料) 他人의 生命을 害한 者는 被害者의 直系尊屬 直系卑屬 및 配偶者에 對하여는 財産上의 損害없는 境遇에도 損害賠償의 責任이 있다

第753條 (未成年者의 責任能力) 未成年者가 他人에게 損害를 加한 境遇에 그 行爲의 責任을 辨識할 知能이 없는 때에는 賠償의 責任이 없다

第754條 (心神喪失者의 責任能力) 心神喪失中에 他人에게 損害를 加한 者는 賠償의 責任이 없다 그러나 故意 또는 過失로 因하여 心神喪失을

招來한 때에는 그러하지 아니하다

第755條 ( 責任無能者의 監督者의 責任 ) ① 前2條의 規程비 依하여 無能力者에게 責任없는 境遇에는 이를 監督할 法定義務있는者가 그 無能力者의 第三者에게 加한 損害를 賠償을 責任이 있다 그러나 監督義務를 懈怠하지 아니한 때에는 그러하지 아니하다

② 監督義務者에 가름하여 無能力者를 監督하는者도 前項의 責任이 있다

第756條 ( 使用者의 賠償責任 ) ① 他人을 使用하여 어느 事務에 從事하게 한 者는 被用者가 그 事務執行에

—31—

-37-

關하여 第三者에게 加한 損害를 賠償할 責任이 있다. 그러나 使用者가 被用者의 選任 및 그 事務監督에 相當한 注意를 한때 또는 相當한 注意를 하여도 損害가 있을 境遇에는 그러하지 아니하다.

② 使用者에 가름하여 그 事務를 監督하는 者도 前項의 責任이 있다.

③ 前2項의 境遇에 使用者 또는 監督者는 被用者에 對하여 求償權을 行使할 수 있다.

第757條(都給人의 責任) 都給人은 受給人이 그 일에 關하여 第三者에게 加한 損害를 賠償할 責任이 없다.

0177

한·미국 간의 상호방위조약 제4조에 의한 시설과 구역 및 한국에서의 미국군대의 지위에 관한 협정(SOFA)
전59권. 1966.7.9 서울에서 서명 : 1967.2.9 발효(조약 232호) (V.53 민사청구권 관계자료, 1964-66) 183

第ク60條 ( 共同不法行爲者의 責任 ) ①

數人이 共同의 不法行爲로 他人에게

損害를 加한때에는 連帶하여 그 損

害를 賠償할 責任이 있다

② 共同아닌 數人의 行爲中 어느者의

行爲가 그 損害를 加한것인지를 알

수 있는 때에도 前項과 같다

③ 敎唆者나 幇助者는 共同行爲者로

본다

第ク61條 ( 正當防衛 緊急避難 ) ① 他人

의 不法行爲에 對하여 自己 또는

第二者의 利益을 防衛하기 爲하여

不得己 他人에게 損害를 加한 者는

0178

~33~

賠償할 責任이 없다

그러나 被害者는 不法行爲에 對하여

損害의 賠償을 請求할수 있다

② 前項의 規定은 急迫한 危難을 避

하기 爲하여 不得己 他人에게 損害

를 加한 境遇에 準用한다

第762條 (損害 賠償請求權에 있어

서의 胎兒의 地位) 胎兒는 損害賠償

의 請求權에 關하여는 이미 出生한

것으로 본다

第763條 (準用規定) 第393條 第

394條、第396條 第399條의

規定은 不法行爲로 因한 損害賠償에

0173

準用한다.

第764條 (名譽毁損의 境遇의 特則)
他人의 名譽를 毁損한 者에 對하여
는 法院은 被害者의 請求에 依하여
損害賠償에 갈음하거나 損害賠償과
함께 名譽回復에 適當한 處分을 命
할 수 있다

第765條 (賠償額의 輕減請求) ① 本章
의 規定에 依한 賠償義務者는 그
損害가 故意 또는 重大한 過失에
依한 것이 아니고 그 賠償으로 因하
여 賠償者의 生計에 重大한 影響을
미치게 될 境遇에는 法院에 그 賠

-35-

0180

償額의 輕減을 請求할수 있다

② 法院은 前項의 請求가 있는 때에
는 債權者 及 債務者의 經濟狀態와
損害의 原因 等을 參酌하여 賠償額을
輕減할수 있다

第166條 (損害賠償請求權의 消滅時效)

① 不法行爲로 因한 損害賠償의 請求
權은 被害者나 그 法定代理人이 그
損害 및 加害者를 안날로 부터 三
年間 이를 行使하지 아니하면 時效
로 因하여 消滅한다

② 不法行爲를 안 날로 부터 10 年
을 經過한 때에도 前項과 같다

0181

그러나 都給 또는 指示에 關하여 都給人에게 重大한 過失이 있는 때에는 그러하지 아니하다.

第758條(工作物等의 占有者·所有者의 責任) ① 工作物의 設置 또는 保存의 瑕疵로 因하여 他人에게 損害를 加한 때에는 工作物占有者가 損害를 賠償할 責任이 있다 그러나 占有者가 損害의 防止에 必要한 注意를 懈怠하지 아니한 때에는 그 所有者가 損害를 賠償할 責任이 있다 ② 前項의 規定은 樹木의 栽植 또는 保存에 瑕疵있는 境遇에 準用한다.

~37~

0182

㊂ 前2項의 境遇에 占有者 또는 所

有者는 그 損害의 原因에 對한 責

任있는 者에 對하여 求償權을 行使할

수 있다

第759條 (動物의 占有者의 責任)

① 動物의 占有者는 其動物이 他人에

게 加한 損害를 賠償할 責任이 있

다 그러나 動物의 種類와 性質에

따라 그 保管에 相當한 注意를 懈

怠하지 아니한 때에는 그러하지 아

니하다

② 占有者에 갈음하여 動物을 保管한

者도 前項의 責任이 있다.

0183

1963

Claims Adjudicated
Nr. 839

Claims Allowed
Nr. ~~XXXX~~ 680

Claims Disallowed
Nr. 159

Claims Paid
Nr. 649

Amount Paid

$148,185.86    Won 19,264,162

1964 (as of 1 Sept)

Claims Adjudicated
Nr. 911

Claims Allowed
Nr. ~~XXX~~ 589

Claims Disallowed
Nr. 322

Claims Paid
Nr. 576

Amount Paid

$101,433.52    Won 25,865,548

C134

# INTERNATIONAL CLAIMS

## HEARINGS

BEFORE THE

## SUBCOMMITTEE OF THE
## COMMITTEE ON FOREIGN RELATIONS
## UNITED STATES SENATE

EIGHTY-NINTH CONGRESS

FIRST SESSION

ON

### S.J. Res. 13 and S.J. Res. 32

RYUKYUAN CLAIMS

AND

### EXECUTIVE C, 89TH CONGRESS, 1ST SESSION

GUT DAM CLAIMS AGREEMENT WITH CANADA

AND

### S. 1826, S. 1935, S. 2064

BILLS TO AMEND THE INTERNATIONAL CLAIMS
SETTLEMENT ACT OF 1949

AUGUST 4 AND 5, 1965

Printed for the use of the Committee on Foreign Relations

U.S. GOVERNMENT PRINTING OFFICE
WASHINGTON : 1965

52-255

0185

0186

# CONTENTS

III

0187

# INTERNATIONAL CLAIMS

## WEDNESDAY, AUGUST 4, 1965

UNITED STATES SENATE,
SUBCOMMITTEE ON CLAIMS LEGISLATION,
OF THE COMMITTEE ON FOREIGN RELATIONS,
*Washington, D.C.*

The committee met, pursuant to notice, at 10 a.m., in room 4221, New Senate Office Building, Senator John Sparkman presiding.

Present: Senator Sparkman.

Senator SPARKMAN. Let the committee come to order, please.

The Subcommittee on Claims Legislation is meeting this morning to receive testimony on Senate Joint Resolutions 13 and 32, both of which would authorize a contribution of not to exceed $22 million to certain inhabitants of the Ryukyu Islands for claims based on death or injury, and for use of and damage to private property, arising from acts and omissions of members of the U.S. Armed Forces after August 15, 1945, and before April 28, 1952.

(S.J. Res. 13 and S.J. Res. 32 follow:)

[S.J. Res. 13, 89th Cong., 1st sess.]

JOINT RESOLUTION To authorize a contribution to certain inhabitants of the Ryukyu Islands for death and injury of persons, and for use of and damage to private property, arising from acts and omissions of the United States Armed Forces, or members thereof, after August 15, 1945, and before April 28, 1952.

Whereas certain persons of the Ryukyu Islands suffered damages incident to the activities of the Armed Forces of the United States, or members thereof, after the surrender of Japanese forces in the Ryukyu on August 15, 1945, and before the effective date of the Treaty of Peace with Japan on April 28, 1952; and

Whereas article 19 of the Treaty of Peace with Japan extinguished the legal liability of the United States for any claims of Japanese nationals, including Ryukyuans, with the result that the United States has made no compensation for the above-mentioned damages (except for use of and damage to land during the period from July 1, 1950, to April 28, 1952); and

Whereas the High Commissioner of the Ryukyu Islands has considered the evidence regarding these claims, and has determined, in an equitable manner, those claims which are meritorious, and the amounts thereof: Therefore be it

*Resolved by the Senate and House of Representatives of the United States of America in Congress assembled,* That the United States should make an ex gratia contribution to the persons determined by the High Commissioner of the Ryukyu Islands to be meritorious claimants, in the amounts determined by him, and that the Secretary of the Army or his designee should, under regulations prescribed by the Secretary of Defense, pay such amounts to the claimants or their legal heirs, as a civil function of the Department of the Army; and be it further

*Resolved,* That no funds appropriated under this authorization shall be disbursed to satisfy claims, or portions thereof, which have been satisfied by contributions made by the Government of Japan.

SEC. 2. There is authorized to be appropriated not to exceed $22,000,000 to carry out this joint resolution, which funds are authorized to remain available until expended.

1

0188

SEC. 3. No remuneration on account of services rendered on behalf of any claimant in connection with any claim filed with the Commission under this subchapter shall exceed 5 per centum of the total amount paid pursuant to any award certified under the provisions of this subchapter on account of such claim. Fees already paid for services performed in submitting a claim to the Joint American-Ryukyuan Commission shall be deducted from the amounts authorized under this legislation. Any agreement to the contrary shall be unlawful and void. Whoever, in the United States or elsewhere, demands or receives, on account of services so rendered, any remuneration in excess of the maximum permitted by this section, shall be guilty of a misdemeanor, and, upon conviction thereof, shall be fined not more than $5,000 or imprisoned not more than twelve months, or both.

---

[S.J. Res. 32, 89th Cong., 1st sess.]

JOINT RESOLUTION To authorize a contribution to certain inhabitants of the Ryukyu Islands for death and injury to persons, and for use of and damage to private property, arising from acts and omissions of the United States Armed Forces, or members thereof, after August 15, 1945, and before April 28, 1952

Whereas certain persons of the Ryukyu Islands suffered damages incident to the activities of the Armed Forces of the United States, or members thereof, after the surrender of Japanese forces in the Ryukyus on August 15, 1945, and before the effective date of the Treaty of Peace with Japan on April 28, 1952;

Whereas article 19 of the Treaty of Peace with Japan extinguished the legal liability of the United States for any claims of Japanese nationals, including Ryukyuans, with the result that the United States has made no compensation for the above-mentioned damages (except for use of and damage to land during the period from July 1, 1950, to April 28, 1952);

Whereas it is particularly consonant with the concern of the United States, as the sole administering authority in the Ryukyu Islands, for the welfare of the Ryukyuan people, that those Ryukyuans who suffered damages incident to the activities of the United States Armed Forces, or members thereof, should be compensated therefor;

Whereas payment of ex gratia compensation, by advancing the welfare of the Ryukyuan people, will promote the security interest, foreign policy, and foreign relations of the United States; and

Whereas the High Commisisoner of the Ryukyu Islands has considered the evidence regarding these claims, and has determined, in an equitable manner, those claims which are meritorious, and the amounts thereof: Therefore be it

*Resolved by the Senate and House of Representatives of the United States of America in Congress assembled,* That the United States should make an ex gratia contribution to the persons determined by the High Commissioner of the Ryukyu Islands to be meritorious claimants, in the amounts determined by him, and that the Secretary of the Army or his designee should, under regulations prescribed by the Secretary of Defense, pay such amounts to the claimants or their legal heirs, as a civil function of the Department of the Army; and be it further

*Resolved,* That no funds appropriated under this joint resolution shall be disbursed to satisfy claims, or portions thereof, which have been satisfied by contributions made by the Government of Japan.

SEC. 2. There is authorized to be appropriated not to exceed $22,000,000 to carry out the provisions of this joint resolution, which funds are authorized to remain available for two years from the effective date of their appropriation. Any funds unobligated by the end of that period shall be covered into the Treasury of the United States.

SEC. 3. No remuneration on account of services rendered on behalf of any claimant in connection with any claim shall exceed 5 per centum of the total amount paid, pursuant to the provisions of this joint resolution, on such claim. Fees already paid for such services shall be deducted from the amounts authorized under this joint resolution. Any agreement to the contrary shall be unlawful and void. Whoever, in the United States or elsewhere, demands or receives, on account of services so rendered, any remuneration in excess of the maximum permitted by this section, shall be guilty of a misdemeanor, and, upon conviction thereof, shall be fined not more than $5,000 or imprisoned not more than twelve months, or both.

0189

Senator SPARKMAN. The subcommittee also expects to receive testimony on the Gut Dam Claims Agreement between the United States and Canada which provides for the establishment of a three-member international arbitral tribunal to receive, determine, and make awards on claims of U.S. nationals for damage to their properties on the shores of Lake Ontario resulting from the construction and maintenance by Canada of Gut Dam in the St. Lawrence River.

Our first witness this morning is Senator Daniel K. Inouye, who will testify on the Ryukyuan claims legislation. Senator Inouye, we are glad to have you.

Please proceed in your own way.

## STATEMENT OF HON. DANIEL K. INOUYE, A U.S. SENATOR FROM THE STATE OF HAWAII

Senator INOUYE. Mr. Chairman, I appear before this committee in support of Senate Joint Resolution 13 and Senate Joint Resolution 32, which would authorize a contribution to certain inhabitants of the Ryukyu Islands for death and injury to persons, and for use of and damage to private property, arising from acts and omissions of the U.S. Armed Forces, or members thereof, after August 15, 1945, and before April 28, 1952.

I am gratified to have this opportunity to speak on behalf of this resolution, the purpose of which I have supported since I was a Representative and which I am happy to see is finally receiving the close attention which it merits. I hope that with the matter before you now, the committee will act on these Department of Defense recommendations and fulfill an obligation to the people of the Ryukyu Islands.

### EXECUTIVE BRANCH SUPPORTS THESE CLAIMS

I am happy to support the Defense Department's proposal to secure compensation for the inhabitants of Okinawa who have suffered from acts arising from the presence of U.S. armed services there in the pretreaty period. The efforts of the Department are necessary, thoughtful and timely.

The distinguished members of this committee are quite familiar with the main issues involved, I am sure, and it will not be necessary to speak at length on the work of the Joint United States-Ryukyuan Committee. At this particular time I would like to discuss the major points of the Defense Department's case and to place the entire matter in historical perspective, emphasizing again the need for this Government to effect compensation.

### BACKGROUND TO PRESENT SITUATION

The years following the battle of Okinawa were ones of extreme hardship for the people of the Ryukyu Islands. Like many other areas in the world, their economy was badly dislocated. The ravages of war leveled most of the island's buildings, and the lives of these people were changed considerably. The social, economic, and political disruption meant a profound transformation in their lives, and it required many years for the situation to assume a normal state.

0190

Beyond the suffering caused by war. Okinawa was permanently altered by the necessity to retain our bases there to deter totalitarian aggression. Japanese administration was removed, and control passed to the United States which had early recognized the strategic significance of the area and which continues to do so. The 1952 Peace Treaty with Japan gave to the United States the right to continue exercising control over Okinawa, thus retaining the status quo which had existed since 1945.

During the period between the cessation of hostilities and the signing of the peace treaty; that is, 1945-52, there existed a situation in which no provision was made to cover any accidents which naturally arise anywhere when Armed Forces are stationed in great numbers and assigned numerous functions under trying circumstances. Although the United States adheres to the provisions of the Hague Convention No. IV of 1907, which requires occupation forces to compensate individuals or municipalities for property taken or used, this provision was unfortunately ignored in the military buildup. Since there was no authorized local government which could be held responsible for the claims for the use of land by the military, thus increasing the scarcity of land available for agriculture, these claims have remained unsettled until the present day.

### EXAMPLES OF HARDSHIPS

I would like to cite two cases which I hope will suffice to demonstrate the hardships created by the lack of a provision to enable the settlement of claims.

Saburo Nagamine heads a family of six persons, only two of whom work to contribute to the family's income. After the war, all of his land was seized for military purposes. In June 1952, some 60 percent of the relatively small amount of land was returned to him and the remainder is under lease by the United States.

Mr. Nagamine's claim for pretreaty rental is $593.44. In addition, he seeks an additional $960.32 in restoration compensation to make his land fit again for other purposes. He has had to clear concrete and stone from the land, and the work is still incomplete. Because his claim belongs to the pretreaty category, he has had to borrow against his military rent to finance the operation.

Shunko Nakamura owns a grocery shop but was formerly engaged in agriculture until the military appropriated his land. His wife works as a housekeeper, and of his six children, only one, his oldest daughter, is engaged in gainful employment. His older son goes to college and the others go to high school or primary school; this education requires some $700 per year.

Mr. Nakamura has had to rent the land on which his present house stands and pays $144 for the lot. Their house is old and decrepit and is in danger of collapse in a typhoon. If the claim is paid, the Nakamuras will finally be able to repair their home.

These cases are fairly representative of many others. The claims are esentially relatively small but affect families whose livelihood depends on every available resource.

0191

## EARLY NEGLECT BY UNITED STATES TO ACT

It is unfortunate that nothing was done to effect compensation at the time of the signing of the Japanese Peace Treaty in 1952, or even before. Such an oversight is particularly distressing since no one has ever denied the justice of these claims or the moral obligation for someone to pay. Perhaps it was Okinawa's unique status as a nominal Japanese possession under American administration which resulted in the unfortunate situation. However, at last the U.S. Government has, under a plan submitted by the Defense Department, proposed to right a very old wrong.

Thirteen years have passed since the signing of the peace treaty. That some of these claims will be almost 20 years old is a sorry reflection of the initial confusion which surrounded the original claims issue. The passing of the years, however, has allowed us to see this matter in clearer perspective. The removal of Japanese authority and the concomitant creation of Okinawa as the major cornerstone in our Far East Military Establishment has meant that the United States is fully responsible to the inhabitants of Okinawa to see that their interests are protected.

## NO LEGAL OBLIGATION OF THE UNITED STATES

It is, of course, true that the United States is bound by no legal convention that requires us to settle these claims. Japanese sovereignty ceased to exist with the signing of the peace treaty. Any responsibility to effect compensation also ceased at that time. Such fine points of international law should not, however, obscure the fact that the United States did in 1945 assume full responsibility for the protection and administration of the islands. In the process we, as the occupying force, were clearly answerable to a number of accidents and unfortunate incidents. Justice and simple morality demands redress for the Okinawan people.

I am not here to describe the settlement process. I understand that the representatives from the Department of Defense are fully prepared to do so. The sum is not a large one, but its payment will nevertheless have a great impact on future American-Okinawan relations. Affecting almost half the people of Okinawa directly or indirectly, the settlement of the claims issue will provide ample proof that the United States is indeed morally responsible and concerned with their welfare. It is no secret that our relations with the Okinawans have at times been strained, and I believe it is imperative that this measure be approved as further demonstration of our good will. Just compensation requires no defense, and I believe that we shall benefit enormously from the renewed faith in America among the Okinawan people.

I thank you, Mr. Chairman, once again, for this opportunity to appear before this committee, sir.

Senator SPARKMAN. Thank you, Senator Inouye.

Senator INOUYE. Thank you, sir.

Senator SPARKMAN. The next witness will be Secretary Stanley Resor, Secretary of the Army.

Mr. Secretary, we are glad to have you with us this morning. We also have General Watson, the High Commissioner, and we have Am-

0192

bassador Berger, Deputy Assistant Secretary for Far Eastern Affairs of the Department of State.

I presume that all of you will be at the table at the same time. Which one proceeds first?

Mr. Secretary.

## STATEMENT OF HON. STANLEY R. RESOR, SECRETARY OF THE ARMY, DEPARTMENT OF DEFENSE

Secretary RESOR. If it is agreeable to you, sir, I would like to proceed first.

Senator SPARKMAN. We will be very glad to hear from you.

By the way, let me say that you may treat your statement as you see fit. I say this for the benefit of all witnesses. Any prepared statement will be carried in the printed record in full; and then you can either read or discuss it in any way you wish.

Secretary RESOR. I think inasmuch as my prepared statement lays out the situation, it might be helpful if I read it.

Senator SPARKMAN. We will be very glad to have you do so.

Secretary RESOR. Mr. Chairman, I welcome this opportunity of appearing in support of the Senate Joint Resolution 32.

This is an administration proposal; it is part of the program of the President, and it is supported by the Secretary of Defense and the Secretary of State.

### SETTLEMENTS TO BE SUPERVISED BY THE DEPARTMENT OF THE ARMY

Since the Department of the Army has been designated as the executive agency of the Department of Defense for the civil administration of the Ryukyu Islands, I am representing the Department of Defense at this hearing.

The joint resolution before you would authorize the payment of approximately 180,000 claims, submitted by the inhabitants of Okinawa for damages arising from acts or omissions of the U.S. Armed Forces, during the 7-year period following the armistice and prior to the treaty of peace with Japan. This is not a war-claims bill. It does not involve payment for damages which occurred during the war nor for the postwar rehabilitation of war-damaged areas.

On the contrary, these claims fall into two familiar peacetime categories: first, claims for torts committed by U.S. military personnel resulting in injury to or the death of Okinawans or damage to their private property.

Second, claims for the requisitioning of their property—mostly agricultural land—for use by the military.

Normally, under international law and practice, just compensation in such circumstances would be required, by or on behalf of the occupation forces. Surprising though it may seem, not a single cent of compensation (other than a few rental payments made by us at the end of the occupation, and a relatively small Japanese gratuitous payment made in 1957) has been received by any of the approximately 80,000 Okinawans who suffered injury or death or whose property was, in effect, confiscated by U.S. Armed Forces during the occupation of Okinawa.

0193

## U.S. CLAIMS WAIVED BY 1952 PEACE TREATY WITH JAPAN

The failure of the United States to pay these claims stems from the fact that all such claims were waived in the Japanese Peace Treaty of 1952. In the administration's judgment, however, the equitable and moral obligation of the United States continues unsatisfied. The purpose of the bill before you is to correct this injustice.

Certain background information will place this matter in proper focus. The Ryukyu Islands extend southwesterly from Japan to Taiwan. Okinawa is the largest of these islands. It has about 85 percent of the total Ryukyuan population of almost a million persons. All the claims covered by the proposed resolution relate to Okinawa.

## BACKGROUND TO AMERICAN ADMINISTRATION OF RYUKYU ISLANDS

The U.S. forces seized Okinawa in the last battle of World War II. Following up the policy first expressed in the Cairo Declaration, on July 26, 1945, the Potsdam Declaration announced that Japan would be stripped of its former imperial holdings, and that its sovereignty would be limited to the four main islands of the Japanese mainland, including such minor offshore islands as the Allied Powers should determine. The Ryukyus were not among these islands. They were therefore administered by the United States—separately from Japan itself.

Although consideration was given, during the late forties, to retaining U.S. bases in the Ryukyus, the future status of these islands remained in limbo until January 1950. At that time, Secretary of State Acheson stated that the United States would continue to hold important defense positions in the Ryukyus, as part of the defense perimeter running along the Aleutians to Japan and thence to the Ryukyus.

The outbreak of the Korean war in June 1950 underscored the importance of our Ryukyuan base for the defense of the free world, and confirmed our determination that Okinawa should be retained under U.S. control for an indefinite period. The value of this base has been vindicated by the important role which it played in the Korean war and is now playing in support of the free world's commitments in southeast Asia.

Because of such strategic considerations, the treaty of peace with Japan provided that the United States would retain full jurisdiction over the Ryukyu Islands, for an indefinite period. The Government of Japan has stated its desire for the reversion of administrative control over Okinawa, and the U.S. Government has repeatedly stated that it looks forward to the day when the security interests of the free world in the Far East will permit their restoration to full Japanese sovereignty.

Meanwhile, however, Presidents Eisenhower, Kennedy, and Johnson have all given public notice that, in order to protect the security of the free world, the political status of this area will remain unchanged, as long as conditions of threat and tension continue to exist in the Far East.

Thus, for the last 20 years, the United States has held and exercised all powers of administration, legislation, and jurisdiction over the

0194

territory and inhabitants of these islands. Our announced policy is that the United States intends to continue to retain these powers as long as our military bases are needed there.

I turn now to the specific matter covered by the resolution which is before your committee. The surrender of all Japanese forces and the resultant general armistice took place on August 14, 1945, and the military occupation period encompassed by this resolution starts from that date.

Certain damages were caused to residents of the Ryukyu Islands during the almost 7 years between the armistice and the peace treaty of 1952. These damages were caused by various acts and omissions of the U.S. forces. They ranged from the uncompensated use of real and personal property (taken over for occupation requirements) to tortious acts committed by members of the U.S. forces.

It is a generally recognized principle of international law, particularly as reflected in the provisions of Hague Convention Number IV of 1907 (which has been ratified by both Japan and the United States), that individuals or municipalities whose property is used or taken by occupation forces should be fairly compensated for such use.

In practice, occupation authorities have usually transferred to the local governments the burden for making such payments, either at the time of requisition or in the peace settlement. This was U.S. policy in both world wars.

Even though the precise obligation in international law for paying claims arising from death or personal injury suffered by residents of occupied territories, due to acts or omissions of occupation forces or their members, is less clear than that concerning requisitioned property, U.S. policy has also been to transfer this obligation to the local governments in both world wars.

Why were these policies not followed in Okinawa?

It was due to a unique combination of circumstances, resulting largely from the fact that, pursuant to the Potsdam Declaration, Okinawa was removed from Japanese control at the end of the war and administered directly by the United States during the entire period of the occupation.

Thus, the Japanese Central Government was stripped of its powers in Okinawa and could not logically be held responsible for paying claims. On the other hand, there was no financially responsible indigenous governmental authority on Okinawa which could conceivably have paid them.

It was not possible to use funds authorized by the Foreign Claims Act, because this statute specifically precludes making any payments to enemy nationals, which the Ryukyuans were during the entire period of the occupation.

International custom provides that any deferred obligations incurred by an occupying power should be ultimately resolved in the peace settlement. Nevertheless, the treaty of peace with Japan did not provide for such a settlement.

Article 19a of the treaty waived the claims of Japanese nationals (which include Ryukyuans) against the United States, but failed to make any provision for how these claims should be honored.

The United States has taken the position that article 19a absolved us from legal liability with regard to these claims. We therefore

0195

denied payment for them, except for certain claims relating to rentals for land and payments for damages caused thereto during the last part of the occupation period, as I should now like to explain.

## U.S. RECOGNITION OF STRATEGIC IMPORTANCE OF ISLANDS

A number of factors converging in early 1950 (including our decision to maintain a worldwide defense perimeter, as reflected by the above-noted remark of Secretary Acheson) resulted in the U.S. decision that, beginning with fiscal year 1951, we would pay our own way in the Ryukyus. Thus, as of July 1, 1950, the principle of uncompensated requisitioning of Ryukyuan private property was abandoned in favor of leasehold arrangements, with rentals to be paid by the U.S. Government; and with correlative provisions for compensating landowners for damages caused to their property during that period. From that date on, we paid rentals from appropriated funds for all real estate held by U.S. forces in the Ryukyus.[1]

Some of these rentals were paid before the treaty entered into force; the remainder have been paid subsequently.[2]

The Government of Japan similarly has denied any legal liability on its part for pretreaty claims in Okinawa. Nevertheless, in 1957 it made gratuitous payments of about $2.8 million to these claimants. These payments have been deducted from the claims covered by the proposed legislation, and a specific provision has been included, precluding disbursement of funds appropriated thereunder for claims already satisfied by the Government of Japan.

Some 180,000 claims are covered by the proposed legislation, involving a total of about 80,000 individual Okinawan claimants—representing, with an average of 5 persons to a family, about 400,000 ultimate beneficiaries. The fact that almost half of the population of the Ryukyus is involved in this matter reveals the widespread interest in the proposed joint resolution, throughout the entire archipelago.

The vast majority of the claims are for small amounts. The average amount to be received by an individual claimant is $275 ($22 million divided by 80,000). However, compared with the yearly per capita income of $319 in Okinawa, this is a significant amount.

The bulk of the claims were submitted to the U.S. High Commissioner during the early years after the peace treaty. The claimants were reminded of article 19a of the treaty, and told that the claims could not be honored, because the U.S. Government had no legal liability for them. These consistent turndowns resulted in the presentation of numerous petitions, requesting the U.S. Government to modify its position.

In 1960, acting on the High Commissioner's continued recommendations, the Department of the Army, with the approval of the Secretary of Defense and the concurrence of both the Secretary of State and the Director of the Bureau of the Budget, directed the High Com-

---

[1] These rental arrangements were undertaken on the basis of implied leases, ultimately executed in the post-treaty period by virtue of the retroactive provisions of Civil Administration Proclamation No. 26, dated Dec. 5, 1953.
[2] The above-mentioned proclamation qualifies, under art. 19b of the treaty, as exempting these particular pretreaty claims from the waiver provisions of art. 19a thereof. The already satisfied pretreaty claims, of course, are not included among the claims covered by the proposed joint resolution, which covers land claims for only the three-and-a-half year period from Jan. 1, 1947, through June 30, 1950.

0196

missioner to review the entire subject and to hold discussions with the Ryukyuan claimants, their representatives, and the government of the Ryukyu Islands.

In his public announcement to this effect in April 1961, General Caraway, the then High Commissioner, noted that the United States thereby assumed no legal responsibility to settle these claims; and stated that they were being reviewed because of the concern of the United States, as the administering authority in Okinawa, for the well-being of the Okinawan people. Advance copies of this announcement were distributed to the President of the Senate, Speaker of the House, members of the concerned committees in both the Senate and House, including the Senate Foreign Relations Committee.

### COMMITTEE ESTABLISHED TO REVIEW CLAIMS

The High Commissioner subsequently established a Joint Ryukyuan-American Committee which reviewed the evidence in accordance with standards that had previously been developed with regard to claims submitted to the U.S. Government by residents of other areas in the Far East. The committee submitted a unanimous report to the High Commissioner. He transmitted it to the Department of the Army, fully supporting the Committee's conclusions and recommending that appropriate action be taken to seek congressional authorization to pay those claims which were adjudged meritorious.

The legislative proposal now before you is a direct result of the Committee's study and of the High Commissioner's approval.

Although amounts totaling about $53 million were originally claimed, the total amount of meritorious claims was adjudged, in the course of the Joint Committee's review, to be slightly under $22 million—a reduction of about 60 percent.

In summary, during the 7-year military occupation of the Ryukyus by the U.S. Armed Forces, approximately 80,000 Ryukyuans suffered damages arising from the acts or omissions of the U.S. Armed Forces. To date, with minor exceptions, these individuals have received no compensation. It is clear that under international law and practice, these persons would normally be entitled to just compensation by or on behalf of the occupying forces. It has been the general practice of the United States to transfer this obligation to the local government. But, in the Ryukyus, from the beginning of the occupation to the present day, the United States has had the sole jurisdictional authority and continues to have.

Accordingly, it is the view of the administration that the United States has an equitable and moral obligation, although not a legal obligation, in this case, to pay for the damages caused by the Armed Forces. This committee's favorable consideration of the resolution now before you and its ultimate passage by the Congress would satisfy this equitable and moral obligation.

To assist today in this presentation, Lt. Gen. Albert Watson II, has come from his assigned post in Okinawa. General Watson has been High Commissioner of the Ryukyu Islands (as well as Commanding General of the Army forces in that area) and has been so since August 1 of last year. He is thus thoroughly familiar with the feelings and needs of the Ryukyuan people, as well as of the military im-

0197

portance of these islands to our national security and to the security of the free world.

General Watson is accompanied by two members of his staff, who served on the Joint Committee which reviewed these claims. Mr. Eugene V. Slattery is an attorney of the Legal Affairs Department of the U.S. Civil Administration of the Ryukyus. The other is Mr. Felipe T. Santos, a supervisor in the Real Estate Division of the U.S. Army Engineer District on Okinawa.

Because this proposal may involve questions relating to foreign policy considerations and to the interpretation of relevant provisions of the Treaty of Peace with Japan, the Department of State is represented here by the Honorable Samuel D. Berger. He is formerly U.S. Ambassador to Korea and now Deputy Assistant Secretary of State for Far Eastern Affairs.

Subject to your desires, Mr. Chairman, I would like to ask General Watson to speak next, to describe how the Joint Committee conducted its review and what were its principal findings. Ambassador Berger would then cover the peace treaty and foreign policy implications.

Mr. Chairman, I thank you and the members of the committee for the privilege of appearing before you.

This, sir, completes my statement.

Senator SPARKMAN. Thank you very much, Mr. Secretary.

Senator Fong has come in, and I know he has other committees to attend. Therefore, I will ask him to testify at this time.

## STATEMENT OF HON. HIRAM L. FONG, A U.S. SENATOR FROM THE STATE OF HAWAII

Senator FONG. I will only take a minute, Mr. Chairman.

I would like to have my statement received in the record. I will not read it.

Senator SPARKMAN. It will be received in full.

Senator FONG. I have just listened with great interest to the statement of the Honorable Stanley R. Resor, Secretary of the Army. I believe he has covered the question very fairly, and I would like to recommend that these claims be paid because it will promote good will and friendship for us in that part of the Pacific. Okinawa is a bastion of our defense in the Far East. We need to maintain the good will of the people there. Since these claims would be paid to about 400,000 of the 800,000 people there, almost one-half of the people of the Ryukyu Islands would be benefited. The claims, on the average, are small. Under international law, we are obligated to pay these claims, and I therefore ask that they be paid without further delay.

Senator SPARKMAN. Thank you, Senator Fong.

We appreciate your appearance, and your statement will be received.

Senator FONG. I want to say also, Mr. Chairman, I have received many, many letters from mayors and legislators of the various cities, towns, and villages and from many of the residents in Okinawa asking that these long-delayed claims be paid.

Senator SPARKMAN. Thank you.

We appreciate your coming.

Senator FONG. Thank you.

0198

(Senator Fong's statement referred to follows:)

STATEMENT OF U.S. SENATOR HIRAM L. FONG, REPUBLICAN, OF HAWAII

Mr. Chairman, I appreciate the opportunity to appear before your distinguished committee today to testify in behalf of Senate Joint Resolution 13, which I introduced on January 6, 1965, and Senate Joint Resolution 32, introduced by the chairman and my colleague, Senator Inouye, on January 22. Both resolutions provide for payment to inhabitants of Okinawa for deaths, injuries, property damage, and land use that occurred after the termination of hostilities with Japan before the effective date of the Japanese Peace Treaty in 1952. Both resolutions are substantially the same. Both resolutions request authorization for $22 million. The only difference is that Senate Joint Resolution 13 has been revised in Senate Joint Resolution 32 by the Secretary of the Army. As the changes are of a technical nature, I request to be a cosponsor of the Fulbright resolution, Senate Joint Resolution 32.

The legislative proposal of the Department of Defense, Senate Joint Resolution 32, is based on an extensive study and review in the field by the Joint Ryukyuan-American Committee. The Committee consisted of representatives of the U.S. Civil Administration of the Ryukyu Islands and of the government of the Ryukyu Islands working together. This Committee reported its findings to the High Commissioner of the Ryukyu Islands. He, in supporting the report, recommended that the Department of the Army take appropriate steps to obtain congressional authority to pay the claims which were adjudged meritorious.

The joint resolution seeking $22 million would authorize the payment of about 180,000 claims submitted by the people of Okinawa, primarily for deaths and injuries to persons, for use of land, for destruction of personal and real property, for damage to agricultural crops, and for loss of fishing rights during the period subsequent to actual war hostilities.

Briefly, these claims may be classified as follows:

1. Land rentals comprising about 141,600 claims, totaling about $15 million.
2. Restoration of lands for any damage done to property, amounting to about $2.5 million.
3. Fruit trees, timber, bamboo, etc., totaling about $1,030,000.
4. Personal injuries and death caused by personnel of the U.S. Armed Forces, involving about $830,000.
5. Destruction of buildings valued at about $610,000.
6. Loss of inshore fishing rights, amounting to about $500,000.

In addition, there are 14 or 15 other classes of meritorious claims making up the balance of the $22 million.

Out of the 180,000 claims covered by the proposed resolution, about 80,000 individual claims are for smaller amounts. Each of these may average about $275 ($22 million divided by 80,000). But each claim may represent an average family of 5 persons, or about 400,000 ultimate beneficiaries. This is about half of the total population of the Ryukyu Islands.

This proposed legislation, therefore, directly affects the well-being of many people. These are people, as I know very well from those whom I have known in Hawaii, and those I have contacted during my trip to Okinawa in 1959, whose life for many generations has been attached to the soil and for whom their farm, however small, represents not only their livelihood but a settled, stable, traditional way of life. Despite the changes wrought by war and the existence of our bases there, Okinawa remains essentially an agrarian society. Despite the improved conditions of recent years, it remains comparatively poor in rural villages. The several hundred dollars (on an average) that these payments will help per family will mean a great deal in terms of the necessities of a household, for the improvement of their home, for the education of their children. Among the payments that are provided are claims for loss of life and for personal injuries to their loved ones. These are small in total but they are big in terms of maintaining our good will and understanding with these most gracious, cultured, and friendly people.

In view of the fact that Okinawa is of great strategic importance to the United States, this continued friendly relation with the local people is vital and significant. The main island of Okinawa is a bastion of our strength in the Far East where we can move with freedom of action. In these moments of airstrikes in Vietnam, the importance of that establishment should need no further emphasis.

In the Japanese Peace Treaty of 1952, Japan waived all claims against the

0199

United States of Japanese nationals, and this has been regarded as removing any legal liability of the United States to the inhabitants of the Ryukyu Islands who suffered injury or death, or whose property was damaged by the U.S. Armed Forces during the occupation of Okinawa. The treaty, also, granted the United States full administrative, legislative, and judicial powers over the inhabitants of the islands, leaving Japan with residual sovereignty.

For all intents and purposes, the United States has exercised exclusive powers of administration since the Japanese surrendered in 1945.

In paying claims arising from death or personal injury suffered by residents of occupied countries, due to acts or omissions of occupation forces, the U.S. policy in both World Wars has been to transfer the burden to the local governments to make such payment. But in the case of Okinawa, pursuant to the Potsdam Declaration, the Japanese Government was stripped of its power over the islands. The U.S. Government then did not have any government to arrange for the payment. There was no local sovereign power in Okinawa which could be financially responsible. Had Japan retained administrative jurisdiction over these island inhabitants, the Japanese Government would have effected payments under the supervision of the Supreme Command. But this was not the situation. The United States, as the administering authority in Okinawa, has the responsibility of seeing that these claims are paid direct.

I urge the committee to act quickly and favorably on the joint resolutions pending before you.

Senator SPARKMAN. General Watson, we are delighted to have you here, and we will be delighted to hear from you.

## STATEMENT OF GEN. ALBERT WATSON II, HIGH COMMISSIONER FOR THE RYUKYUAN ISLANDS

General WATSON. Mr. Chairman, I appreciate this opportunity to appear before this committee.

My purpose is to provide you with additional background information regarding the Joint United States-Ryukyuan Committee and its deliberations, together with some detailed information regarding the categories of pretreaty claims.

My service as High Commissioner, as was noted earlier, of the Ryukyu Islands dates back to August 1, 1964. Nevertheless, the present legislative proposal began to take shape back in 1961.

As stated by Secretary Resor, this matter came about because of the fact that all claims against the United States, arising out of actions of the U.S. forces in the Ryukyus during the occupation, were waived in the treaty of peace with Japan—signed at San Francisco—which entered into force on April 28, 1952. On April 6, 1961, the then High Commissioner—General Caraway—announced that the U.S. Government was prepared to review this matter in detail. He announced that he would establish a joint committee, whose mission would be to conduct this review, to assemble and evaluate all pertinent information, and to make recommendations to the High Commissioner.

### ACTIVITIES OF JOINT UNITED STATES-RYUKYUAN COMMISSION

Pursuant to this announcement, as Secretary Resor mentioned, the High Commissioner appointed four U.S. members, while the chief executive of the government of the Ryukyu Islands appointed four Ryukyuan members. The U.S. members included Mr. John P. King. then President of the U.S. Land Tribunal in USCAR; Mr. Eugene Slattery, an attorney of USCAR's Legal Affairs Department, here present; Mr. Felipe T. Santos, a supervisor in the Real Estate Divi-

52-255—65——2

0200

sion of the U.S. Army Engineer District on Okinawa, here present; and Mr. Richard Rose, then Chief of the Land Section in USCAR's Legal Affairs Department.

Heading the Ryukyuan membership was Mr. Ryojun Kugai, director of the legal affairs department of the government of the Ryukyu Islands. The other three Ryukyuan members were Mr. Choko Kuwae, a member of the Ryukyuan Legislature and president of the association which was formed by the pretreaty claimants to advance their cause; Mr. Hiroshi Makino, a prominent Ryukyuan attorney; and Mr. Ibi Nakamoto, formerly mayor of the city of Naha.

I might say here parenthetically that the city of Naha is the largest city in the Ryukyuan Islands.

This Committee met 19 times, between May 10 and December 29, 1961, and reviewed, in detail, the written evidence in support of these claims, which had been assembled over a period of several years by representatives of the claimants.

Claims for the rental of real property are supported by oral and written evidence of use and occupation of the involved lands by the U.S. Government. Claims for personal injury or death and damage to personal or real property are supported by written evidence of claimants and Ryukyuan officials; this written evidence is largely in the form of statements, affidavits, investigative reports, and police records made at the time the damages were suffered. All of the voluminous documentary evidence has been preserved and is on file in the Ryukyu Islands. The Committee also made numerous on-site inspections of the claimed damages, particularly in connection with released lands.

The Committee agreed that the United States would incur no cost or liability whatsoever regarding the handling or disposal of these claims, and that, should the United States make ex gratia payments for them, the disbursements would be made by the government of the Ryukyu Islands, at no expense to the United States. All of the Joint Committee's decisions were unanimous, and I believe that the conclusions reached are fair and equitable. The then High Commissioner approved the conclusions and recommendations of the Joint Committee which have been incorporated in the administration's proposal which you are now considering.

### CATEGORIES OF CLAIMS

The meritorious claims fall into 21 distinct categories, which are recapitulated in the tabulation attached to my statement. It is that page 11. Perhaps it would be helpful if I were to comment briefly on these categories.

First, land rentals: This is by far the largest of all the categories, comprising about 141,600 claims and totaling almost $15 million. I should perhaps elaborate on why the pretreaty period during which the Committee found rental claims to be meritorious was limited to the three and a half years from January 1, 1947, through June 30, 1950. The Joint Committee did not accept rental claims for the latter part of 1945 and all of 1946, because the Ryukyuan inhabitants were still dispersed during this period, the lands were vacant, and no crops were planted. The loss of crop production is the agreed

0201

basis for calculating all rentals of agricultural lands, and there was
no gainful use to which nonagricultural lands could have been put
during this period of almost total disruption. The Committee therefore established January 1, 1947, as a somewhat arbitrary, but roughly
accurate, beginning date of the period during which it regarded
rental claims as having merit.

Further, as Secretary Resor has explained, the Committee regarded
this period as terminating on June 30, 1950, because of the fact that
the U.S. forces, as of July 1 of that year, began to pay for real estate
used by them, under leasehold arrangements. The meritorious pretreaty land-rental claims therefore encompass a period of only three
and a half years, or just about half of the occupation period.

I shall not attempt to detail for you at this point the somewhat complicated method developed for determining the productivity of the
various agricultural lands held by the U.S. forces during the pretreaty period, and the relative evaluation of other lands. This method
can be explained now, should you wish to explore this matter.

In any event, I believe that the formulas established by the Joint
Committee for the rental value of both agricultural and commercial
lands are fair, practical, and in accordance with objective values in the
Ryukyu Islands at the time. It is my understanding that the same
standards have been successfully applied in many other situations in
the Far East, particularly in Korea and Japan, in resolving legal
claims with regard to land rented by U.S. forces.

2. Restoration of lands: The claims in this category amount to
slightly over $2.5 million. These particular claims are based on the
principle (which is observed by U.S. forces throughout the world)
that any person or organization leasing or renting real estate is obliged
to restore the property involved to its condition when leased, or to
make appropriate reimbursement for any damage done thereto during
the period of the lease. Fee value of the land was the basis when the
cost of restoration would equal or exceed the fee value.

As with the land-rental claims of the first category, we are likewise
concerned here only with damages caused during the 3½ years between January 1, 1947, and June 30, 1950.

Further, we are dealing only with damages caused during that
period to lands which have subsequently been released. The Joint
Committee decided not to regard any alterations caused during the pretreaty period to lands which are still under lease to U.S. forces as
constituting meritorious claims—because, in its opinion, these alterations (such things as housing areas, hospitals, airbases, roadways,
pipelines, and other permanent-type installations) should not be regarded as "damages," but rather as definite improvements, increasing
the value of the lands. I concur in this view.

All of the restoration claims relate to lands which have already been
released by the U.S. forces to their owners. As already indicated, the
Joint Committee found no meritorious claims to be supported by reason of the alterations caused to lands still under lease to the U.S.
forces.

3. Water rights: The U.S. forces took over two water points, or
large springs, without compensation. They have a combined flow of
1,500,000 gallons of water per day. The owners of the water points
formerly used the water for irrigation of crops, for domestic purposes,

0202

and for generating small amounts of electricity. The monetary damages suffered by the water owners amount to about $50,000.

The last category I would like to describe specifically is the fourth category; personal injuries and death.

Damages in the amount of about $830,000 for personal injuries and deaths were caused by personnel of the U.S. forces. These tortious damages resulted from accidents (involving motor vehicles, aircraft, and marine vessels), ammunition and gasoline explosions, and physical violence. From August 15, 1945, to April 28, 1952, 346 Ryukyuans were killed and 382 injured in such ways. Although no official compensation has been paid for these damages, donations amounting to about $7,000 were paid by American personnel to the victims of an explosion of ammunition; these gifts have been deducted from the meritorious claims approved by the Joint Committee for said deaths and injuries.

I would just like to briefly remark on the remaining categories. They total some $3.6 million. They include destruction of growing crops. Growing crops, valued at about $5,000, were destroyed on lands taken over by U.S. forces.

6. Fruit trees, mulberry trees, and teaplants: These damages amounted to about $430,000. The trees and plants were several years of age, and bearing. The cost of each tree or plant was based upon its fair market value at the time of destruction.

7. Standing trees and bamboos: Timber trees (pine, bamboo, et cetera) were damaged, in the amount of about $600,000.

8. Firewood and charcoal material: Hardwood trees, suitable for firewood and charcoal, were damaged, in the amount of about $18,000. This category involves almost 16 million board feet of wood.

9. Rental for buildings: 604 buildings were occupied by U.S. forces, without compensation, from August 15, 1945, to April 28, 1952. These rentals total about $74,000.

10. Buildings destroyed: 3,255 buildings, having at the time of destruction a reasonable value of about $610,000, were destroyed by U.S. forces in making lands available for U.S. housing and other necessary buildings.

11. Wells: 1,332 wells were destroyed, with a total value of about $110,000.

12. Tombs: 941 tombs were destroyed, with a total value of about $80,000.

13. Reservoirs: 52 reservoirs were destroyed, with a total value of about $65,000.

14. Stone walls: 1,994 stone walls were destroyed, with a total value of about $390,000.

15. Water tanks: 219 water tanks were destroyed, with a total value of about $14,000.

16. Collapsed and destroyed lands: Extensive amounts of land were destroyed by tidal and water action, arising from the destruction of seawalls and the diversion of natural watercourses by U.S. Forces. The lost land had a reasonable value of about $235,000.

17. Destruction of sugar mill: A sugar mill was destroyed by U.S. Forces, causing a loss to the owners in the sum of about $8,000.

18. Loss of inshore surface fishing rights: The U.S. Forces excluded nine fishing cooperatives from taking fish in inshore waters. The

020:

cooperatives had been licensed to fish in these waters for many years. They utilized 243 fishing vessels, and 712 fishermen. The Committee found that the fishing cooperatives had suffered damage in the sum of about $560,000, for which they have received no compensation.

19. Removal and relocation of buildings: The U.S. Forces requisitioned certain lands, from which the owners were compelled to remove 3,751 buildings, at their own expense, in the sum of about $220,000.

20. Severance damage: Many pipelines, powerlines, and other utilities required the taking of lands consisting of only a portion of the individual holdings. In many cases, this caused measurable damage to the landowner, because of the resultant severance of one portion of his property from the remainder.

Damages caused by this piecemeal taking of land amounts to about $14,000.

21. Property damages by tortious acts: Because of negligence on the part of U.S. Forces, or their personnel, damages in the amount of about $80,000 were caused to buildings and other property in connection with 257 incidents, such as aircraft accidents and ammunition explosions—the most notable of which was the explosion of an ammunition-laden LCT at a wharf on Ie-Jima Island during August 1948.

### COMMENTS ON CHAIRMAN OF JOINT COMMITTEE TO REVIEW RYUKYUAN CLAIMS

This completes my comments on the various categories of meritorious claims. I trust that my remarks will give you a general idea of how the Joint Committee went about its work, and of what findings it reached. I deeply regret that Judge King, who chaired the Joint Committee, is not here personally to give you more details of the Committee's work and to answer such questions as you may have about this portion of our presentation. He is an authority without challenge on all matters which are covered in our proposal insofar as the processing of the claims, their validity and so on are concerned. He has had a long career of public service with the U.S. Government and had hoped to be able to be present here as his final official act before retiring from active work. He has been suffering from a serious heart condition for some time and it has recently worsened to the point where the doctors have determined that it would be medically imprudent for him to come back to Washington, as had been planned, to participate in these hearings.

I would like to briefly summarize his background.

Judge King's background and experience amply justify his selection by the then High Commissioner to chair the Joint Committee. Prior to becoming a civilian official of the U.S. civil administration of the Ryukyu Islands some 8 years ago, he had had 40 years of distinguished service with the Regular Army, from which he retired in the rank of colonel in 1956. His military experience covers the Mexican border incident of 1916, World War I, World War II, and the Korean war.

He graduated from Stanford University Law School with the degree of juris doctor, and has been an active member of the California bar since 1925. Most of his military career was spent as an attorney

0204

in the Judge Advocate General's Corps, and, for the last 22 years in the service, most of his professional time was devoted to reviewing claims submitted by foreigners against the United States.

During 1943, when stationed in Hawaii, he personally reviewed claims involving loss of and damage to crops and trespass upon lands.

From 1944 to 1945, he was in New Guinea and the Philippines, reviewing claims relating to damage to and loss of trees, crops, and personal property.

From 1945 to 1951, as President of Foreign Claims Commission No. 173, he reviewed such claims in Korea; and from 1951 to 1956 he was similarly engaged in Japan.

During his more than 8 years of civilian service with USCAR, his regular assignment has been President of the U.S. Land Tribunal, which adjudicates matters relating to the valuation of all lands leased by the U.S. forces in the Ryukyus. At the same time, he also served as associate justice of USCAR's appellate court. In assuming the chairmanship of the Joint Committee, Judge King brought to this task not only demonstrated legal competence and extensive experience in the claims field, but also knowledge of the Japanese language and wide-ranging familiarity with the laws and customs of various peoples of the Far East.

I have taken the time to give you this thumbnail sketch of Judge King, in his unfortunate absence, because I believe that you should know the kind of man who chaired this important Committee and guided it in reaching conclusions, findings, and recommendations based on solid factual analysis and endorsed by the High Commissioner and the executive branch.

In conclusion, I believe that favorable consideration of this resolution by your committee and by the Congress would discharge an equitable obligation of the United States in the Ryuku Islands and throughout the free world.

Mr. Chairman, this concludes my statement.

(The attachment referred to follows:)

### Recapitulation of meritorious claims

| Category | Amount |
|---|---|
| 1. Land rentals | $14,939,539.00 |
| 2. Restoration of lands | 2,518,718.71 |
| 3. Water rights | 50,377.00 |
| 4. Personal injuries and death | 831,032.69 |
| 5. Growing crops | 5,019.00 |
| 6. Fruit trees, mulberry trees, and tea plants | 431,066.00 |
| 7. Standing trees and bamboos | 609,834.00 |
| 8. Firewood and charcoal material | 18,399.00 |
| 9. Rentals for buildings | 73,908.00 |
| 10. Building destroyed | 610,982.00 |
| 11. Wells | 111,281.00 |
| 12. Tombs | 81,468.00 |
| 13. Reservoirs | 65,569.00 |
| 14. Stone walls | 393,423.00 |
| 15. Water tanks | 13,807.00 |
| 16. Collapsed and destroyed lands | 236,469.00 |
| 17. Destruction of sugar mill | 8,376.00 |
| 18. Loss of inshore surface fishing rights | 562,607.00 |
| 19. Removal and relocation of buildings | 219,259.00 |
| 20. Severance damage | 13,293.00 |
| 21. Property damages by tortious acts | 80,097.00 |
| Total damages | 21,874,524.40 |

0205

Senator SPARKMAN. Thank you very much, General, for a very clear statement.

Does Ambassador Berger have a statement?

Mr. Ambassador, we will be glad to hear from you.

## STATEMENT OF HON. SAMUEL D. BERGER, DEPUTY ASSISTANT SECRETARY OF STATE FOR FAR EASTERN AFFAIRS, DEPARTMENT OF STATE

Mr. BERGER. Yes, sir.

Mr. Chairman, I have been asked to appear before you today to provide the views of the Department of State on Senate Joint Resolution 32, authorizing an ex gratia contribution to Ryukyuan inhabitants for death and injury of persons, and for use of and damage to private property, arising from acts and omissions of the U.S. Armed Forces before the entry into force of the peace treaty with Japan.

As you know, the President has delegated to the Secretary of Defense the responsibility for the administration of the Ryukyu Islands as long as the United States finds it necessary to govern them. To the extent that the pretreaty claims question is an internal Ryukyuan matter, the Department of State supports the views of the Department of Defense expressed earlier by Secretary Resor and General Watson.

### FOREIGN POLICY IMPLICATIONS OF CLAIMS SETTLEMENT

There are, however, two foreign policy questions raised by the proposed legislation on which the Department of State wishes to comment.

First, there is the relationship of the proposed legislation to the treaty of peace with Japan (TIAS 2490). Article 19(a) of that treaty reads as follows:

Japan waives all claims of Japan and its nationals against the Allied Powers and their nationals arising out of the war or out of actions taken because of the existence of state of war, and waives all claims arising from the presence, operations, or actions of forces or authorities of any of the Allied Powers in Japanese territory prior to the coming into force of the present treaty.

It is our view that residents of Ryukyu Islands are nationals of Japan and that the Ryukyu Islands were Japanese territory in the period "prior to the coming into force of the present treaty" as specified in this paragraph. We therefore believe that the United States has no legal obligation to pay the claims of Ryukyuans arising from the presence, operations, or actions of U.S. forces in the Ryukyus in the pretreaty period.

The Japanese Government similarly denies any legal liability, on its part, for pretreaty damages in the Ryukyus, since it had no administrative authority in this area during the pretreaty period and continues, under article 3 of the treaty, to have no administrative authority there. It further denies that the waiver provision of article 19(a), which established that the United States not be liable for such claims, generated any corresponding liability for them on the part of Japan.

Since both the United States, in its capacity as the former occupying authority, and Japan, in its capacity as nominal sovereign, deny

0206

legal liability for the claims of Ryukyuans for damages suffered in the pretreaty period, individual Ryukyuans would appear to have no recourse but to appeal, through the government of the Ryukyu Islands, for redress to the United States as the present administering authority. The Department of Defense has already commented on the validity of these claims and their relationship to other U.S. programs in the Ryukyus.

## CONTRIBUTION OF JAPANESE GOVERNMENT

Second, I call the committee's attention to the fact that the Japanese Government, while denying legal liability, appropriated 1 billion yen ($2.8 million) in 1957 as an ex gratia payment to Ryukyuans having claims for damages suffered in the pretreaty period. This payment was made by the Japanese Government as an "advance" against future payment in full by the United States, and a Japanese Cabinet decision was made to the effect that the 1 billion ex gratia payment would be considered reimbursable to Japan in the event of a later U.S. settlement covering losses sustained by Ryukyuans during the pretreaty period.

Both the United States and Japan are now contributing to the economic development and social welfare in the Ryukyus, and we expect that the settlement by the United States of these pretreaty claims will contribute substantially to our common objectives. Utilization of a part of such settlement to reimburse the Japanese Government for its earlier ex gratia payment would reduce by that much the effectiveness of the U.S. payment in stimulating economic growth in the islands.

In connection with the preparation of the administration's proposal on the settlement of these claims, the Department of State has brought these considerations to the attention of the Japanese Government, requesting that it now waive its claim to reimbursement for its 1957 payment.

Although the Japanese Government is in sympathy and agreement with the objectives underlying the U.S. request that it waive these claims, it informs us that it can reverse its earlier Cabinet decision only through certain legislative action which would adversely affect its legal position with regard to oustanding claims in areas other than the Ryukyus.

Because the Government of Japan considers it should be reimbursed if full payment is made by us, a provision has been inserted to provide that U.S. payment not cover payment already made by Japan. We anticipate no reaction from the Government of Japan as a result of its inclusion which would adversely affect the close, amicable relations which exist between our countries.

In summary, the Department strongly supports the proposed legislation as being a fair and equitable settlement of a longstanding grievance of the people of the Ryukyu Islands and in the best foreign relations interests of the United States.

That concludes my statement, Senator.

Senator SPARKMAN. Thank you very much, Mr. Ambassador. Does that conclude the statements of the proponents?

Secretary RESOR. Yes, sir.

0207

Senator SPARKMAN. I would like to ask a few questions, not a great many.

You have made a very clear and very full statement. But I believe, General, you said that all of the findings and recommendations were made on a unanimous basis, is that right?

General WATSON. That is correct, sir; yes.

Senator SPARKMAN. That applies to the amounts to be paid and everything?

General WATSON. Yes, sir. Amounts and the details of the claim itself, the validity of the claim.

## OTHER FINANCIAL COMPENSATION TO CLAIMANTS

Senator SPARKMAN. One statement I don't quite understand. You say that $7,000 had been paid for death and injury from private sources.

Did you mean that that much covers all of the death claims or just that certain cases were compensated for?

General WATSON. Sir, this was done in certain specific cases, out of the good will of the Americans there. We have a people-to-people program there which is designed to improve our relations with the Ryukyuan people.

Senator SPARKMAN. The reason I was curious was because I notice there were about 700 of those cases, and $7,000 would not have covered very much.

General WATSON. No, sir; this was a specific instance connected with the explosion of an ammunition ship.

Senator SPARKMAN. We do propose to reimburse Japan, is that correct?

Secretary RESOR. No, we do not.

General WATSON. We do not.

Senator SPARKMAN. I thought it was stated that we would reimburse them, but not pay for any of the damages that Japan had paid for.

Mr. BERGER. No, sir. The Japanese, when they made this ex gratia payment, stipulated that they should be reimbursed, but that was a unilateral action by the Japanese Government, and in the proposed legislation, we stipulate that no part of our payment shall be used for reimbursement.

Senator SPARKMAN. For repayment to Japan?

Mr. BERGER. Quite right.

Senator SPARKMAN. Or for the payment of the damages that were covered in the payments by Japan?

Mr. BERGER. That is correct.

Senator SPARKMAN. I am glad to get that straight, because I thought it was something else.

## CONTRACT FOR ATTORNEYS' FEES

Now, are there any intermediaries concerned?

You are familiar, I am sure, with the difficulties we had on the last round of Philippine claims.

Are there any considerations of that kind here?

0208

Secretary RESOR. There is an American law firm which has represented the Ryukyuans: the Washington law firm of Stitt & Hemmendinger. They have received a retainer of approximately $10,000 beginning, I believe, in the year 1958, going down through the current year, and they have a contingent arrangement to be paid an additional fee, if the claims are paid, on a graduated scale. We have a copy of the correspondence which reflects that arrangement, which we would be glad to turn over to the committee. The total fee which they would be paid would come well under the limitation provided in this resolution which, as you will notice, is 5 percent. If the whole sum is paid, I think it works out, including the retainer, to about $260,000, and that is in the range of 1 percent of the total amount.

Senator SPARKMAN. Was that agreement entered into before 1961 or after? It was in 1961, I believe you said that these claims really began to take shape.

Secretary RESOR. The correspondence here indicates that it was originally entered into in 1958, and was later amended to continue it through the current—on a year-to-year basis, so the original letter contract between the law firm and the claimants association was in May of 1958.

### ESTIMATE OF LEGAL COSTS

Senator SPARKMAN. What would be your estimate as to the amount that would be paid if this bill passed in the form in which it has been proposed?

Secretary RESOR. My estimate would be that, in addition to the retainer which has already been paid.

Senator SPARKMAN. That is $10,000.

Secretary RESOR. Annually for 8 years.

Senator SPARKMAN. Then $10,000 annually.

Secretary RESOR. Annually for 8 years.

Senator SPARKMAN. That is $80,000.

Secretary RESOR. Right. Our estimate is, if the full amount of the claims were paid, there would be an additional sum of $180,000.

Senator SPARKMAN. Now, I believe you say that these come out of the claims, they are not added to our bill.

Secretary RESOR. That is correct. The claimants would have to pay the law firm pursuant to their own arrangements, pursuant to this letter agreement, out of the moneys which the claimants received.

So, this would reduce the net amount which the claimants received, assuming that this is all paid and collected.

Senator SPARKMAN. Did the Army approve of this agreement?

Secretary RESOR. No, we had nothing to do with this. This is an agreement between the claimants and the law firm, and we have had nothing to do with it, and we express no opinion with respect to it.

Senator SPARKMAN. Here is this statement in the resolution:

Fees already paid for services performed in submitting a claim to the Joint American-Ryukyuan Commission shall be deducted from the amounts authorized under this legislation.

Have we paid any fees?

Secretary RESOR. No, sir; we have not.

0209

General WATSON. No, sir.

Senator SPARKMAN. What is the meaning of that statement?

Secretary RESOR. Are you reading from section——

Senator SPARKMAN. On page 3 of Senate Joint Resolution 13.

Secretary RESOR. Section 3.

Senator SPARKMAN. Section 3, page 3.

Secretary RESOR. Right.

Senator SPARKMAN. Right in the middle of the section, it is the second sentence.

## LIMIT ON LEGAL FEES

Secretary RESOR. I see now the meaning of it. The first sentence puts a 5-percent limitation on the amount of fees which can be collected in the aggregate or from any individual claimant. This second sentence merely says that, in computing whether or not that 5 percent has been exceeded, you will count in any sums that have already been paid.

In other words, that goes against the 5 percent. Fees already paid for such services——

Senator SPARKMAN. In other words, it is not deducted from the amount we would pay, but it is deducted in calculating the amount that might be collected under the 5-percent provision.

Secretary RESOR. Right. I read it to mean, where it says fees shall be deducted from the amounts authorized under this joint resolution, I take it that means from the amounts of legal-service fees authorized.

In other words, authorized by the preceding sentence.

Senator SPARKMAN. You are not reading the word "authorized" into the resolution, are you? I don't see it.

Secretary RESOR. It is in that sentence you referred to, line 16; that is what gave me difficulty at first. I didn't understand——

Senator SPARKMAN. The last line of my resolution is 15.

Secretary RESOR. Well, you have in section 3, you have a second sentence that reads: "Fees already paid for such services"—for services performed in submitting a claim——

Senator SPARKMAN. It reads, "shall be deducted from the amounts authorized under this legislation".

Secretary RESOR. Joint resolution——

Senator SPARKMAN. I am looking at Senate Joint Resolution 13. You are looking at 32?

Secretary RESOR. Yes, and 32 is the one that we are supporting, the language there I think is slightly different.

Senator SPARKMAN. Yes. I see it.

In other words, a person who might have been receiving only a small compensation would be protected under the 5-percent provision.

Secretary RESOR. That is correct.

Senator SPARKMAN. Regardless of how small it is, 5 percent still applies.

Secretary RESOR. That is correct.

Senator SPARKMAN. And does it graduate downward as it becomes larger?

Secretary RESOR. You are referring now to the Hemmendinger fee?

0210

Senator SPARKMAN. I understood you to state it was a graduated fee.

Secretary RESOR. That is correct; it is an agreement with the association of all the claimants.

Senator SPARKMAN. Yes.

Secretary RESOR. And it says, referring here to the final fee above the retainer, that it will be contingent upon success in obtaining compensation for the landowners and will be 5 percent of the amounts recovered up to $1 million, plus 3 percent of any amount up to the second million, plus one-half of 1 percent of all amounts above $2 million.

Senator SPARKMAN. When you are speaking of those millions are you talking about individual claimants, or the aggregate?

Secretary RESOR. No, this I believe speaks of the aggregate of all claims. But the resolution prevents any individual claimant, no matter how small his claim is, from paying more than 5 percent.

Senator SPARKMAN. In other words, he is protected under the 5-percent limitation.

Secretary RESOR. Correct, as set forth in the resolution.

Senator SPARKMAN. I believe it would be well for us to include this agreement in detail as a part of the hearing.

Secretary RESOR. Right. I understand that it is already on file with the Department of Justice, I believe, under the Foreign Agents Registration Act.

Senator SPARKMAN. We have some material on it. In fact, we have a statement from the law firm regarding it.

General WATSON. Mr. Chairman, may I add one point here?

Senator SPARKMAN. Yes, General.

General WATSON. There is nothing in the proposed resolution that puts a graduated scale.

Senator SPARKMAN. I understand.

General WATSON. Yes.

Senator SPARKMAN. Something was said about it before.

General WATSON. Yes, sir.

Senator SPARKMAN. And I thought it referred to the individual. But it applies to the gross amount.

General WATSON. Yes, sir.

Senator SPARKMAN. With the 5-percent maximum for any individual.

General WATSON. That is right, sir.

Senator SPARKMAN. Yes.

Thank you very much, gentlemen. I cannot think of anything else to ask right now.

I appreciate your coming.

(The following letters pertaining to Ryukyuan claims were received for the record:)

STITT & HEMMENDINGER,
*Washington, D.C., May 8, 1958.*

THE RELIEF ASSOCIATION FOR OKINAWA & OGASAWARA
(Napno Doho Engo Kai);
*22–5 Chome Shiba Shinbashi Minatoku,*
*Tokyo, Japan.*

GENTLEMEN: We have the honor to submit the following proposal (superseding all earlier communications) on the subject of the retainer of our firm to present to the U.S. Government the case of the Okinawan landowners for compensation for use of their land by U.S. military forces before the treaty of peace with Japan.

0211

Stitt & Hemmendinger will be retained through the Relief Association for Okinawa and Ogasawara (Nanpo Doho Engo Kai), acting at the request of and in the interest of the Committee for Compensation for Pre-Treaty Military Land Use (Kowahakkozen Gunyotochito No Sonshitsu Hosho Kakutoku Kiseikai), for the period of 2 years to represent the interests of the latter association, which was formed in Okinawa on March 19, 1958, and which consists of the mayors of towns and villages, the chairmen of town and village councils and village committees on the military use of land in the Ryukyus.

Stitt & Hemmendinger will be compensated at the rate of $10,000 a year, payable $5,000 initially and $5,000 at 6-month intervals. This fee will cover all professional work in the investigation of law and facts and developments of theory and strategy of the case; it will also cover all ordinary expenses such as telephone, correspondence, local travel, entertainment, etc. It will not cover extraordinary expenses such as the retainer of experts on public or congressional relations, the reproduction and dissemination of documents in large numbers, or travel to the Far East. For these aspects of the case, a special budget will be developed as soon as our study of the case warrants.

The final fee, above this retainer, will be contingent upon success in obtaining compensation for the landowners by action of the U.S. Government, and will be 5 percent of the amounts recovered up to $1 million, plus 3 percent of any amount up to the second million dollars, plus one-half of 1 percent (0.5 percent) of all amounts above $2 million.

It is understood, if this proposal is accepted, that we will commence work on the basis of the initial payment of $5,000, and that the whole situation will be reviewed in the light of our initial study before a second payment is made. There will be no obligation to continue the retainer if upon such a review the circumstances do not appear to justify it.

If the above arrangements are acceptable, it is requested that appropriate endorsement confirming such acceptance be made on a copy of this letter and be returned to us. It is further requested that we be furnished in due course a copy of the document evidencing the acceptance of these proposals by the Ryukyuan Committee for Compensation for Pre-Treaty Military Land Use.

Yours sincerely,

NOEL HEMMENDINGER.

The above proposals are hereby accepted.

KEIZO SHIBUSAWA,
(For the Relief Association for Okinawa & Ogasawara)
(Nanpo Doho Engokai).

WASHINGTON, D.C., *June 19, 1958.*

Mr. NOEL HEMMENDINGER,
*Stitt & Hemmendinger,*
*Washington, D.C.*

DEAR MR. HEMMENDINGER: We refer to your letter of May 8, 1958, to the Relief Association for Okinawa & Ogasawara (Nanpo Doho Engokai) in which are set forth your proposals with respect to representation in Washington of the case of the landowners of Okinawa for compensation for use of their land by the U.S. military forces before the treaty of peace with Japan.

We have been informed by the Relief Association for Okinawa & Ogasawara that it has accepted your proposals and we are glad to assure you that for our part these proposals are also accepted.

It is our understanding that you will look to the Relief Association for Okinawa & Ogasawara for the payments which are to be made to you in any event for this work, and that our responsibility is limited to the payments as set forth in your letter of May 8 which are contingent upon your success in obtaining compensation for the landowners by action of the U.S. Government.

GAZEN TOKESHI,

(For the Association To Acquire Compensation for Damages Prior to Peace Treaty) (Kowahakkozen Gunyotochito No Sonshitsu Hosho Kakutoku Kiseikai).

0212

JULY 8, 1960.

Mr. CHOJO OYAMA,
*President, Association To Acquire Compensation for Damages Prior to Peace Treaty, Okinawa Kaikan Hall, Naha, Okinawa.*

DEAR MR. OYAMA: The purpose of this letter is to confirm new contractual arrangements between the law firm of Stitt & Hemmendinger and the Association To Acquire Compensation for Damages Prior to Peace Treaty.

By letter contract of May 8, 1958, between Stitt & Hemmendinger and the Nanpo Doho Engokai the law firm of Stitt & Hemmendinger was retained for the period of 2 years to represent the interests of the Association To Acquire Compensation for Damages Prior to Peace Treaty, by presenting to the U.S. Government the case of the Okinawan landowners to be compensated by some authority for use of their land by U.S. military forces before the treaty of peace with Japan.

The agreement further provided:

"Stitt & Hemmendinger will be compensated at the rate of $10,000 a year, payable $5,000 initially and $5,000 at 6-month intervals. This fee fill cover all professional work in the investigation of law and facts and developments of theory and strategy of the case; it will also cover all ordinary expenses such as telephone, correspondence, local travel, entertainment, etc. It will not cover extraordinary expenses such as the retainer of experts on public or congressional relations, the reproduction and dissemenation of documents in large numbers, or travel to the Far East. For these aspects of the case, a special budget will be developed as soon as our study of the case warrants.

"The final fee, above this retainer, will be contingent upon success in obtaining compensation for the landowners by action of the U.S. Government, and will be 5 percent of the amounts recovered up to $1 million, plus 3 percent of any amount up to the second million dollars, plus one-half of 1 percent (0.5 percent) of all amounts above $2 million."

By letter of June 19, 1958, from Mr. Takeshi to us, the Association To Acquire Compensation for Damages Prior to Peace Treaty accepted our proposals as set forth in the letter of May 8, 1958, on the understanding that we would look to the Nanpo Doho Engokai for the payments to be made to us in any event for this work, and that the responsibility of the association should be limited to the payments as set forth in our letter of May 8 which are contingent upon our success in obtaining compensation for the landowners by action of the U.S. Government.

The 2-year period stipulated in the letter contract of May 8, 1958, has expired, and the last fee we have received covered the period through May 7, 1960.

It is proposed that the Association To Acquire Compensation for Damages Prior to Peace Treaty enter into a direct retainer arrangement with the firm of Stitt & Hemmendinger for the same purposes and same compensation, terminable by either party effective May 7 of each year, and that the Nanpo Doho Engokai henceforth have no connection with Stitt & Hemmendinger.

The fee of $10,000 will be payable in $5,000 installments, commencing May 8, 1960, and will cover all professional work and all ordinary expenses of Stitt & Hemmendinger in accomplishing the purposes of the contract. It will not cover extraordinary expenses for the retainer of experts on public or congressional relations, the reproduction and dissemination of documents in large numbers, or travel to the Far East. If such expenditures should appear desirable in sums that could not reasonably be defrayed by Stitt & Hemmendinger within the stipulated retainer, Stitt & Hemmendinger will make appropriate proposals to the association. Contingent compensation will remain payable as provided in the May 8, 1958, letter and the association's letter of June 19, 1958.

Endorsement of this letter below shall constitute its acceptance of this proposal by the Association To Acquire Compensation for Damages Prior to the Peace Treaty.

Sincerely yours,

NOEL HEMMENDINGER.

Accepted for the Association To Acquire Compensation Prior to Peace Treaty:
CHOJE OYAMA.

Senator SPARKMAN. Next will be Executive C, 89th Congress, 1st session.

0213

(The agreement referred to follows:)

[89th Cong., 1st sess., Executive C]

## GUT DAM CLAIMS AGREEMENT WITH CANADA

MESSAGE FROM THE PRESIDENT OF THE UNITED STATES TRANSMITTING THE AGREE-
MENT BETWEEN THE UNITED STATES AND CANADA CONCERNING THE ESTABLISH-
MENT OF AN INTERNATIONAL ARBITRAL TRIBUNAL TO DISPOSE OF U.S. CLAIMS
RELATING TO GUT DAM, SIGNED AT OTTAWA, MARCH 25, 1965

MAY 17, 1965.—Agreement was read the first time and, together with the message and
accompanying papers, was referred to the Committee on Foreign Relations and was
ordered to be printed for use of the Senate

THE WHITE HOUSE, *May 17, 1965.*

*To the Senate of the United States:*

With a view to receiving the advice and consent of the Senate to ratification,
I transmit herewith the agreement between the Government of the United States
of America and the Government of Canada concerning the establishment of an
International Arbitral Tribunal to dispose of U.S. claims relating to Gut Dam,
signed at Ottawa, March 25, 1965.

I transmit also, for the information of the Senate, the report by the Secretary
of State with respect to the agreement.

This agreement is an outstanding example of the close and friendly cooperation
between us and our good neighbor to the north.

Claims have been made by many nationals of the United States that their
properties on the shores of Lake Ontario have suffered damage or detriment as
a result of high water caused by the construction and maintenance by Canada
of Gut Dam in the St. Lawrence River.

Those claims total approximately $9 million and have been the subject of
discussions and negotiations between the United States and Canada for many
years. The present agreement is the result of those negotiations.

The agreement provides for the establishment of a three-member international
arbitral tribunal with authority to receive, determine, and make awards on
claims of U.S. nationals. The tribunal will determine whether Gut Dam was the
cause of the damage, the nature and extent of the damage, the existence of any
legal liability to pay compensation, and what amount of compensation should be
paid and by whom. The Canadian Government agrees to pay all compensation
for which it is found liable under the agreement.

I recommend that the Senate give early and favorable consideration to this
agreement and to its ratification.

LYNDON B. JOHNSON.

(Enclosures: (1) Report of the Secretary of State; and (2) agreement between
the Government of the United States of America and the Government of Canada
concerning the establishment of an International Arbitral Tribunal to dispose
of U.S. claims relating to Gut Dam, signed at Ottawa, March 25, 1965.)

DEPARTMENT OF STATE, *Washington, May 11, 1965.*

THE PRESIDENT,
*The White House:*

I have the honor to submit to you the agreement between the Government of
the United States of America and the Government of Canada concerning the
establishment of an International Arbitral Tribunal to dispose of U.S. claims
relating to Gut Dam, signed at Ottawa March 25, 1965, with the recommendation that the agreement be transmitted to the Senate for the advice and consent
of that body to ratification.

The purpose of the agreement is to provide for the final disposition of claims
of U.S. nationals against Canada for damage caused by high waters to property
located along the American shores of Lake Ontario. The damage is claimed to
have resulted from the construction and maintenance by Canada of Gut Dam
across the international boundary in the St. Lawrence River. Several hundred
claims of U.S. nationals requesting damages of approximately $9 million are
involved.

By an act of Congress, approved June 18, 1902 (32 Stat. 392), the United States
consented to the construction by Canada of Gut Dam in the St. Lawrence River,
approximately 70 miles below Lake Ontario, provided that the plans and details
of the work were approved by the Secretary of War. On August 18, 1903, and

0214

October 10, 1904, the Secretary of War approved the plans submitted by Canada and agreed that the dam could be built on the following condition:

"That if the construction and operation of the said dam shall cause damage or detriment to the property owners of Les Galops Island, or to the property of any other citizens of the United States, the Government of Canada shall pay such amount of compensation as may be agreed upon between the said Government and the parties damaged, or as may be awarded the said parties in the proper court of the United States before which claims for damage may be brought."

The dam was built in 1903 and removed by the Canadian Government in 1953. In 1952 and 1953 residents of the United States filed several suits against Canada in the U.S. District Court for the Northern District of New York claiming that high waters in Lake Ontario had damaged their abutting properties and that the high waters were caused by Gut Dam, wich had raised the level of the lake and of the St. Lawrence River. The suits were dismissed on the ground that service on the Canadian Government was ineffective. The Supreme Court of the United States refused to review them. Since 1954 the Department of State has negotiated with the Canadian Government for a settlement of the claims or their submission to an arbitral tribunal for adjudication.

During the negotiations the Government of Canada took the position that the Government of the United States may have a partial legal responsibility in connection with the construction of Gut Dam and that Canada was prepared to enter into the agreement only if the tribunal was empowered to consider whether the United States had made itself liable for any of the damage attributable to Gut Dam. Consequently the tribunal has authority to determine "by whom" compensation should be paid, which raises the possibility of a contingent liability on the part of the United States.

The agreement provides in article I for the establishment of a three-member international arbitral tribunal (a chairman and two national members), known as the Lake Ontario Claims Tribunal—United States and Canada, to receive, determine, and make awards on claims of U.S. nationals.

Under article II the tribunal will determine whether Gut Dam was the cause of the damage, the nature and extent of the damage, the existence of any legal liability to pay compensation, and what amount of compensation should be paid and by whom. That article also specifies the legal principles on which determinations are to be made by the tribunal.

Article III requires that the Government of the United States take such action as may be necessary to insure that the Foreign Claims Settlement Commission of the United States shall discontinue its investigation and determination of all claims relating to Gut Dam. The Commission has transmitted to U.S. claimants a letter informing them of the signature of the present agreement and that, in view of the provisions of Public Law 87–587, approved August 15, 1962 (76 Stat. 387), the Commission is discontinuing its investigation and determination of claims regarding Gut Dam and will, at the appropriate time, transfer its records on those claims to the Department of State. A copy of that letter is enclosed.

Article IV provides that each Government shall appoint a secretary of the tribunal, and that those persons shall serve as joint secretaries of the tribunal and be subject to its instructions. The tribunal is authorized to appoint such other persons, including engineers, as it considers necessary in the performance of its duties.

Article V provides that the tribunal shall meet at such times and places as agreed upon by its members, subject to the instructions of the two Governments.

Article VI requires the tribunal to adopt rules for its proceedings, subject to the concurrence of the two Governments.

Article VII specifies that within 90 days after the agreement enters into force the Government of the United States shall file with the Joint Secretaries of the tribunal copies of the claim of each national of the United States and transmit copies of each such claim to the Government of Canada. The Government of Canada is required to file with the Joint Secretaries within 120 days of the receipt of each claim copies of its answer with respect to it and within the same period to submit copies of the answer to the Government of the United States. Provision is made for the filing with the tribunal and the transmission of copies to the Government of Canada of a brief by the United States with

0215

reference to the construction and maintenance of Gut Dam and damage or detriment caused thereby. Reply briefs by Canada are to be filed with the tribunal and copies transmitted to the Government of the United States.

Article VIII provides that each Government shall designate an agent to represent it before the tribunal and that each Government may employ such counsel, engineers, investigators, and other persons to assist its agent as it may desire.

Article IX provides that each Government's agency shall serve as its channel of communication with the tribunal.

Article X requires each Government to facilitate on-the-spot and other investigations by the tribunal, agents, counsel, and other persons with respect to property covered by any claim presented.

Article XI requires that the tribunal keep permanent records of its proceedings.

Article XII requires the tribunal to render its decisions expeditiously, make interim reports, and submit to the agents a copy of each decision when rendered. It permits a minority member to report a dissenting opinion. Decisions of the tribunal are to be made by the majority of its members and are final and binding upon both Governments.

Under article XIII awards of the tribunal are to be entered in U.S. dollars and are to be paid in U.S. dollars within 1 year from the date the tribunal submits to the two Governments its decision to which the award relates.

Article XIV requires that within 2 years from the date of its first meeting the tribunal shall determine and render decisions on all claims submitted to it, unless the two Governments agree to extend the period.

Article XV provides that each Government shall defray expenses incurred by it, pay the salary of its national member, and share equally in all other expenses of the tribunal. It will be necessary to seek appropriations for these expenses which, in view of the number of claims, will be substantial.

The agreement provides in article XVI that it shall be ratified and shall enter into force on the day of the exchange of the instruments of ratification.

It is hoped that the agreement will be given favorable consideration by the Senate.

Respectfully submitted.

DEAN RUSK.

(Enclosures: (1) Agreement between the Government of the United States of America and the Government of Canada concerning the establishment of an International Arbitral Tribunal to dispose of U.S. claims relating to Gut Dam, signed at Ottawa March 25, 1965; and (2) copy of letter dated April 7, 1965, sent by Foreign Claims Settlement Commission to claimants.)

AGREEMENT BETWEEN THE GOVERNMENT OF THE UNITED STATES OF AMERICA AND THE GOVERNMENT OF CANADA CONCERNING THE ESTABLISHMENT OF AN INTERNATIONAL ARBITRAL TRIBUNAL TO DISPOSE OF UNITED STATES CLAIMS RELATING TO GUT DAM

THE GOVERNMENT OF THE UNITED STATES OF AMERICA; and
THE GOVERNMENT OF CANADA

Considering that claims have been made by nationals of the United States of America against the Government of Canada alleging that their property in the United States has suffered damage or detriment as a result of high water levels in Lake Ontario or the St. Lawrence River;

Considering that these claimants have alleged further that the damage or detriment was attributable in whole or in part to the construction and maintenance of a dam in the international section of the St. Lawrence River known as and hereinafter referred to as "Gut Dam" and have claimed compensation for such damage or detriment from the Government of Canada; and

Considering that in the special circumstances associated with these claims the need arises to establish an international arbitral tribunal to hear and dispose of these claims in a final fashion,

Have agreed as follows:

ARTICLE I

1. An international arbitral tribunal, which shall be known as the Lake Ontario Claims Tribunal United States and Canada, hereinafter referred to as "the Tribunal", is hereby established for the purpose of hearing and finally disposing

52-255—65——3

0216

of claims of nationals of the United States of America including juridical persons that are presented to the Tribunal in accordance with the terms of this Agreement.

2. The Tribunal shall consist of the Chairman and two national members. One national member shall be appoonted by the Government of the United States of America within two months after this Agreement enters into force; the other national member shall be appointed by the Government of Canda within the same period; a third member, who shall preside over the Tribunal as Chairman, shall be designated jointly by the two Governments within three months after this Agreement enters into force. If the third member has not been designated within three months after this Agreement enters into force, either Party to this Agreement may request the President of the International Court of Justice to designate such third member. In the event of the inability of any member of the Tribunal to serve, or in the event of a member failing to act as such, his successor shall be chosen in accordance with the same precedure and within the same time limits provided herein for the selection of his predecessor.

3. Each member of the Tribunal shall have one vote. Every decision of the Tribunal shall be reached by a majority vote and shall constitute a full and final determination of the subject matter of the decision.

4. Each member of the Tribunal shall be a judge or a lawyer competent to hold high judicial office in his national State. No member prior to his appointment shall have been associated directly or indirectly with any matter relating to this Agreement.

5. Each member of the Tribunal, before entering upon his duties, shall make and subscribe to a solemn declaration before the Joint Secretaries of the Tribunal stating that he will carefully and impartially examine and decide according to his best judgment and in accordance with the provisions of this Agreement all matters presented for his decision. A duplicate of every such declaration shall be filed with each of the Joint Secretaries of the Tribunal.

### ARTICLE II

1. The Tribunal shall have jurisdiction to hear and decide in a final fashion each claim presented to it in accordance with the terms of this Agreement. Each decision of the Tribunal shall be based on its determination of any one or more of the following questions on the basis of the legal principles set forth in this Article:

(a) Was the construction and maintenance of Gut Dam the proximate cause of damage or detriment to the property that is the subject of such claim?

(b) If the construction and maintenance of Gut Dam was the proximate cause of damage or detriment to such property, what was the nature and extent of damage caused?

(c) Does there exist any legal liability to pay compensation for any damage or detriment caused by the construction and maintenance of Gut Dam to such property?

(d) If there exist a legal liability to pay compensation for any damage or detriment caused by the construction and maintenance of Gut Dam to such property, what is the nature and extent of such damage and what amount of compensation in terms of United States dollars should be paid therefor and by whom?

2. The Tribunal shall determine any legal liability issue arising under paragraph 1 of this Article in accordance with the following provisions:

(a) The Tribunal shall apply the substantive law in force in Canada and in the United States of America (exclusive, however, of any laws limiting the time within which any legal suit with respect to any claim is required to be instituted) to all the facts and circumstances surrounding the construction and maintenance of Gut Dam including all the documents passing between Governments concerning the construction of the dam and other relevant documents.

(b) In this Article the law in force in Canada and the United States of America respectively includes international law.

(c) No claim shall be disallowed or rejected by the Tribunal through the application of the general principle of international law that legal remedies must be exhausted as a condition precedent to the validity or allowance of any claim.

0217

3. In the event that in the opinion of the Tribunal there exists such a divergence between the relevant substantive law in force in Canada and in the United States of America that it is not possible to make a final decision with regard to any particular claim as provided by this Article, the Tribunal shall apply such of the legal principles set forth in paragraph 2 as it considers appropriate, having regard to the desire of the Parties hereto to reach a solution just to all interests concerned.

4. The Tribunal shall not have jurisdiction over any claim presented under this Agreement unless the claim is accompanied by an undertaking, signed by the claimant in a form that is valid and binding under Canadian and United States law on any such claimant and his successors and assigns and indicting that he

    (a) accepts the decision of the Tribunal as final and binding with respect to the matters to which it relates, and

    (b) waives any right he may have to proceed against the Government of Canada otherwise than in a manner consistent with the terms of this Agreement.

5. Nothing in this Article shall be deemed to prevent the Tribunal from making any general finding or findings with respect to all claims submitted to it, or any particular category of claims submitted to it.

## ARTICLE III

1. Any claim presented to the Tribunal under the terms of this Agreement shall be considered and dealt with exclusively in accordance with the procedures set out in this Agreement.

2. The Government of the United States of America shall take such action as may be necessary to insure that the Foreign Claims Settlement Commission of the United States shall discontinue its investigation and determination of all claims relating to Gut Dam.

## ARTICLE IV

1. Each Government shall appoint a Secretary of the Tribunal. The persons so appointed shall act as Joint Secretaries of the Tribunal and shall be subject to its instructions.

2. The Tribunal may appoint such other persons, including engineers, as are considered necessary to assist in the performance of its duties, on such terms and conditions as the Tribunal may see fit, subject only to the availability of funds provided by the two Governments for the expenses of the Tribunal.

## ARTICLE V

The Tribunal shall meet at such times and places as may be agreed upon by the members of the Tribunal, subject to instructions of the two Governments.

## ARTICLE VI

The Tribunal shall, with the concurrence of the two Governments, adopt such rules for its proceedings as may be deemed expedient, and necessary, but no such rule shall contravene any of the provisions of this Agreement. The rules shall be designed to expedite the determination of claims.

## ARTICLE VII

1. Within 90 days after this Agreement enters into force, the Government of the United States of America shall file with the Joint Secretaries of the Tribunal three copies of the claim of each national of the United States of America alleging damage or detriment caused by the construction and maintenance of Gut Dam that it is submitting for adjudication. It shall also within the same period transmit three copies of each such claim to the Government of Canada. The claims shall be accompanied by all of the evidence on which the Government of the United States of America intends to rely.

2. Within 120 days after the receipt of each claim by the Government of Canada, in accordance with the terms of paragraph 1 of this Article, the Government of Canada shall file with the Joint Secretaries of the Tribunal three copies of the answer it is submitting with respect to such claim. It shall also within the same period transmit three copies of each such answer to the Government of the United States of America. The answer shall be accompanied by all of the evidence on which the Government of Canada intends to rely.

0218

3. Within such time as may be prescribed by the rules adopted by the Tribunal:

(a) The Government of the United States of America shall file with the Joint Secretaries of the Tribunal three copies of a brief with reference to the construction and maintenance of Gut Dam and to any damage or detriment caused thereby and three copies of all briefs being submitted in support of the claims;

(b) The Government of the United States of America shall transmit three copies of each such brief to the Government of Canada; and

(c) The Government of Canada shall file with the Joint Secretaries of the Tribunal three copies of one or more briefs in reply to the briefs of the Government of the United States of America and transmit three copies of the brief or briefs of the Government of Canada as so filed to the Government of the United States of America.

With the briefs each Government may submit evidence to rebut evidence submitted by the other Government.

4. No other pleadings or other briefs may be submitted by either Government except at the request of or with the approval of the Tribunal.

### ARTICLE VIII

1. Each Government shall designate an Agent who shall present to the Tribunal all the pleadings, evidence, briefs and arguments of his Government with respect to any claim filed with the Tribunal in accordance with the provisions of this Agreement. To assist the Agent, each Government may employ or appoint such counsel, engineers, investigators and other persons as it may desire.

2. All individual claims shall be presented to the Tribunal through the Agent of the Government of the United States of America.

### ARTICLE IX

Whenever under the terms of this Agreement the approval or other form of instructions of Governments is required, such approval or other form of instructions shall be communicated by the Agent of such Government. All other communications required to be made to or by either Government under the terms of this Agreement shall be channeled through its Agent.

### ARTICLE X

The Governments shall make all reasonable efforts to ensure that the members of the Tribunal, Agents, counsel and other appropriate persons shall be permitted at all reasonable times to enter and view and carry on investigations upon any of the property covered by any claim presented under the terms of this Agreement.

### ARTICLE XI

The Tribunal shall keep accurate, permanent records of all its proceedings.

### ARTICLE XII

1. The Tribunal shall in an expeditious manner render decisions on the matters referred to it and shall from time to time make such interim reports as are requested by the two Governments or as the Tribunal deems advisable.

2. The Tribunal shall submit to the Agents a copy of each decision when rendered. Each such decision shall be supported by reasons in writing and shall be accompanied by a copy of the record of all the proceedings maintained in relation to the hearing of the claim with which the decision is concerned.

3. A minority member may report a dissenting opinion in writing, which shall accompany any decision of the Tribunal submitted under the provisions of paragraph 2 of this Article to the Agents.

4. The decisions of the majority of the members of the Tribunal shall be the decisions of the Tribunal and shall be accepted as final and binding by the two Governments.

### ARTICLE XIII

Awards of the Tribunal shall be entered in United States dollars. Every award made by the Tribunal shall be paid in United States dollars within one year from the date the Tribunal submits the decision to which the award relates to the two Governments in accordance with the provisions of Article XII.

0219

## ARTICLE XIV

The Tribunal shall determine and render decisions on all claims submitted to it within a period of two years from the date of the first meeting of the Tribunal, unless the two Governments agree to extend the period.

## ARTICLE XV

Each Government shall defray the expenses incurred by it in the presentation of claims, pleadings, evidence and arguments to the Tribunal and shall pay the salary of its national member. All other expenses of the Tribunal, including the honorarium of the Chairman of the Tribunal, which shall be fixed by agreement of the two Governments, shall be defrayed in equal portions by the two Governments.

## ARTICLE XVI

1. This Agreement shall be ratified, and the instruments of ratification shall be exchanged at Washington as soon as possible.

2. This Agreement shall enter into force on the day of exchange of the instruments of ratification.

IN WITNESS WHEREOF the respective Plenipotentiaries have signed the present Agreement.

DONE in duplicate at Ottawa, this twenty-fifth day of March, one thousand nine hundred sixty-five.

For the Government of the United States of America:
  W. WALTON BUTTERWORTH
For the Government of Canada:
  PAUL MARTIN

FOREIGN CLAIMS SETTLEMENT COMMISSION,
OF THE UNITED STATES,
*Washington, D.C.,* ————.

DEAR ————: The Governments of the United States and Canada on March 25, 1965, signed an agreement for the final disposition of claims of nationals of the United States against Canada arising out of the construction and maintenance of Gut Dam. A copy of the agreement is enclosed.

The agreement provides for the establishment of a three-member international arbitral tribunal known as the Lake Ontario Claims Tribunal—United States and Canada. The agreement also provides for the designation of an agent for the United States who will present the claims of U.S. nationals to the tribunal. The tribunal will determine whether Gut Dam caused damage to American property holders by raising the water level of Lake Ontario and, if it did, the amount of damages sustained and who is liable for the damage. The Canadian Government agrees to pay for all damages for which it is found liable. The agreement will be submitted to the Senate of the United States for advice and consent to ratification by the President.

Public Law 87-587, approved August 15, 1962, giving the Foreign Claims Settlement Commission authority to receive and determine the validity and amount of claims for damages caused by Gut Dam provides, in part, as follows:

"SEC. 5. If the Government of Canada enters into an agreement with the Government of the United States providing for arbitration or adjudication of the claims filed under this Act, the Commission shall discontinue its investigation and determination of the claims and transfer or otherwise make available to the Secretary of State all records and documents relating to the claims or, on the request of the Secretary of State, return to claimants documents filed in support of their claims."

In view of the foregoing provision of Public Law 87-587, the Commission is discontinuing its investigation and determination of claims. Thus, it will not be necessary to communicate further with the Commission in response to requests for additional evidence and other data in support of your claim. The documents and information already submitted will be transferred to the Secretary of State at the appropriate time.

The Department of State has informed the Commission that as soon as the agreement is ratified and an agent for the handling of claims before the tribunal has been designated all persons who have filed claims with the Commission, or their attorneys, will be informed. The Department of State has further in-

0220

formed the Commission that at least 6 months will be needed to obtain the advice and consent of the Senate and the appropriation of funds for the expenses of the agent and his staff and that no useful purpose could be served by writing the Department of State about their claims before notice is given to claimants or their attorneys that an agent has been designated.

Sincerely yours,

EDWARD D. RE, *Chairman.*

Senator SPARKMAN. Our first witness is Mr. Richard D. Kearney, Deputy Legal Adviser, Department of State. He will be accompanied by Mr. Edward G. Misey of the Department of State.

We are glad to have both you gentlemen.

## STATEMENT OF RICHARD D. KEARNEY, DEPUTY LEGAL ADVISER, DEPARTMENT OF STATE; ACCOMPANIED BY EDWARD G. MISEY, DEPARTMENT OF STATE

Mr. KEARNEY. Thank you.

Senator SPARKMAN. We will proceed with the agreement relating to the Gut Dam.

Mr. KEARNEY. Very good, sir.

I am Richard D. Kearney, Deputy Legal Adviser, Department of State. I am accompanied by Edward G. Misey, who is Deputy Assistant Legal Adviser for International Claims.

Mr. Chairman, I appreciate very much this opportunity of appearing before the subcommittee in order to present the views of the Department of State on the agreement between the United States and Canada for the settlement of claims of American nationals arising out of the construction and maintenance of Gut Dam by Canada. The agreement was signed at Ottawa on March 25, 1965.

The purpose of the agreement is to provide a means for the judicial determination of claims of American nationals who sustained damages to their properties on the south shores of Lake Ontario and the St. Lawrence River in the United States at various times between 1947 and 1952.

The agreement with Canada provides for the establishment of a three-member international arbitral tribunal, known as the Lake Ontario Claims Tribunal, United States and Canada. The tribunal is to decide whether Gut Dam caused damage to American holders of property on Lake Ontario by raising the water level of the lake and, if it did, the amount of damages sustained and who is liable for the damage. The Canadian Government agrees to pay for all damages for which it is found liable.

### BACKGROUND

Gut Dam was constructed in 1903 by Canada across the international boundary in the St. Lawrence River near Ogdensburg, N.Y., from Adams Island in Canada to Les Galops Island in the United States, approximately 70 miles below Lake Ontario, in order to improve navigation in the river.

0221

An act of Congress, approved June 18, 1902 (32 Stat. 392), authorized the United States to give its consent to the construction by Canada of the dam with the condition:

* * * That the type of the proposed dam and the plans of construction and operation thereof shall be such as will not, in the judgment of the Secretary of War, materially affect the water level of Lake Ontario or the Saint Lawrence River or cause any other injury to the interests of the United States or any citizen thereof: *And provided further*, That the work of construction on United States territory shall not be commenced until plans and details of the work shall have been submitted to and approved by the Secretary of War.

Subsequently, the Secretary of War, on August 18, 1903, and October 10, 1904, executed formal documents approving plans submitted by the Canadian Government and agreeing that the dam could be built on the following condition:

That if the construction and operation of the said dam shall cause damage or detriment to the property owners of Les Galops Island, or to the property of any other citizens of the United States, the Government of Canada shall pay such amount of compensation as may be agreed upon between the said Government and the parties damaged, or as may be awarded the said parties in the proper court of the United States before which claims for damage may be brought.

The dam was built in 1903 and remained in place until early 1953, when it was removed by Canada in connection with preparations for the St. Lawrence Seaway project.

The claims were first brought to the attention of the Department of State in 1951. In 1952 and 1953, several persons who claimed damages filed suits against Canada in the U.S. District Court for the Northern District of New York alleging that high waters in Lake Ontario had damaged their abutting properties and that the high waters were caused by Gut Dam, which had raised the level of the lake and of the St. Lawrence River.

In July 1953, the Canadian Government made an offer directly to representatives of the claimants to submit the matter to arbitration. The claimants were unable to effect an agreement with the Canadian Government and on May 10, 1954, requested the assistance of the Department of State.

Negotiations thereafter between the two Governments for an arbitration progressed satisfactorily until the U.S. District Court for the Northern District of New York ordered hearings in the above-mentioned lawsuits. The Canadian Government then declined to continue with the negotiations until the suits were disposed of by the courts. The suits were dismissed on the ground that service on the Canadian Government was ineffective. The Supreme Court on April 22, 1957, refused to review the cases.

### U.S. DESIRE TO SETTLE THESE CLAIMS

The Department of State had continued to press the Canadian Government for a settlement of the claims or their submission to a tribunal for adjudication. One step which was taken was a reference to the International Joint Commission by the Governments of the United States and Canada to conduct an engineering investigation regarding the effect of Gut Dam on the water level of Lake Ontario.

In 1958 the Commission reported that Gut Dam raised the water level of Lake Ontario at intermediate flows of 240,000 and 267,000 cubic feet per second, 3½ and 4 inches, respectively.

0222

The engineers also reported that the mean level of the lake at Oswego varied from a low elevation above sea level in November 1934 of 242.68 feet to a high elevation in June 1952 of 249.29 feet or a variance of 6.61 feet. The report stated further that changes and fluctuations in the lake are attributable to quantity of water in the lake, wind, barometric pressure, and manmade changes, such as Gut Dam.

On the basis of the report, the Department of State concluded that abutting property owners had sustained damage to their properties as a result of the several factors mentioned, but the report did not permit a determination of the amount of the damage which is attributable to Gut Dam.

Another element in the sequence of events is the work that has already been done by the Foreign Claims Settlement Commission of the United States on these claims.

### ACTION OF FOREIGN CLAIMS SETTLEMENT COMMISSION

Public Law 87-587, approved August 15, 1962, gave the Foreign Claims Settlement Commission authority to receive and determine the validity and amount of claims of American nationals for damages attributable to Gut Dam.

We are informed by the Foreign Claims Settlement Commission that 539 claims aggregating approximately $8.5 million were filed under the law.

Public Law 87-587 did not provide funds for the settlement of these claims. Instead, the law required the Foreign Claims Settlement Commission to submit to the President a report on all claims determined for such action by the President as he may deem appropriate.

Section 5 of the law, however, provided that if Canada enters into an agreement with the United States providing for arbitration or adjudication of the claims, the Commission should discontinue its investigation and determination of the claims.

Accordingly, after the United States and Canada agreed on March 25, 1965, to arbitrate the claims, the Foreign Claims Settlement Commission discontinued its investigation and determination of them and informed claimants to that effect on April 7, 1965.

The Commission's work however, will be of valuable assistance in connection with the presentation of the claims to the tribunal.

### PROVISIONS OF AGREEMENT

With respect to the agreement itself, article I establishes the Lake Ontario Claims Tribunal, United States and Canada. It will receive, determine, and make awards on claims of American nationals. The tribunal will consist of a Chairman, plus a member appointed by the Government of the United States, and a member appointed by the Government of Canada.

The Chairman will be designated jointly by the two Governments within 3 months after the agreement enters into force. If the third member has not been designated by that time, either the United States or Canada may request the President of the International Court of Justice to designate the third member.

0223

Article I also provides that each member of the tribunal shall be a judge or a lawyer competent to hold high judicial office in his national state.

Under article II the tribunal will determine whether Gut Dam was the cause of the damage, the nature and extent of the damage, the existence of any legal liability to pay compensation, and what amount of compensation should be paid and by whom. During the negotiations Canada took the position that the United States may have some legal responsibility in connection with the construction of Gut Dam and that it was prepared to enter into the agreement only if the tribunal were empowered to consider whether the United States had made itself liable for any of the damage attributable to Gut Dam.

While the U.S. negotiators insisted that there was no legal basis for asserting any liability on the part of the United States in order to secure arbitration of the claims of the American property holders, the tribunal was given authority to determine by whom compensation should be paid, which gives the tribunal the possibility of finding some liability on the part of the United States.

Article II also outlines the general legal principles to be applied by the tribunal in determining the claims.

Article III requires the United States to take steps to insure that the Foreign Claims Settlement Commission discontinue its investigation and determination of all claims relating to Gut Dam. As mentioned above, the Foreign Claims Settlement Commission on April 17, 1965, discontinued its work on the claims.

The succeeding articles are concerned with matters pertaining to overall organization of the tribunal, the requirements for filing claims, payment of awards, and provisions for the exchange of ratifications.

The agreement represents the successful result of discussions and negotiations over several years with Canada on the claims. We consider this agreement a further demonstration of the close and friendly ties which characterize the relationship between the two Governments.

Further, the reference of these claims of American nationals against Canada to an international arbitral tribunal for final disposition will be a reaffirmation by the United States of its commitment to the settlement of such disputes by international adjudication.

Finally, the decisions of the Lake Ontario Claims Tribunal, United States and Canada, should make a substantial contribution to the development of international law in the important field of boundary waters.

The Department of State respectfully recommends favorable consideration by the subcommittee of this agreement.

Senator SPARKMAN. Thank you very much.

Will there be any statement from your associate?

## ADMINISTRATIVE EXPENSES

How much is this going to cost the United States?

Mr. KEARNEY. The administrative expenses for the tribunal and presenting the claims?

0224

Senator SPARKMAN. Well, I notice that article 15 provides that each Government shall defray expenses incurred by it, pay the salary of its national member and share equally in all other expenses of the tribunal.

Mr. KEARNEY. Yes.

Senator SPARKMAN. It says it will be necessary to seek appropriations for these expenses, which in view of the number of claims, will be substantial.

Mr. KEARNEY. Yes, Senator.

Senator SPARKMAN. But I don't see any figure.

Mr. KEARNEY. We have estimated that the overall amount will probably come to about $250,000.

Senator SPARKMAN. It says we pay for our national member. What about the Chairman? How are his expenses paid?

Mr. KEARNEY. We will pay one-half.

Senator SPARKMAN. And Canada one-half?

Mr. KEARNEY. And Canada one-half.

Senator SPARKMAN. And Canada pays for the expenses of its nationals?

Mr. KEARNEY. It will pay for the expenses of its nationals and then we, the United States, will have to pay for the expenses of the U.S. agent who presents the cases, and he will undoubtedly have to have an assistant in view of the number of cases involved, possibly two assistants. There will also be on each side a secretary to the tribunal, a U.S. secretary, a Canadian secretary. The U.S. secretary salary will be paid by the United States and the Canadian secretary salary paid by the Canadians.

There will be office rental probably and normal expenses of running an office like furniture and office supplies and that sort of thing.

Senator SPARKMAN. You would estimate the total appropriation of $250.000, or do you mean that amount per year?

Mr. KEARNEY. No. I mean during the life of the——

Senator SPARKMAN. It should be of relatively brief existence.

### TRIBUNAL ESTABLISHED FOR 2 YEARS

Mr. KEARNEY. We have a provision in the treaty which requires the tribunal to finish up its work within 2 years after it gets started. However, there are bound to be preliminary expenses. For example, we will have to get our agent and his helpers on the payroll before the tribunal gets started because they will have to prepare all these cases and get them in to the tribunal.

Senator SPARKMAN. Canada asked us for permission to build the dam; is that correct?

Mr. KEARNEY. Yes, sir.

Senator SPARKMAN. In fact we both had to agree to it. It crossed the international boundary, didn't it?

Mr. KEARNEY. It did.

Senator SPARKMAN. In the agreement Canada promised to pay all damages that occurred?

Mr. KEARNEY. That is our position; yes, sir. Although the wording is not exact on this point.

0225

Senator SPARKMAN. Then why in a case like that do we have to pay anything? It seems to me that the total expense should fall on Canada. Do we do this as a service to our own nationals who are claimants?

Mr. KEARNEY. That is the reason for it. The position of the Canadians is that they are not liable for any damages. They do not consider that Gut Dam was the proximate cause of the injury to the property which our people own on Lake Ontario, and the——

Senator SPARKMAN. This becomes more or less then a friendly suit between the two governments to determine liability?

Mr. KEARNEY. That is correct, sir.

Senator SPARKMAN. We are very glad to have had you, and we appreciate your giving us the presentation that you have.

Mr. KEARNEY. Thank you very much.

Senator SPARKMAN. I may say before we recess, that tomorrow we shall have another meeting of the subcommittee to consider S. 1826, S. 1935, and S. 2064, bills to amend the International Claims Settlement Act of 1949.

There being no further business the subcommittee stands in recess until 10 o'clock tomorrow morning.

Thank you, gentlemen.

(Whereupon, at 11:10 a.m., the subcommittee recessed, to reconvene at 10 a.m., Thursday, August 5, 1965.)

0226

# INTERNATIONAL CLAIMS

---

## THURSDAY, AUGUST 5, 1965

UNITED STATES SENATE,
SUBCOMMITTEE ON CLAIMS LEGISLATION
OF THE COMMITTEE ON FOREIGN RELATIONS,
*Washington, D.C.*

The subcommittee met, pursuant to notice, at 10 a.m., in room 4221, New Senate Office Building, Senator John Sparkman presiding.

Present: Senators Sparkman and Clark.

Senator SPARKMAN. Let the committee come to order, please.

I hope other Senators may be able to come in for the subcommittee meeting but we have several witnesses this morning, and I think we had better get started.

The Subcommittee on Claims of the Committee on Foreign Relations is meeting this morning to receive testimony on the following three bills to amend the International Claims Settlement Act of 1949:

S. 1935, which I introduced by request, relating to Polish, Bulgarian, Rumanian, and Yugoslav claims;

S. 1826, which was introduced by Senator Smathers, relating to Cuban claims; and

S. 2064, introduced by Senator Morse, which would permit the return of indirect interests in certain enemy corporations vested by the U.S. Government.

(S. 1935, S. 1826, and S. 2064 follow:)

[S. 1935, 89th Cong., 1st sess.]

A BILL To amend the International Claims Settlement Act of 1949, as amended, to provide for the timely determination of certain claims of American nationals settled by the United States-Polish Claims Agreement of July 16, 1960, and for other purposes

*Be it enacted by the Senate and House of Representatives of the United States of America in Congress assembled,* That the International Claims Settlement Act of 1949, as amended, is further amended as follows:

(1) Subsection (f) of section 4, title I, is hereby amended to read as follows:

"(f) No remuneration on account of services rendered on behalf of any claimant in connection with any claim filed with the Commission under this title shall exceed 10 per centum of the total amount paid pursuant to any award certified under the provisions of this title, on account of such claim. Any agreement to the contrary shall be unlawful and void. Whoever, in the United States or elsewhere, demands or receives, on account of services so rendered, any remuneration in excess of the maximum permitted by this section, shall be fined not more than $5,000 or imprisoned not more than twelve months, or both."

(2) Section 6, title I, is amended by inserting "(a)" after the section number and adding at the end thereof the following subsection:

"(b) The Commission shall complete its affairs in connection with the settlement of United States-Polish claims arising under the Polish Claims Agreement of July 16, 1960, not later than March 31, 1966."

41

0227

(3) Subsection (b) of section 7, title I, is amended by inserting "(1)" after the subsection letter, and adding at the end thereof the following paragraphs:

"(2) The Secretary of the Treasury shall deduct from the undisbursed balance in the Polish claims fund, created pursuant to section 8, as of the date of enactment of this paragraph and from each payment thereafter into that fund, 5 per centum thereof as reimbursement to the Governor of the United States for expenses incurred by the Commission and by the Treasury Department in the administration of this title. The amounts so deducted shall be covered into the Treasury to the credit of miscellaneous receipts. The Secretary shall make payment to the person or persons entitled thereto out of the Polish claims fund on account of any amounts deducted pursuant to subsection (b) of section 7 from payments made pursuant to section 8(c) (1) and (2) prior to the enactment of this paragraph.

"(3) The Secretary of the Treasury shall deduct from each payment into any other special fund created pursuant to section 8, subsequent to November 4, 1964, 5 per centum thereof as reimbursement to the Government of the United States for the expenses incurred by the Commission and by the Treasury Department in the administration of this title. The amount so deducted shall be covered into the Treasury to the credit of miscellaneous receipts."

(4) Paragraph (1) of subsection (c), section 7, title I, is hereby amended to read as follows:

"(1) If any person to whom any payment is to be made pursuant to this title is deceased or is under a legal disability, payment shall be made to his legal representative, except that if any payment to be made is not over $1,000 and there is no qualified executor or administrator, payment may be made to the person or persons found by the Comptroller General to be entitled thereto, without the necessity of compliance with the requirements of law with respect to the administration of estates."

(5) Subsection (c) of section 8, title I, is amended by striking out the phrase "any of the funds" and inserting in lieu thereof "the Yugoslav claims fund", and by inserting the phrase "paragraph (1) of" after the phrase "pursuant to" and before the words "subsection (b)".

(6) Section 8, title I, is hereby further amended by adding at the end thereof the following subsection:

"(e) The Secretary of the Treasury is authorized and directed out of the sums covered into the Polish claims fund and into any other special fund created pursuant to this section subsequent to November 4, 1964, to make payments on account of awards certified by the Commission pursuant to this title with respect to claims included within the terms of the Polish Claims Agreement of 1960 and of any other similar agreement entered into subsequent to November 4, 1964, as follows and in the following order of priority:

"(1) Payment in the amount of $1,000 or in the principal amount of the award, whichever is less;

"(2) Thereafter, payments from time to time on account of the unpaid principal balance of each remaining award which shall bear to such unpaid principal balance the same proportion as the total amount in the Polish claims fund and in any other special fund created pursuant to this section subsequent to November 4, 1964, available for distribution at the time such payments are made bears to the aggregate unpaid principal balance of all such awards; and

"(3) Thereafter, payments from time to time on account of the unpaid balance of each award of interest which shall bear to such unpaid balance of interest, the same proportion as the total amount in the Polish claims fund and in any other special fund created pursuant to this section subsequent to November 4, 1964, available for distribution at the time such payments are made bears to the aggregate unpaid balance of interest of all such awards."

(7) Section 302, title III, is amended by inserting "(a)" after the section number and adding at the end thereof the following subsection:

"(b) The Secretary of the Treasury shall cover into each of the Bulgarian and Rumanian claims funds, such sums as may be paid by the Government of the respective country pursuant to the terms of any claims settlement agreement between the Government of the United States and the Government of such country."

(8) Section 303, title III, is amended by striking out the word "and" at the end of paragraph (2), and by striking out the period at the end of paragraph (3) and inserting in lieu thereof a semicolon and immediately thereafter, the word "and".

0228

(9) Section 303, of title III, is further amended by adding at the end thereof the following new paragraph:

"(4) Pay effective compensation for the nationalization, compulsory liquidation, or other taking of property of nationals of the United States in Bulgaria and Rumania, between August 9, 1955, and the effective date of the claims agreement between the respective country and the United States."

(10) Section 304 of title III is amended by inserting "(a)" after the section number and adding at the end thereof the following subsections:

"(b) The Commission shall receive and determine, or redetermine as the case may be, in accordance with applicable substantive law, including international law, the validity and amounts of claims owned by persons who were nationals of the United States on August 9, 1958, which arose out of the war in which Italy was engaged from June 10, 1940, to September 15, 1947, and with respect to which provision was not made in the treaty of peace with Italy: *Provided*, That no awards shall be made to persons who have received compensation in any amount pursuant to subsection (a) of this section or under section 202 of the War Claims Act of 1948, as amended, or to persons whose claims have been denied by the Commission for reasons other than that they were not filed within the time prescribed by section 306.

"(c) The Commission shall receive and determine, or redetermine as the case may be, in accordance with applicable substantive law, including international law, the validity and amounts of claims owned by persons who were nationals of the United States on September 3, 1943, and the date of enactment of this subsection, against the Government of Italy which arose out of the war in which Italy was engaged from June 10, 1940, to September 15, 1947, in territory ceded by Italy pursuant to the treaty of peace with Italy: *Provided*, That no awards shall be made to persons who have received compensation in any amount pursuant to the treaty of peace with Italy or subsection (a) of this section."

"(d) Within thirty days after enactment of this subsection, or within thirty days after the date of enactment of legislation making appropriations to the Commission for payment of administrative expenses incurred in carrying out its functions under subsections (b) and (c) of this section, whichever date is later, the Commission shall publish in the Federal Register the time when and the limit of time within which claims may be filed with the Commission, which limit shall not be more than six months after such publication.

"(e) The Commission shall certify awards on claims determined pursuant to subsections (b) and (c) of this section to the Secretary of the Treasury for payment out of remaining balances in the Italian claims fund in accordance with the provisions of section 310 of this tile, after payment in full of all awards certified pursuant to subsection (a) of this section.

"(f) After payment in full of all awards certified to the Secretary of the Treasury, pursuant to subsections (a) and (d) of this section, the Secretary of the Treasury is authorized and directed to transfer the unobligated balance in the Italian claims fund into the war claims fund created by section 13 of the War Claims Act of 1948, as amended."

(11) Section 306, title II, is amended by inserting "(a)" after the section number and adding at the end thereof the following subsection:

"(b) Within thirty days after enactment of this subsection or the enactment of legislation making appropriations to the Commission for payment of administrative expenses incurred in carrying out its functions under paragraph (4) of section 303 of this title, whichever is later, the Commission shall publish in the Federal Register the time when and the limit of time within which claims may be filed under paragraph (4) of section 303 of this title, which limit shall not be more than six months after such publication."

(12) Section 310, title III, is amended by adding at the end of subsection (a) thereof the following paragraph:

"(6) Whenever the Commission is authorized to settle claims by the enactment of paragraph (4) of section 303 of this title with respect to Rumania and Bulgaria, no further payments shall be authorized by the Secretary of the Treasury on account of awards certified by the Commission pursuant to paragraphs (1), (2), or (3) of section 303 of the Bulgarian or Rumanian claims funds, as the case may be, until payments on account of awards certified pursuant to paragraph (4) of section 303 with respect to such fund have been authorized in equal proportion to payments previously authorized on existing awards certified pursuant to paragraphs (1), (2), and (3) of section 303."

0229

(13) Section 316, title III, is amended by inserting "(a)" after the section number and adding at the end thereof the following subsection:

"(b) The Commission shall complete its affairs in connection with the settlement of claims pursuant to paragraph (4) of section 303 and subsections (b) and (c) of section 304 of this title not later than two years following the date of enactment of such paragraph, or following the enactment of legislation making appropriations to the Commission for payment of administrative expenses incurred in carrying out its functions under paragraph (4) of section 303 and subsections (b) and (c) of section 304 of this title, whichever is later."

---

[S. 1826, 89th Cong., 1st sess.]

**A BILL To amend title V of the International Claims Settlement Act of 1949 relating to certain claims against the Government of Cuba**

*Be it enacted by the Senate and House of Representatives of the United States of America in Congress assembled,* That section 501 of the International Claims Settlement Act of 1949 (22 U.S.C. 1643) is amended—

(1) by striking out "which have arisen out of debts for merchandise furnished or services rendered by nationals of the United States without regard to the date on which such merchandise was furnished or services were rendered or"; and

(2) by striking out the last sentence thereof.

SEC. 2. Section 503(a) of such Act (22 U.S.C. 1643b(a)) is amended by striking out "arising out of debts for merchandise furnished or services rendered by nationals of the United States without regard to the date on which such merchandise was furnished or services were rendered or".

SEC. 3. Section 506 of such Act (22 U.S.C. 1643e) is amended by striking out ": *Provided,* That the deduction of such amounts shall not be construed as divesting the United States of any rights against the Government of Cuba for the amounts so deducted".

SEC. 4. Section 511 of such Act (22 U.S.C. 1643j) is amended to read as follows:

"APPROPRIATIONS

"SEC. 511. There are hereby authorized to be appropriated such sums as may be necessary to enable the Commission to pay its administrative expenses incurred in carrying out its functions under this title."

---

[S. 2064, 89th Cong., 1st sess.]

**A BILL To amend the International Claims Settlement Act of 1949, as amended, relative to the return of certain alien property interests**

*Be it enacted by the Senate and House of Representatives of the United States of America in Congress assembled,* That the International Claims Settlement Act of 1949, as amended, is further amended by adding section 216 at the end of title 11 thereof, as follows:

"SEC. 216. (a) Notwithstanding any other provision of this Act or any provision of the Trading With the Enemy Act, as amended, any person—

"(1) who was formerly a national of Bulgaria, Hungary, or Rumania, and

"(2) who, as a consequence of any law, decree, or regulation of the nation of which he was a national discriminating against political, racial, or religious groups, at no time between December 7, 1941, and the time when such law, decree, or regulation was abrogated enjoyed full rights of citizenship under the law of such nation, shall be eligible hereunder to receive the return of his interest in property which was vested under section 202(a) hereof or under the Trading With the Enemy Act, as amended, as the property of a corporation organized under the laws of Bulgaria, Hungary, or Rumania if 25 per centum or more of the outstanding capital stock of such corporation was owned at the date of vesting by such persons and nationals of countries other than Bulgaria, Hungary, Rumania, Germany, or Japan, or if such corporation was subjected after December 7, 1941, under the laws of its country, to special wartime measures directed against it because of the enemy or alleged enemy character of some or all of its stockholders; and no certificate by the Department of State as provided under section 207(c) hereof shall be required for such persons

0230

"(b) An interest in property vested under the Trading With the Enemy Act, as amended, as the property of a corporation organized under the laws of Bulgaria, Hungary, or Rumania shall be subject to return under subsection (a) of this section only if a notice of claim for the return of any such interest has been timely filed under the provisions of section 33 of that Act. In the event such interest has been liquidated and the net proceeds thereof transferred to the Bulgarian Claims Fund, Hungarian Claims Fund, or Rumanian Claims Fund, the net proceeds of any other interest transferable but not yet transferred to the same Fund may be used for the purpose of making the return hereunder.

"(c) Determinations by the designee of the President or any other officer or agency with respect to claims under this section, including the allowance or disallowance thereof, shall be final and shall not be subject to review by any court."

SEC. 2. The first sentence of section 207(c) of the International Claims Settlement Act of 1949, as amended, is amended to read as follows:

"(c) The sole relief and remedy of any person having any claim to any property vested pursuant to section 202(a), except a person claiming under section 216, shall be that provided by the terms of subsection (a) or (b) of this section, and in the event of the liquidation by sale or otherwise of such property, shall be limited to and enforced against the net proceeds received therefrom and held by the designee of the President."

Senator SPARKMAN. Our first witness this morning is Mr. Andrew T. McGuire, the General Counsel of the Foreign Claims Settlement Commission. Mr. McGuire, I believe you have a prepared statement. Please proceed in your own way.

I will say this for the benefit of all the witnesses. If you have prepared statements, they will be published in full regardless of how you may proceed.

We are glad to have you, Mr. McGuire.

## STATEMENT OF DR. EDWARD F. RE, CHAIRMAN, FOREIGN CLAIMS SETTLEMENT COMMISSION, PRESENTED BY ANDREW T. McGUIRE, GENERAL COUNSEL

Mr. McGUIRE. Thank you, Mr. Chairman.

First of all, may I express the regrets of Dr. Re, the Chairman of the Commission, for being unable to be here this morning. He has asked me to present the following statement in his behalf.

Mr. Chairman and members of the subcommittee, it is a pleasure and a privilege to appear before you this morning in behalf of the Chairman of the Foreign Claims Settlement Commission in support of S. 1935 entitled "A Bill To Provide for the Timely Determination of Certain Claims of American Nationals Settled by the United States-Polish Claims Agreement of July 16, 1960, and for Other Purposes," and S. 1826 which is designed to amend title V of the International Claims Settlement Act of 1949, as amended, relating to claims against the Government of Cuba.

### S. 1935

The bill, S. 1935, proposes amendments to titles I and III of the International Claims Settlement Act which directly affect the activities of the Foreign Claims Settlement Commission.

#### GENERAL SCOPE OF S. 1935

This bill is similar to S. 1987 and H.R. 10712 in the 87th Congress and S. 947 in the 88th Congress, none of which were enacted. With the exception of new Bulgarian, Rumanian, and Italian claims, S.

52Z255—65——4

0231

1935 is workaday legislation that does not engender much appeal. It involves technicalities designed principally to put the business of the Commission in order and constitutes good administration.

The bill, if enacted, would provide further compensation to Americans who have received only partial payments on their awards, provide for the filing of new claims by citizens whose losses occurred after the execution of international agreements or enactment of enabling legislation, and provide compensation for a small group found to have been excluded from coverage under treaties on the one hand and statutes on the other.

These potential claimants have been corresponding individually, and through their Senators and Congressmen, with the Commission constantly during the past 5 or more years, urging that the executive as well as the legislative branch support enactment of legislation included in S. 1935.

For the most part, this bill would update the International Claims Settlement Act of 1949, as amended, in light of the recent claims agreements which have been concluded between the United States and the Governments of Poland, Bulgaria, Rumania, and Yugoslavia, and to reopen, to a certain extent, the Italian Claims program as provided under title III of the act.

## POLISH CLAIMS PROGRAM

Under the Polish Claims Agreement of July 16, 1960, the Governments of the United States and the Polish People's Republic entered into an en bloc settlement of claims of nationals of the United States against Poland for the nationalization or other taking by Poland of property and rights or interests therein; the deprivation of use or enjoyment of property; and debts of nationalized enterprises. Under this agreement the Polish Government agreed to pay to the United States Government an aggregate of $40 million in 20 equal installments—$10 million has been paid thus fair. The next installment of $2 million is due January 10, 1966.

The Commission commenced the Polish claims program on September 1, 1960, under the provisions of title I of the International Claims Settlement Act of 1949, as amended, which established the procedures for the administration of such a program by the Foreign Claims Settlement Commission.

Section 4 of title I of this statute authorizes the Commission to receive, examine, and adjudicate claims immediately upon the signing of a claims agreement with any government with which the U.S. Government was not at war during World War II. In determining such claims the Commission is directed to apply the provisions of the claims settlement agreement and the applicable principles of international law, justice, and equity. However, the time limitations, as contained under this title of the statute with respect to the completion date of the programs authorized, applied only to claims under the Yugoslav Claims Agreement of 1948. That claims program was completed on December 31, 1954, pursuant to such limitations.

A total of 10,239 claims have been filed under the Polish agreement. In relation to programs previously administered by the Commission, this one is more than six times the size of the Yugoslav program, equal to the size of the program under title III of the act, which pro-

0232

vided for certain claims against the Governments of Bulgaria, Hungary, Italy, Rumania, and the Soviet Union, and more than twice the size of the Czechoslovakian program under title IV of the act. Four years were allowed for the completion of each of those programs. Accordingly, the Commission proposes that the period for processing claims against Poland be no greater than 4 years from the last day for filing timely claims, which was March 31, 1962. The bill, consequently, provides for a completion of the program on March 31, 1966.

Of the 10,239 claims filed, proposed decisions have been entered on 9,111 claims and 7,673 final decisions have been issued as of July 30, 1965.

## PROVISIONS FOR ATTORNEYS' FEES

With respect to other sections of title I of the International Claims Settlement Act of 1949, a proposal is made under the bill to amend subsection (f) of section 4 which would have the effect of relieving the Commission of the burden of determining attorneys' fees and to make title I consistent with the attorney fee provisions of titles III and IV of the act.

Section 4(f) presently provides for a limitation on attorneys' fees of 10 percent of any payment on an award made by the Commission but authorizes the Commission to set the amount of such fee within the 10-percent limitation. Further provision is made for deduction by the Secretary of the Treasury of the amount of the fee and for payment directly to the attorney. Titles III and IV of the act simplify this procedure by authorizing a flat 10-percent fee and leaves the settlement to the attorney and client.

## DEDUCTION OF 5 PERCENT

An amendment is also proposed to change the existing procedures under section 7(b) which presently provides for a direct deduction of 5 percent of any payment made on an award. This procedure was changed under titles III and IV by providing for a direct deduction of 5 percent from each deposit into the respective funds thus eliminating an extensive administrative burden for the Treasury Department.

S. 1935 proposes to incorporate the provisions comparable to those of title IV to apply (1) to the undisbursed balance of the Polish claims fund as of the date of enactment and to the future payments received from the Polish Government under the terms of the agreement to be completed in 1980; (2) to payments into the fund contemplated by the new Yugoslav Claims Agreement of November 5, 1964, which calls for five annual payments of $700,000 to be completed in 1970; and (3) to payments into any other similar fund.

The Treasury Department has deducted from each Polish payment of up to $1,000 already made on account of the principal of awards, 5 percent for administrative expenses. Under the present priority of payments, holders of awards in the principal amount of $1,000 or less have not, therefore, received payment in full. The amendment would authorize the Treasury Department to make payment of the amount previously deducted.

0233

48    INTERNATIONAL CLAIMS

## PRO RATA PAYMENT ON AWARDS

Unlike the Yugoslav agreement of 1948 whereby a lump-sum settlement was made, the Polish agreement of 1960 provided payment in installments. Therefore, the present provisions of section 8(b) which deals with payment priorities was geared to the Yugoslav settlement by providing for additional payments up to 25 percent of the unpaid principal of awards in amounts in excess of $1,000 after payments of awards in the amount of $1,000 or less have been paid in full. Money thus far received for transfer into the Polish claims fund has only been sufficient to pay awards less than $1,000 in full and an initial payment of $1,000 in those cases where the award exceeded $1,000. The payments, of course, have been subjected to the 5-percent deduction for administrative expenses.

The bill proposes to retain the present language of section 8(c) in the event future prorated payments are made under the Yugoslav Claims Agreement of 1948 and to add a new subsection (e) to apply to the Polish Claims Agreement of 1960, the Yugoslav Claims Agreement of 1964, and any other similar agreement made subsequently with respect to payment priorities. The new subsection is similar to the language of title III of the act which provides payment in the amount of $1,000 or in the principal amount of the award, whichever is less, and thereafter, payments on a prorated basis on account of the unpaid principal balance of each remaining award. After payment in full of the principal amount of awards, payment is authorized on account of the unpaid balance of each award of interest under the same prorated basis.

## PAYMENT TO LEGAL REPRESENTATIVES

The bill further provides for an amendment to paragraph (1) of subsection (c) of section 7 of title I which deals with payments to a legal representative where the person to whom any payment is made is deceased or is under a legal disability. This section presently provides that where the award does not exceed $500, requirements with respect to the appointment of a qualified executor or administrator are waived and payment may be made to the person or persons found by the Comptroller General to be entitled thereto. This amendment raises the limit from an award not in excess of $500 to any payment not in excess of $1,000. A similar change was made regarding claims under title IV of the act against the Government of Czechoslovakia.

## BULGARIAN AND RUMANIAN CLAIMS PROGRAMS

The bill contains certain amendments to title III of the International Claims Settlement Act of 1949 with respect to claims against Bulgaria, Rumania, and Italy.

The first amendment to title III relates to section 302 by adding subsection (b).

This new subsection permits the transfer into the Rumanian and Bulgarian claims funds of money derived from the Rumanian Claims Agreement of March 30, 1960, and the Bulgarian agreement of July 2, 1963. The statute now provides that the Rumanian and Bulgarian

0234

funds shall be comprised only of sums blocked and vested and transferred by the Attorney General. The additional funds realized from the respective agreements cannot be transferred into these funds unless the act is amended. S. 1935 proposes such an amendment. The additional net amount available to be transferred into the Rumanian fund is $2.5 million. Under the Bulgarian agreement the Bulgarian Government agreed to pay $400,000, of which $200,000 was paid on July 1, 1964, and the balance was paid on July 1, 1965.

Certain technical changes are also proposed under section 303 to permit the disposition of a small number of claims against Rumania, included within the agreement of March 30, 1960, and against Bulgaria included within the agreement of July 2, 1963. These claims, which have arisen since August 9, 1955, are based upon the nationalization, compulsory liquidation, or other taking of property of nationals of the United States by those countries. Claims of this nature arising prior to August 9, 1955, were disposed of by the Commission in a prior program completed on August 9, 1959. An amendment is also proposed to permit a 6-month filing period for these new claims and a 2-year settlement period. Also included under the bill is an amendment to revamp the award payment provisions with respect to claims against Rumania and Bulgaria in order to insure that the new awardees will not obtain a pecuniary advantage over previous awardees. Awardees under the Rumanian program have received approximately 35 cents on the dollar in payment on their awards. Awardees under the Bulgarian program have received approximately 50 cents on the dollar in payment on their awards. This amendment would limit payments on new awards to a like extent, and then permit the residual balance to be distributed proportionately among all awardees.

## ITALIAN CLAIMS PROGRAM

The most significant difference in the present measure and those bills introduced in prior Congresses deals with the residual balance in the Italian claims fund.

For background information concerning these claims, the attention of the committee is invited to the provisions of article 78 of the Treaty of Peace with Italy under which the Italian Government was required to restore all rights and interests to property in Italy belonging to United States nationals. If the property could not be returned or if, as a result of the war a United States national had suffered a property loss, he was entitled to compensation in lire to the extent of two-thirds of the sum necessary, at the date of payment, to purchase similar property or indemnified for the loss suffered.

In 1947, under the Lombardo agreement, the Italian Government paid the United States the sum of $5 million, to be utilized in such manner as the Government of the United States might deem appropriate, to be applied to claims of United States nationals arising out of the war with Italy and for which no other provision had been made. Subsequently, Public Law 285, 84th Congress, was enacted on August 9, 1955, which authorized the settlement of those claims against Italy for which no provision had been made under the Treaty of Peace with Italy.

0235

By August 8, 1958, it was apparent that the Italian Claims Fund would be more than sufficient to pay anticipated awards against the Government of Italy. On that date the statute was amended by Public Law 85-604, section 2, to permit awards to persons who were nationals of the United States on August 9, 1955, the date of enactment of title III of the act, even though their claims were based upon property losses occurring at an earlier date. The amendment, in effect, broadened the international law principle requiring continuous U.S. nationality of a claim from the date of loss to the date of filing. Thus all claims previously denied under the original provisions of section 304 of the act because of failure to qualify under the international law principle, but which would be eligible for awards under the amendment, had to be reconsidered. Under this amendment over 100 claims were reconsidered and the amounts of the awards totaled $606,464. In order to permit the Commission to complete its determinations with respect to these claims, the time limitation under section 316 was waived and the program was completed on May 1, 1960. No amendment, however, was made to section 306 or any other section of the act providing for the filing of new claims.

The bill, S. 1935, would reopen and extend the Italian Claims program to cover claims under section 304 of the act, not previously compensable because of late filing, and claims of persons who had become nationals of the United States on or before August 9, 1955, who had not filed under the original statute.

The proposal would also include claims arising in territory ceded pursuant to the Treaty of Peace with Italy, including the Dodecanese Islands which were heretofore excluded under the provisions of the act. Excluded from consideration are claims of persons who have received compensation previously pursuant to section (a) of section 304, section 202 of the War Claims Act of 1948, as amended, or under the Treaty of Peace with Italy. Any balance remaining in the Italian Claims Fund after payment of claims as proposed under these amendments is to be transferred into the War Claims Fund created under section 13 of the War Claims Act of 1948, as amended. The present balance in the Italian Claims Fund is approximately $1,088,000.

### CONCLUSION

Mr. Chairman, at line 19, page 6 of the bill the date "August 9, 1958" has been included erroneously. The correct date is "August 9, 1955". This was the date of enactment of title III of the International Claims Settlement Act of 1949, as amended, and constitutes the date on which the various interested agencies of the executive branch agreed. The 1955 date is the date used in the sectional analysis submitted with the draft bill by the executive branch.

The cost of administering the proposals under this amendment will be borne by the claims fund concerned and not the U.S. Government.

The Commission cannot proceed in the orderly administration of the Polish, Rumanian, Bulgarian, and Yugoslav claims programs unless the items pertaining to them are enacted. The remaining items reflect good administrative practice. Moreover, it is important that this legislation be enacted promptly because installment payments aggregating $10 million have already been made by the Government

0236

of Poland. On July 1, 1964, the Government of Rumania made its final installment payment of $500,000 under the terms of the agreement of March 30, 1960. On July 1, 1965, the Government of Bulgaria made its lump-sum settlement final installment payment in the amount of $200,000.

For the foregoing reasons the Commission urges early and favorable action on S. 1935.

S. 1826

S. 1826 proposes to amend title V of the International Claims Settlement Act of 1949 relating to certain claims against the Government of Cuba.

During the 88th Congress, title V was added to the act by Public Law 88-666, approved October 16, 1964. This statute provided for the presettlement adjudication of claims of Americans against the Government of Cuba in the following categories: (1) Claims which have arisen out of debts for merchandise furnished or services rendered by nationals of the United States without regard to the date on which such merchandise was furnished or services rendered; (2) claims arising since January 1, 1959, for losses resulting from the nationalization, expropriation, intervention, or other taking of, or special measures directed against, property owned by nationals of the United States; and (3) claims for disability or death resulting from actions taken by or under the authority of the Government of Cuba.

RECOMMENDED REPEAL OF VESTING PROVISIONS

Section 511 of title V provides for the vesting and sale of property of the Government of Cuba blocked in the United States and authorizes the appropriation of such sums as may be necessary to pay the administrative expenses of this Commission and the Treasury Department in carrying out their functions in connection with this program.

The purpose of S. 1826 is to obviate the correlation of the administrative expenses of the Foreign Claims Settlement Commission and the Treasury Department to the proceeds of vested and liquidated assets of the Cuban Government. Specifically, the bill would eliminate the present provisions for the vesting of Cuban Government-owned property located in the United States which is currently blocked under the Cuban assets control regulations enforced by the Treasury Department under both section 620(a) of the Foreign Assistance Act of 1961 and section 5(b) of the Trading With the Enemy Act.

When the President signed Public Law 88-666 on October 16, 1964, he expressed certain misgivings concerning the vesting provisions of that statute, stating in part:

> The United States strongly adheres to the sanctity of property. The vesting of the property of foreign governments or nationals is not a step that we should undertake without careful consideration.

The President then requested that a study and report be made by the Secretary of State and the Attorney General. This study has been completed and in consequence the executive branch has concluded to recommend that the vesting provisions be deleted from Public Law

0237

88-666. Thus, the Foreign Claims Settlement Commission joins with the other interested agencies of the executive branch in support of S. 1826.

## ADMINISTRATIVE EXPENSES

S. 1826 would authorize a direct appropriation for the administrative expenses of the Commission. During the course of the hearings preceding the enactment of Public Law 88-666, the Commission compared the Cuban program to the previously completed Czechoslovakian claims program from the standpoint of cost. State Department representatives have estimated that approximately 4,000 claims would be filed against Cuba. The Czechoslovakian program had a similar number of claims that may be deemed to be of a comparable degree of complexity. The Czechoslovakian program was administered by the Commission at the cost of about $1 million. The Commission estimates that the cost of administering the Cuban claims program would also cost $1 million.

Authorization of an appropriation for administrative expenses now will enable the Commission to commence the adjudication of the claims and provide for a liquidation of the total amount due from the Castro government. Upon settlement, an appropriate sum can be deducted for reimbursement to the general fund of the Treasury as has been done in all previous programs.

S. 1826 would also amend the statute by (1) omitting reference to claims which have arisen out of debts for merchandise furnished or services rendered by nationals of the United States which arose prior to and after January 1, 1939; (2) deleting the provisions precluding the authorization for the payment of claims; and (3) omitting the right of the United States to espouse a claim for an amount equal to the deductions made on the approved amount of awards.

Senator SPARKMAN. By the way, right in the middle of that paragraph, January 1, 1959, I understand you to say "1939"; 1959 is correct.

Mr. McGUIRE. 1959 is what I intended to say, Mr. Sparkman.

## DEBT CLAIMS

The language "without regard to the date on which such merchandise was furnished or services were rendered" appears to be unnecessary. The term "property" under Public Law 88-666 is defined as "any property, right, or interest, including any leasehold interest, and debts owed by the Government of Cuba or by enterprises which have been nationalized, expropriated, intervened, or taken by the Government of Cuba and debts which are a charge on property which has been nationalized, expropriated, intervened, or taken by the Government of Cuba."

Thus, if a debt arose prior to January 1, 1959, for failure of the Cuban Government enterprises to pay nationals of the United States for goods or services, such unpaid debt would still exist after January 1, 1959, and, therefore, may have been subjected to confiscatory measures imposed upon property by the Cuban Government.

0238

## DENIAL OF APPROPRIATIONS FOR PAYMENT OF CLAIMS

The elimination of the language in the present statute precluding the authorization of an appropriation for the purpose of paying claims may be misleading. By reference over from title I of the act U.S. liability for payment of claims is expressly denied. Therefore, the last sentence of section 501 is unnecessary. Nevertheless, it is felt that deletion of the language at this stage may be misconstrued and it is therefore recommended that the sentence not be omitted.

## OFFSETS

Finally, S. 1826 proposes repeal of that portion of section 506 of Public Law 88-666 which reads:

*Provided,* That the deduction of such amounts shall not be construed as divesting the United States of any rights against the Government of Cuba for the amounts so deducted.

The Commission favors enactment of this amendment inasmuch as this appears to be a matter more appropriate for future negotiation.

However, mention is made of a difference in concept contained in the House and Senate reports that accompanied Public Law 88-666. The House report (No. 1759) states that section 506 is designed to prevent duplication in the amount of any award and that the Commission is to deduct all amounts the claimant has received from other sources on account of the same loss. The Senate report (Rept. No. 1521) refers, as an example, to a tax writeoff on a claim by an American citizen. The Commission has never construed this "offset" language to refer to tax writeoffs inasmuch as this factor is covered by the Internal Revenue Code. The overall analysis of this section makes it appear that this section combines two features which have been handled separately in past claims legislation. For example, section 206 of title II of the War Claims Act of 1948, as amended, treats the matter separately. I think that the legislative history should be clarified in this respect.

## UNNECESSARY LANGUAGE

The Commission feels that it would be remiss in its duty to this committee if it failed to refer to the language contained in section 507 of Public Law 88-666 which provides that the Commission certify to the Secretary of State the amount and the basic information underlying an award together with a statement of the evidence relied upon and the reasoning employed in reaching its decisions with respect to each claim determined by the Commission. The latter part of that sentence commencing with the word "together" is unnecessary. The Commission presently sets forth such information in its written decisions to the extent possible and such decisions are available to the Department of State as well as any other interested party.

The attention of the committee is invited to the fact that appropriate provisions are contained in title I of the International Claims Settle-

0239

ment Act and are incorporated by reference in title V. They provide as follows:

Subsection 4(b) of title I of the act provides in part:

* * * All decisions shall be upon such evidence and written legal contentions as may be presented within such period as may be prescribed therefor by the Commission, and upon the results of any independent investigation of cases which the Commission may deem it advisable to make. Each decision by the Commission pursuant to this Act shall be by majority vote, and shall state the reason for such decision, and shall constitute a full and final disposition of the case in which the decision is rendered.

Subsection 4(h) provides:

The Commission shall notify all claimants of the approval or denial of their claims, stating the reasons and grounds therefor, and, if approved, shall notify such claimants of the amount for which such claims are approved * * *. The action of the Commission in allowing or denying any claim under this Act shall be final and conclusive on all questions of law and fact and not subject to review by the Secretary of State or any other official, department, agency, or establishment of the United States or by any court by mandamus or otherwise.

The Commission recommends repeal of the language to which I have referred.

Mr. Chairman, S. 1826 is a good bill, and the Commission strongly recommends its enactment.

S. 2064

Also before your committee for consideration today is the bill designated S. 2064 entitled "A bill to amend the International Claims Settlement Act of 1949, as amended, relative to the return of certain alien property interests."

This bill proposes to eliminate certain inequities between the vesting provisions of title II of the International Claims Settlement Act and the Trading With the Enemy Act with respect to the return of certain vested property to former Bulgarian, Hungarian, and Rumanian owners who were subjected to discriminatory measures during World War II.

In effect, S. 2064 would equate the provisions of both acts by placing a persecutee, with an indirect interest in a vested property, in the same status as a persecutee with a direct interest in such property.

This bill would have no effect upon the completed Bulgarian, Hungarian, and Rumanian claims programs administered by the Commission pursuant to title III of the International Claims Settlement Act of 1949, as amended, which were completed on August 9, 1959, nor would the bill affect directly in any other manner the functions of the Commission including those contained in S. 1935 with respect to claims under the Bulgarian Claims Agreement of July 2, 1963, and the Rumanian Claims Agreement of March 30, 1960.

### BILL WITHIN JURISDICTION OF DEPARTMENT OF JUSTICE

Title II of the International Claims Settlement Act and the Trading With the Enemy Act are administered by the Department of Justice. Consequently, the Commission takes no position in regard to the enactment of S. 2064.

Senator SPARKMAN. Thank you, Mr. McGuire. You have given a very clear and succinct statement. I shall ask very few questions.

Taking up S. 1935 first, do you know of any opposition to this bill in its present form?

0240

Mr. McGUIRE. No, sir; I do not.

Senator SPARKMAN. As I understand it, this applies to the countries named therein, and it more or less brings it in line with the basic act already passed.

Mr. McGUIRE. Yes.

Senator SPARKMAN. And also with action taken on various other claims settlement agreements, is that not correct?

Mr. McGUIRE. That is correct, Mr. Chairman.

### PERCENTAGE OF AWARDS TO BE PAID

Senator SPARKMAN. On the Polish claims, in terms of percentage, how much do you estimate each claimant will receive on his award under that program?

Mr. McGUIRE. You are asking me a question, Mr. Chairman, that I am not in a position to respond to at this time. I think I testified that we have completed action on proposed decisions on 9,111 claims out of some 10,239. Obviously, in the early stages of a program of this nature, the obvious denials usually fall out first, so that the greater percentage of the denials in this program have been met.

Now, of the 9,111 proposed decisions that have issued, as of July 31 the proposed awards constituted an aggregate of some $50 million. It seems reasonable to assume that with approximately 1,000 claims remaining, that the awards will not be quite as high as we had first thought, and it seems to me that, at this juncture, a "guesstimate" could be made that a fairly reasonable percentage will be paid on the awards made by the Commission.

In other words, it is difficult to estimate just what percentage, but it would seem as of right now that there is the possibility of at least a 50-percent payment on the awards.

Senator SPARKMAN. Fifty percent?

Mr. McGUIRE. That would be my best guess at this time, yes.

Senator SPARKMAN. 9,111 are proposed for settlement.

Mr. McGUIRE. They have been disposed of, that is right.

Senator SPARKMAN. Have they been paid?

Mr. McGUIRE. No.

Senator SPARKMAN. They have been decided by the Foreign Claims Settlement Commission.

Mr. McGUIRE. That is right.

Senator SPARKMAN. That leaves about 1,000.

Mr. McGUIRE. That is right.

Senator SPARKMAN. How many have been declined?

Mr. McGUIRE. I am not prepared to answer that question, Mr. Chairman. I can furnish that information for you though.

Senator SPARKMAN. It is just a matter of interest. If it is not too difficult, you might supply it for the record.

(The information referred to follows:)

There have been 5,881 proposed denials and 3,230 proposed awards.

Mr. McGUIRE. I can say this as a general rule, and it is not a rule, it is a happening, these programs seem to fall out at about 60-percent denials.

Senator SPARKMAN. About how much?

Mr. McGUIRE. About 60 percent.

0241

Senator SPARKMAN. Sixty percent fall out.

Mr. McGUIRE. Approximately that percentage are not able to qualify for one reason or another; yes, sir.

Senator SPARKMAN. How many claims did you have?

Mr. McGUIRE. We had 10,239.

Senator SPARKMAN. Does the 9,111 include denials as well as approvals?

Mr. McGUIRE. Denials and awards.

Senator SPARKMAN. That is where I misunderstood. I thought you meant that that many had been approved. That includes the denials as well as the approvals.

Mr. McGUIRE. That is correct.

### ATTORNEY FEES

Senator SPARKMAN. By the way, with reference to the 10-percent attorney's fee, is that without any graduation, regardless of how large or how small the claim?

Mr. McGUIRE. What we propose is to leave it up to the attorney and client.

Senator SPARKMAN. You are really proposing to split that, are you not? Is that a deduction for attorneys' fees, or is that a deduction for attorney's fees and administrative expenses?

Mr. McGUIRE. No. The 10 percent relates to the attorneys' fees.

Senator SPARKMAN. In other words, they are allowed not to exceed 10 percent for attorneys' fees.

Mr. McGUIRE. That is correct.

Senator SPARKMAN. Is that true regardless of the size of the claim?

Mr. McGUIRE. Yes, sir.

Senator SPARKMAN. How large are the largest claims?

Mr. McGUIRE. The largest award that we have made to date is in the claim of the Silesian-American Corp., and my recollection is that that award, proposed award, was for about $16 million, and I understand that this is the largest claim that we had in this program.

Senator SPARKMAN. The 10 percent is a part of the basic law, is it not?

Mr. McGUIRE. That is correct.

Senator SPARKMAN. And you have no discretion with reference to that, except to see that it does not exceed that.

Mr. McGUIRE. That is correct, but under title I of the act, under which we are administering this Polish program, the Commission presently has the authority to graduate the amount of a fee within the 10 percent.

Senator SPARKMAN. But you are asking that that be changed to make it conform to all other statutes.

Mr. McGUIRE. That is correct.

Senator SPARKMAN. Certainly I think attorneys ought to be adequately paid, but it seems to me a little strange that $1,600,000 would be paid for that claim, whereas one for $1,000 would only get a $100 fee. There may not necessarily be more work for a larger claim.

Mr. McGUIRE. Not necessarily. Mr. Chairman, what we propose here is to leave this matter for negotiation between the attorney and client. I am certain that no client with an award of $16 million would be too happy about paying a $1.6 million fee.

Senator SPARKMAN. Well, perhaps that particular claimant might

0242

not be, but you know when you put a ceiling in, it usually becomes the floor as well as the ceiling.

Mr. McGuire. That is absolutely true.

Senator Sparkman. Do they show what the attorney's fee is?

Mr. McGuire. No.

Senator Sparkman. In other words, you have no knowledge.

Mr. McGuire. We have no policing function.

Senator Sparkman. You do not go into that at all.

Mr. McGuire. No, sir.

Senator Sparkman. You approve of S. 1935 with certain changes.

Mr. McGuire. That is right.

Senator Sparkman. And you approve of S. 1826.

Mr. McGuire. I beg your pardon, we approve 1935.

Senator Sparkman. S. 1826, relating to the Cuban claims, you suggest certain changes there.

Mr. McGuire. That is correct.

Senator Sparkman. By the way, do you have Cuban funds available for settlement of those claims, or is this something in the future?

Mr. McGuire. This is something in the future. This is what we call a presettlement adjudication. In other words, this is to liquidate the damages that Cuba owes the United States.

Senator Sparkman. In other words, when they settle, they get your certificate.

Mr. McGuire. That would be correct.

Senator Sparkman. Which can be cashed in.

Mr. McGuire. If, as, and when there is a settlement.

Senator Sparkman. You leave S. 2064 up to the Justice Department.

Mr. McGuire. That is correct. This is a function of the Justice Department.

Senator Sparkman. On all of them except Cuba, the funds are available, is that right?

Mr. McGuire. That is correct, sir; yes.

Senator Sparkman. And in most of them the full payment is already in hand.

Mr. McGuire. With respect to Bulgaria and Rumania, yes. With respect to Poland and Yugoslavia, they are paying in future installments.

Senator Sparkman. Thank you very much, Mr. McGuire.

Mr. McGuire. Thank you, Mr. Chairman.

Senator Sparkman. The next witness will be Mr. Andreas F. Lowenfeld, Deputy Legal Adviser of the Department of State.

Mr. Lowenfeld, we have your prepared statement. You may proceed as you see fit.

## STATEMENT OF ANDREAS F. LOWENFELD, DEPUTY LEGAL ADVISER, DEPARTMENT OF STATE; ACCOMPANIED BY ELY MAURER, ASSISTANT LEGAL ADVISER; EDWARD G. MISEY, DEPUTY ASSISTANT LEGAL ADVISER; AND FABIAN A. KWIATEK, ATTORNEY, OFFICE OF THE LEGAL ADVISER

Mr. Lowenfeld. Thank you, Mr. Chairman.

I am pleased to appear before this subcommittee to present the views of the Department of State on S. 1826, a bill to amend title V of the International Claims Settlement Act of 1949 relating to certain claims

0243

against the Government of Cuba. The State Department strongly supports this bill.

I am appearing only on S. 1826.

Senator SPARKMAN. I understand that.

Mr. LOWENFELD. We do support the other bills before the committee, and if you have any questions of the State Department, Mr. Misey here is prepared to answer them.

Senator SPARKMAN. Very well. Does that include S. 2064?

Mr. LOWENFELD. Mr. Maurer will answer the questions, but the general statement is, yes, we are in support of them.

Senator SPARKMAN. Very well.

Mr. LOWENFELD. The principal purpose of S. 1826 is to repeal the vesting provision of the Cuban Claims Act as passed last fall. We believe this vesting provision could have unfortunate effects on the overall position of the United States in endeavoring to protect foreign investment. We believe that the position of the United States as a defender of international law would be strengthened by repeal of this provision. We see no disadvantages to repeal from the point of view of American claimants.

In addition to this principal purpose, S. 1826 also would clear up an ambiguity concerning the scope of the claims against Cuba which may be considered by the Foreign Claims Settlement Commission, which I shall discuss later on. Finally, I should like to comment briefly on a point of difference between S. 1826 and the corresponding bill, H.R. 9336, which was reported out favorably August 2 by the Committee on Foreign Affairs of the House of Representatives.

### VESTING PROVISIONS IN CUBAN CLAIMS

The most significant result of S. 1826, as I have said, would be to eliminate the vesting provision of the act contained in present section 511. Under that section any property of the Government of Cuba which was blocked in accordance with the Cuban assets control regulations, issued July 8, 1963, and which remains so blocked 6 months after enactment of the section, shall vest in an officer of the U.S. Government to be designated by the President. Vested property is to be sold or otherwise liquidated as expeditiously as possible after vesting, and the proceeds are to be used for the administrative expenses of the U.S. Government in administering the Cuban claims program.

Senator SPARKMAN. Is it limited to that?

Mr. LOWENFELD. Yes, sir; it is.

Senator SPARKMAN. In other words, even if you had blocked funds beyond that amount, they could not go into this fund for the settlement of claims.

Mr. LOWENFELD. That is correct, if there are additional funds they would be covered over into miscellaneous receipts of the Treasury.

Under the proposed amendment, present section 511 would be repealed, and in its place there would be inserted a simple authorization for an appropriation to cover the Claims Commission's administrative expenses under the Cuban claims program.

The Department of State strongly supports this amendment.

You may recall that last August, when the Cuban claims legislation was under consideration by the Congress, the Department supported the principal purpose of the then proposed legislation, but opposed the vesting and sale of any Cuban assets. As Mr. Meeker, the De-

0244

partment's Legal Adviser, wrote to the chairman of the Foreign Relations Committee, traditionally vesting and sale of foreign assets have been measures applied only to wartime enemies of the United States and have been carried out for the purpose of paying war reparations. The seizure of alien property in peacetime anywhere is contrary to our fundamental beliefs and, we believe, is contrary to our national interests.

In signing the Cuban Claims Act last October, President Johnson expressed his misgivings about the wisdom of the vesting provision. and requested the Secretary of State to make a full study to determine the effect of that provision on American interests abroad and its implications for the conduct of our foreign relations. Accordingly, we made a thorough study of the issues raised by the vesting provision. Our conclusion was that the vesting provision of the Cuban Claims Act could set an unfortunate example for countries less dedicated than the United States to the preservation of property rights; that it would raise serious questions under international law; and that it would hamper, rather than aid, any future settlement of claims of American citizens arising out of the actions of the present Government of Cuba.

Americans own billions of dollars' worth of property in foreign countries. The U.S. Government as a matter of policy encourages business investment in many countries throughout the world. To protect such property and investments, the U.S. Government adheres to and advocates the principle of international law that states have an obligation to pay prompt, adequate, and effective compensation for any taking of property. Were Cuban property now to be vested and sold by the U.S. Government, our effectiveness in upholding this important principle of international law could be seriously weakened and our efforts to protect American-owned property abroad could well be impaired.

#### DISTINCTION BETWEEN GOVERNMENT AND PRIVATE PROPERTY

We recognize, of course, that the vesting and sale of assets of the Cuban Government is not the same as the vesting and sale of property of Cuban individuals and corporations. But distinctions which seem clear to us are not always accepted and understood by others. States less dedicated to the preservation of property rights could cite our action in the case of Cuba as justification for the taking of American-owned private property.

Moreover, the U.S. Government itself holds many billions of dollars' worth of assets abroad, including embassy buildings, deposits of funds, property on military bases, and others. Thus, if a distinction were to be drawn between protection accorded to private property and protection accorded to Government property, the United States would probably be the principal loser.

In this connection, two points are worth noting. First, as I have stated, the proceeds of the properties to be vested and sold are to be used, under the existing law, not for the purpose of paying claims of American citizens, but merely to defray the expenses of processing such claims. Moreover, the amount that would be derived from the vesting and sale of Cuban Government assets would be insignificant. It has been estimated by the Treasury and Justice Departments that Cuban Government property subject to vesting under title V of the International Claims Settlement Act amounts to only $350,000 to

0245

$400,000. That sum would cover less than half of the expenses of the Foreign Claims Settlement Commission and the Treasury Department in processing claims of American nationals against Cuba. The insignificant amount of Federal funds thus saved could not in our view justify impairment of an important, traditional, and far-reaching position of the United States.

In short, the United States stands for the protection of property rights. We should not be diverted from this position by any argument that we are doing to Cuba only what Cuba has done to us.

We therefore urge passage of section 4 of S. 1826 which would repeal all of section 511 and would authorize an appropriation to enable the Foreign Claims Settlement Commission to pay the necessary expenses of administering the Cuban claims program.

### SCOPE OF CLAIMS

Let me turn next to sections 1 and 2 of S. 1826, relating to the scope of the claims against Cuba that may be presented to the Commission under the act.

Under the present law, there may be ambiguity as to whether debt claims against the Government of Cuba are, like other claims against that Government, limited to those arising after the coming to power of the Castro regime. The present bill, S. 1826, would remove such ambiguity by eliminating, in the passage of sections 501 and 503(a) describing claims covered by the act, the words "which have arisen out of (or 'arising of') debts for merchandise furnished or services rendered by nationals of the United States without regard to the date on which such merchandise was furnished or services were rendered or".

The Department of State supports this amendment. We do not believe it was the intention of the Congress to make a distinction between debt and property claims. We believe the object of the Cuban claims bill was to authorize the filing and determination of claims against the Castro regime, and not to provide a forum for other kinds of claims including those that might have been barred by statutes of limitations or that were not paid for other reasons having nothing to do with the present political status of Cuba.

Finally, I should like to comment briefly on an amendment to section 507(a) of the Cuban Claims Act, which appears in H.R. 9336 as reported out by the House Committee on Foreign Affairs but does not appear in S. 1826. Section 507(a) of the present act provides:

The Commission shall certify to each individual who has filed a claim under this title the amount determined by the Commission to be the loss or damage suffered by the claimant which is covered by this title. The Commission shall certify to the Secretary of State such amount and the basic information underlying that amount, together with a statement of the evidence relied upon and the reasoning employed in reaching its decision.

We could have thought that this provision—a simple statement consonant with usual concepts of judicial or quasi-judicial procedure—would cause no difficulty. The Foreign Claims Settlement Commission, however, proposes to strike out from the second sentence of this subsection everything after the word "amount," so that there would be no statutory requirement for supplying to the Secretary of State the basic information underlying the amount or a statement of the evidence and reasoning supporting the Commission's decision.

On the basis of our experience in negotiating past claims settlements, we believe that well-reasoned and documented explanations of claims

0246

determinations are essential to any successful negotiation of a claims settlement; this will be true in the case of Cuba, whenever negotiation should become possible. We believe that the provision of section 507(a) is particularly appropriate where, as in claims against Cuba today, much of the inquiry must be ex parte and without opportunity to investigate on the scene.

## UNNECESSARY LANGUAGE

The Chairman of the Foreign Claims Settlement Commission has stated in his letter of June 2—and Mr. McGuire repeated it here this morning—that the Commission considers the words in question to be unnecessary, since section 4(b) of title I of the International Claims Settlement Act already sets down the requirement that each decision by the Commission shall state the reason for such decision. We believe, however, that the formulation in the present statute is more explicit and will provide greater assurance that when the time comes for a claims negotiation with some government of Cuba, the State Department will be as fully equipped as possible. We therefore support S. 1826 in its present form, without any deletion from the second sentence of section 507(a) either as proposed by the Commission or as reported out by the House committee as H.R. 9336.

In conclusion, Mr. Chairman, the Department of State believes that S. 1826 is an important bill in the field of international law and administration of claims. We support the bill fully in the form it is before you.

Senator SPARKMAN. Going back to section 507(a), your quotation of it on page 7 is as it appears in present law.

Mr. LOWENFELD. That is correct.

Senator SPARKMAN. And S. 1826 would not disturb that.

Mr. LOWENFELD. Correct.

Senator SPARKMAN. The House provision would follow the suggestion of the Foreign Claims Settlement Commission.

Mr. LOWENFELD. Not quite, Mr. Chairman.

Senator SPARKMAN. Well, it would make changes.

Mr. LOWENFELD. The House bill would leave out starting with the word "together".

Senator SPARKMAN. Yes; I understand, after the word "amount".

Mr. LOWENFELD. No; the Commission would stop at "amount" but what the House did—the first time the word "amount" appears, and what the House did was to stop the second time the word "amount" appears, so it just deleted from "together with a statement" and thereafter. There is that difference.

Senator SPARKMAN. It would seem to me that your argument is good. As I understand it, the Claims Commission hands down what is, in essence, a decision.

Mr. LOWENFELD. Yes.

Senator SPARKMAN. And I see no reason why that should not become a part of the record furnished to the State Department. That is all you are asking for.

Mr. LOWENFELD. That is correct, and we are asking that the decision state the reasons.

Senator SPARKMAN. And, of course, the Commission has not testified here suggesting any change.

Mr. LOWENFELD. I understand the Commission to suggest a change.

52-255—65——5

0247

Senator SPARKMAN. I believe it did.   I wonder if it becomes a little difficult when you have two departments of the Government, differing on a sensitive point of this kind.  Has there been any discussion between the State Department and the Claims Commission on this?

Mr. LOWENFELD. Yes, Mr. Chairman.  There has been a good deal of discussion.

Senator SPARKMAN. You just do not agree, is that right?

Mr. LOWENFELD. Well, as I understand it, the Commission says, "We do this anyway so why put it in the statute," and our experience has been that most of the time they do it, and sometimes they do not, and there is no harm in making sure.

Senator SPARKMAN. You would like to have consistency.

Mr. LOWENFELD. That is correct, Mr. Chairman.

Senator SPARKMAN. Thank you very much.  Are there any other statements from any of you?

Thank you very much, gentlemen.  We appreciate your presentation.

Our next group of witnesses are public witnesses.  First, Mr. Kenneth Sprague, vice president of the American & Foreign Power Co., Inc., New York City.

Mr. Sprague, will you come around please, sir.

## STATEMENT OF KENNETH B. SPRAGUE, VICE PRESIDENT OF AMERICAN & FOREIGN POWER CO., INC.; ACCOMPANIED BY WENDELL LUND, COMPANY COUNSEL

Mr. SPRAGUE. I have with me Mr. Wendell Lund, counsel for the company.

Senator SPARKMAN. Very good to have you both.  I have your statement, and the same thing applies to it as I have said to the others. Proceed as you see fit.

Mr. SPRAGUE. Mr. Chairman, my name is Kenneth B. Sprague.  I am vice president of American & Foreign Power Co., Inc.  I appreciate the opportunity of appearing before your committee to comment upon S. 1826, which sets forth certain proposed changes in the Cuban Claims Act.

American & Foreign Power Co., Inc., is the principal holder of the outstanding securities of Cuban Electric Co., which, until August 1960, when the Castro government of Cuba confiscated its properties in the island, provided over 90 percent of all of the electric power sold to the public in Cuba.  Cuban Electric Co. rendered electric service to the principal cities of Cuba, including Havana and Santiago de Cuba, and it owned and operated the gas system in the city of Havana. The total stated value of the outstanding securities of Cuban Electric Co. is approximately $280 million of which 72 percent is owned by U.S. interests including American & Foreign Power Co., Inc.  At the end of 1959, Cuban Electric Co.'s gross assets amounted to $365 million.

First, I wish to state that American & Foreign Power Co., Inc., and Cuban Electric Co. fully support the principal objective of the Cuban Claims Act (Public Law 88–666), namely, the determination and certification by the Foreign Claims Settlement Commission of the amounts of the claims of U.S. nationals against the Government of Cuba.  The suggestions which I shall offer go primarily to the administration of the claims program and are in no way intended to reflect doubt upon the correctness of the act's basic purpose.

0248

The points that I should like to make relate to: (1) the question of the presentation of claims by creditors of U.S. nationals who are themselves claiming under the law—a procedure which I do not believe advisable; and (2) the effect to be given—insofar as the certification of claims is concerned—to any U.S. tax benefits that may be derived by claimants.

CREDITORS' CLAIMS

Under section 502(3) of Public Law 88–666 it appears that creditors of enterprises that are submitting claims for expropriation losses are entitled to make independent filings based upon the liabilities of the claimant enterprises to such creditors. To take a concrete, though hypothetical, illustration: "X" Corp., which qualifies as a "national of the United States" under section 502(1) and, thus, as a claimant, presents its claim for the value of its assets confiscated by the Castro government in the amount of $10 million. "X" Corp.'s American creditors, to whom it owes, say, $2 million, also file claims. Under these circumstances the Foreign Claims Settlement Commission might have to certify total claims of $12 million although it is evident that the true situation is that "X" Corp. is entitled to $10 million of which $2 million, when and if recovery is had, may be payable to its creditors. Public Law 88–666, like prior claims acts administered by the Foreign Claims Settlement Commission, is written so as to preclude a similar result in the case of stockholders of a claimant corporation. Section 505(a) provides that, where a corporation qualifies in its own right as a claimant, its stockholders are not also entitled to present claims.

If both the companies themselves and their creditors are permitted to file, the result would be an overlapping of claims and a consequent increase in the size and scope of the Commission's task. It cannot be expected that there will be payment in full of claims representing both confiscated assets and indebtedness that normally would be satisfied out of such assets or out of compensation paid for them, and the aggregate amount of claims to be certified by the Commission would be unrealistic. Another practical objection to this procedure is that in some cases the creditor's claim might be defective and subject to a defense or even a counterclaim which the corporation would feel compelled to assert. In such an event the Commission might be placed in the difficult position of having to rule upon legal questions that are far removed from those normally entrusted to it.

It is believed that section 502(3) was drafted in a very broad way in order to assure that all Americans with legitimate claims against the Cuban Government would have an opportunity to present them, and that the wording was based upon a section found in the 1960 United States-Polish Claims Agreement. We take no issue with the proposition that, if a company which has lost its property to the Cuban Government does not qualify to claim in its own behalf because, for example, it is incorporated in Cuba, its creditors should be allowed to present their own claims against the Cuban Government which has seized the property out of which their debts would normally be paid. However, I submit that, when a company itself lodges a claim, the same rule of exclusion that applies to its stockholders should also apply to its creditors. The Foreign Claims Settlement Commission— a body with preeminent expertise in valuation and international legal matters—is not the appropriate forum for the adjudication of creditors' rights. It is my understanding that the problem which I am

0249

posing did not arise under the Polish Claims Agreement, presumably because few U.S.-incorporated companies were directly engaged in business in that country so that corporations qualifying as nationals of the United States did not present claims simultaneously with American creditors. This was not the case in Cuba where there were a number of American corporations which were doing business directly in Cuba and which had American creditors who, under the present drafting of the act, might feel compelled to file their own independent claims.

A change in the wording of section 505(a) of the act that would, it is believed, leave the way open for the filing of claims by creditors whose rights are not otherwise protected and which would eliminate the duplication of claims discussed above is as follows (additions to present text of section 505(a) underlined):

SEC. 505. (a) A claim under section 503(a) of this title based upon an ownership interest in any corporation, association, or other entity which is a national of the United States shall not be considered.

We would propose to add the following:

A claim under section 503(a) of this title based upon a debt or other obligation owing by any corporation, association, or other entity which is a national of the United States shall not be considered if such corporation, association, or other entity files a claim under section 503(a) of this title for losses resulting from the nationalization, expropriation, intervention or other taking of, or special measures directed against, its property.

## TAX BENEFITS

Section 506 of the act (entitled "Offsets") states that the Commission shall deduct from the amount of any claim "all amounts the claimant has received from any source on account of the same loss or losses." The legislative history of this provision does not clearly answer the question of whether any U.S. tax benefits that may have been derived by a claimant as a result of a Cuban loss were intended to be deducted as an amount "received" by the claimant. It would seem that the correct administration of the claims program requires that this doubt be resolved by amendatory legislation.

I would like to add I was pleased this morning to hear Mr. McGuire say that this matter should be clarified.

For the reasons that I am about to mention it is suggested that the question of tax benefits should be eliminated entirely from the purview of the present act.

Public Law 88–666 provides only for the evaluation, not the payment, of claims. As I understand it, the sole intention is to make a record of the total sum owed U.S. nationals by the Cuban Government and the introduction of U.S. tax benefits serves only to confuse and unduly complicate the picture.

Under present law, any recovery which a claimant may obtain on his Cuban loss must be taken into his income and U.S. income tax paid on it at least to the extent that the claimant realized a tax benefit by deducting the loss. In order to treat each claimant equitably, each should be permitted to resubmit his claim as increased by the additional taxpayments he was required to pay upon recovery on his initial claim and this process in theory would be continued indefi-

0250

nitely as each recovery is obtained. It is suggested that this procedure is impractical and should not be adopted.

Under the normal rule applicable where a U.S. taxpayer has incurred a loss (for example, a bad debt loss) and thereafter has recovered such loss (for example, by receipt of payment from the debtor) the recovery is taxable to the extent that the deduction resulted in a tax benefit (sec. 111 of the Internal Revenue Code of 1954). If this rule were followed as to Cuban claims, the claimant would receive the amount of recovery to which he was entitled insofar as recovery was possible, and the U.S. Government would receive any additional tax to which it was entitled by reason of recovery of the loss. There appears to be no valid reason for departing from this rule.

Another difficulty with combining the matter of tax benefits with the claims program under Public Law 88–666 is that a provision calling for the deduction of tax benefits from the amounts of the claims to be certified cannot be fully implemented at this time for the reason that the extent of any tax benefits that may be derived as a result of Cuban losses may not presently be known by the claimants themselves. For example, a claimant that is carrying forward its Cuban loss for a period of 10 years from the date of loss, as it is permitted to do under section 172 of the Internal Revenue Code, cannot furnish a meaningful statement of tax benefits until at least 1969.

It is recommended that section 506 of Public Law 88–666 be amended to provide as follows: This is the way section 506 reads at the present time:

SEC. 506. In determining the amount of any claim, the Commission shall deduct all amounts the claimant has received from any source on account of the same loss or losses.

We would propose to add the following:

For the purpose of the certification of claims under this title, tax benefits, if any, resulting from a loss which is the subject of a claim under section 503(a) shall not be deducted.

STATUS OF AMERICAN PROPERTY IN CHINA

There is another related matter to which I should like your committee to give serious consideration. This matter is the loss of U.S. property to Communist China. The Shanghai Power Co., a subsidiary of our company, lost properties valued in the neighborhood of $70 million when the Communists took over in China. It seems evident that, if the timely determination of claims is desirable in the case of Cuba, it is equally imperative in the case of China where large losses were suffered by U.S. nationals some 15 years ago. Although the prospect for the redress of such damage may be remote at present, the documentation of claims while witnesses and records are still available would serve to facilitate their eventual settlement. I am hopeful that your committee will consider this problem and that it can be included in any bill reported out by your committee.

Thank you very much, Mr. Chairman.

Senator SPARKMAN. Thank you, Mr. Sprague.

Let me ask you just one thing. Perhaps I do not fully understand the import of your suggestion with reference to not allowing creditors to file the claim. Is your company injured in any way by the filing of claims by a creditor that you may have in this country?

0251

Mr. SPRAGUE. No; except that I feel it would confuse and complicate the filing of the claim, and would add a lot of additional work.

Senator SPARKMAN. If they are excluded, then they become wholly dependent upon the action taken by the principal company.

It seems to me a good rule of law that the creditors should be allowed to take such steps as may be necessary to protect their own interests. We do that in ordinary law practice, do we not?

Mr. SPRAGUE. Yes, sir; but would the other creditors not have all rights against the company in any event? As long as the company has assets.

Senator SPARKMAN. Against the company but not necessarily against assets that may become available for the settlement of claims. If they are excluded from filing, I do not see how they could ever file. If X contracts with Y, for instance, to build a house, and Y has various subcontractors, it is my understanding of the law that those subcontractors can go in and file lien against the property for the settlement of their claims regardless of what the principal creditor does.

Mr. SPRAGUE. That is true.

Senator SPARKMAN. That is domestic law. I do not see why it is not a good rule in international law. It seems to me that application of good every day practice of statutory law would permit the creditors to file a claim. However, with reference to all amendments that are suggested, I shall ask the agencies concerned to comment on them before the record is closed.

Mr. SPRAGUE. I understand.

Senator SPARKMAN. Thank you.

Mr. SPRAGUE. It just seemed to us that the creditors were more or less in the same position as public stockholders.

Senator SPARKMAN. Well, it does not quite seem that way to me. The stockholders are part owners. The creditors are dependent on the assets available to the corporation for the satisfaction of their debt. I think there is a distinction. But thank you very much, both of you.

Mr. SPRAGUE. Thank you, Mr. Chairman.

Senator SPARKMAN. Next will be Mr. Robert Reiter, attorney at law of Washington, D.C.

Come around, Mr. Reiter. Mr. Reiter, we have your statement. What I said about the others will apply to you.

## STATEMENT OF ROBERT REITER, ATTORNEY AT LAW, WASHINGTON, D.C.

Mr. REITER. Thank you very much. I will just say a few words rather than reading the statement.

Senator SPARKMAN. Very well.

Mr. REITER. I am an attorney here in Washington, and there are two amendments we want to suggest to the legislation proposed by the Foreign Claims Settlement Commission. The first relates to an Ohio man, and I am sorry that Senator Lausche is not here this morning. I want to mention it at least.

Senator SPARKMAN. I will see that it is called to his attention.

Mr. REITER. Fine. I would appreciate that, Mr. Chairman.

We testified at the original hearings on the International Claims Settlement Act amendments in 1955 with respect to certain Americans

0252

who were hurt in Italy during the war, particularly one Cincinnati man who was captured while he was helping the Allies and sent to a prison and suffered complete breakdown in his health. He thereafter served with the Americans at the close of the war, and was decorated by both the Americans and the Italian democratic authorities after the war. This man has been in very bad shape ever since, and as a result, perhaps to some extent of our testimony, a provision was added, was put into the International Claims Settlement Act regarding the Italian claims to provide for personal injury cases. However, when this case and a number of others were brought up before the Commission, the Commission in this case established a rule that since there was an armistice in Italy in 1943, any claim which occurred after that in northern Italy, where the Germans and the Italians were really fighting until the end of the war in 1945 or at least until 1944, were not compensable.

In other cases, at least one case of the same kind, where the injuries occurred in the same period, the Dayton Daily News in Dayton, Ohio, discovered that the Commission made an award. The matter was taken up by the newspaper with the legal staff of the Foreign Claims Settlement Commission who could not account for the difference, but said that, unfortunately, there was no legislation which permitted the reopening of these claims and therefore there was nothing they could do about it.

### REOPENING ITALIAN CLAIMS

Well now, at this point we have over $1 million left in the Italian Claims Fund. The Commission is proposing to reopen that with respect to certain late filed claims which I do not believe will take care of the whole $1 million. The rest they would propose to use to pay into the Treasury to take care of certain prisoner-of-war claims.

I would suggest that if, in fact, there was this inconsistency in treatment, and if, in fact, this Commission—and let me say the present Commission was not setting at that time—if there was an inconsistency, I suggest that it would take just a few words to permit these cases now to be reconsidered and perhaps compensated before this money is paid for a use which is really not in accordance with the Lombardo agreement under which Italy deposited certain funds with the Treasury to pay an American claim which was not compensated under the peace treaty between the United States and Italy.

That is my first suggestion.

Senator SPARKMAN. Now, let me see if I understand that correctly. Your contention is that since there was actually a condition of war in Italy extending beyond 1943——

Mr. REITER. The treaty was in 1947 in fact, and the statute specifically says the war starting in 1939 and going to 1947.

Senator SPARKMAN. There was actual fighting in Italy—1943 was the date.

Mr. REITER. The armistice in southern Italy was in 1943, yes.

Senator SPARKMAN. That was the cutoff date.

Mr. REITER. No cutoff date but they just applied——

Senator SPARKMAN. Under the decision of the Claims Commission.

Mr. REITER. In this particular case they applied the cutoff date.

Senator SPARKMAN. Yes. Of course, the fighting in Italy beyond that time was between German and Allied forces.

Mr. REITER. And the Italians, too.

0253

Senator SPARKMAN. And the Italians?

Mr. REITER. They were really fighting hard. That is right. The Fascist Italians up in northern Italy were fighting pretty hard during that period.

I might say that Senator Young, of Ohio, was involved in that fighting. I discussed this with him, and he told me that that was the worst part of the war, fighting around Milan and Turin. He was involved in it.

May I continue?

Senator SPARKMAN. Yes, go ahead.

Let me say it is a good point that you make, and I would be interested in knowing—and we shall certainly ask the Claims Commission for comment on that as well as other agencies, perhaps the State Department—with reference to the situation that did exist. I know there was fighting over there. I was there. But I did not know that the Italians were engaged.

Mr. REITER. It was the Italians who finally captured this man and put him in prison.

My second proposal for amendment covers this situation. In this same amendment to the International Claims Settlement Act of 1955, after providing for the vesting of satellite assets which had been blocked during the war and not seized during the war the provision was made if any natural person had an interest, he could then apply to the Office of Alien Property for the divesting of his property and it would be divested to him, since the purpose, the clearly stated purpose of the legislation was not to use private individually owned funds for the payment of nationalization claims. It was for the purpose of using governmental funds and funds of corporations which, for all practical purposes, in these Iron Curtain countries had been nationalized.

The 1-year period expired, and thereafter presumably all the funds would thereafter be used to pay American claims against these countries. This program, as you have heard, has been completed, and at least with respect to two of these three classes of claims, Bulgaria and Rumania, there has been payment in full or pretty close to full. And yet there are certain people who have still managed to get out from behind the Iron Curtain, particularly Rumania, in the past few years, and who are in no different position from those who managed to escape a few years ago within the 1-year divesting period.

Now I realize there has to come an end to these divesting claims, and there has to come a final disposition of them. However, in cases where these people have come out, these natural persons, and have the same essential rights to claim as natural owners, private persons, and where there are still funds remaining in the hands of the Office of Alien Property which have not been turned over to these funds in the Treasury Department and used to pay the claims of American award holders of the Foreign Claims Settlement Commission, it seems to me that it would be desirable to add a provision that these people, if they do come out while there are still funds available, should have the right to apply for divesting.

0254

My understanding is that the people in these countries have had no basis whatever for knowing about the divesting possibilities, and if they did know about it, if their governments ever learned that they had moneys over here, they would probably be in even more trouble.

So the only practical hope of their getting their money back would have been to escape, and if they have been able to escape, and there are still funds available, I have suggested perhaps that they should be permitted to make claim and receive the return of their funds.

Senator SPARKMAN. Have you, in your statement, included suggested language?

Mr. REITER. I have, Mr. Chairman.

Senator SPARKMAN. Well, we shall be very glad to consider this, and, as I said, I will ask the interested agencies and departments to comment.

Mr. REITER. Thank you very much.

Senator SPARKMAN. Thank you, Mr. Reiter.

(Mr. Reiter's statement in full follows:)

### STATEMENT OF ROBERT REITER

#### ITALIAN CLAIMS

Under the terms of an agreement between the United States and Italy in 1947, Italy deposited $5 million in the Italian claims fund in the U.S. Treasury. The purpose of this deposit was explained in the staff memorandum of the Senate Committee on Foreign Relations published in March 1963 on the claims programs administered by the Foreign Claims Settlement Commission, as follows:

"The purpose of the money in the Italian claims fund was, in general, to compensate claimants for losses relating to property located outside of Italy and attributable to Italian military action (e.g., losses on the high seas, in Greece, Yugoslavia, and other areas in which Italy engaged in military action), and certain personal injury and similar nonproperty losses which arose in Italy."

The Commission's consideration of claims under this agreement was completed, and the awards paid in full, and $1,088,623.53 remains in the fund, which under the agreement is to be used solely for the payment of claims against Italy during the war. Under section 10 of S. 1935, the Commission proposes to reopen the program with respect to claims rejected because they were not timely filed.

However, there is another class of claims which should be reconsidered, based on what appears to be a clear error in carrying out the congressional mandate, and resulting in discrimination in treatment between claimants in the identical legal position. This is in the area of claims for personal injury and suffering. Section 304 of the International Claims Settlement Act, as amended, provided for the payment of claims arising "out of the war in which Italy was engaged from June 10, 1940, to September 15, 1947," and the reports of the congressional committees specifically stated that "claims for personal injury, suffering, and other losses would be compensable," following testimony during the hearings on the legislation regarding the imprisonment, injury, and suffering of Americans in Italy.

Yet it appears that in a number of personal injury and suffering cases, the Commission as then constituted (none of the present members were then serving) refused to consider such claims compensable, on technical grounds not supported by the statute. Under the statute their action is unreviewable by any court, and with the end of the program could not be corrected, short of reopening of the program, as now proposed by the Commission.

As one example, the Dayton Daily News of Dayton, Ohio, discovered a situation where an Ohio man's claim was denied because he was captured and imprisoned on November 20, 1943, after the armistice in southern Italy, but while we were still fighting the Italians and Germans in northern Italy, and long before the date specified in the statute as the end of the Italian war—September 15, 1947. This man, Carl L. Hauss, a native-born American citizen, performed valiant service

52-255—65——6

0255

to this country, both during and after the war. He was captured by the Italians and held for 6 months in isolation in prison, without any consideration of the requirements of international law governing such imprisonment, and resulting in the complete breakdown of his health. Yet the Commission found his case uncompensable.

What is more, the Dayton Daily News discovered that in at least one other case, the Commission made an award based on imprisonment which occurred in the same area of Italy, and in December 1943, 3 months after Mr. Hauss was imprisoned. A Commission representative, when asked to explain the difference in treatment accorded the two cases, admitted that the injuries in both cases took place after the armistice, and was unable to account for the granting of one claim and rejection of the other. He simply stated that it was then too late to do anything for Mr. Hauss.

Now, however, that the Commission itself proposes to reopen the Italian claims program, and there is over a million dollars remaining in the Italian claims fund established for the specific purpose of paying American claims of this type, there seems no reason why this inequity cannot be remedied. For this purpose, the following language should be added to the Commission's proposal to amend section 304 of the International Claims Settlement Act, as amended, at the end of section 304(b) as proposed in S. 1935: (after substituting a comma for the period) "and claims for personal injury and suffering."

This addition would occur at the end of the third line of page 7 of S. 1935 as printed.

Copies of the Commission decisions in the Hauss and Leoni cases are being submitted for the record, together with the Dayton Daily News articles dealing with the subject, and an affidavit of Mr. Hauss indicating the meritoriousness of his claim.

0256

FOREIGN CLAIMS SETTLEMENT COMMISSION
OF THE UNITED STATES
WASHINGTON 25, D. C.

IN THE MATTER OF THE CLAIM OF

CARL L. HAUSS
Via Plutarch 2
Milan, Italy

Claim No. IT-10,863

Decision No. IT-859

Under the International Claims Settlement
Act of 1949, as amended

Attorney for Claimant:

ROBERT H. REITER, Esquire
Spaulding, Reitor & Ross
Suite 601, 1311 G Street, N. W.
Washington 5, D. C.

FINAL DECISION

The Commission issued its Proposed Decision on this claim on December 15, 1958, a certified copy of which was duly served upon the claimant. Thereafter, objections were filed and evidence and arguments were presented by counsel at a hearing held on May 21, 1959.

The Commission finds that claimant was arrested on or about November 20, 1943 at San Matino (Luino), Italy, during a skirmish between partisans and the Forces of Germany, and that he was imprisoned at San Vittore Prison, Milan, Italy, at the disposition of the German police. Thus, the Commission also finds that the claim herein asserted under Section 304 of the Act is not compensable since the alleged injuries, if any, for which claim was made were sustained by German action and subsequent to the capitulation during World War II of the Forces of Italy, on September 3, 1943. The Commission finds it unnecessary to make determinations with respect to other elements of the claim.

General notice of the Proposed Decision having been given by posting for thirty days, it is

ORDERED that such Proposed Decision be and the same is hereby entered as the Final Decision on this claim.

Washington 25, D. C.

JUN 8 1959

*Whitney Gillilland*

*Ewil Rice*

*Robert L. Kunzig*

COMMISSIONERS

0257

FOREIGN CLAIMS SETTLEMENT COMMISSION
OF THE UNITED STATES
WASHINGTON 25, D. C.

IN THE MATTER OF THE CLAIM OF

ALESSANDRA BORRIONE LEONI
PATRICIA AGNES LEONI
CARLO ALESSANDRO LEONI
7 Via Marcora
Milan, Italy

Claim No. IT-10,833

Decision No. IT- *879*

Under the International Claims Settlement
Act of 1949, as amended

Attorney for Claimant:

AVV. GUIDO FRATI
10 Via C. Mayr
Milan, Italy

PROPOSED DECISION

This is a joint claim for $33,440.00 by Alessandra Borrione
Leoni (married to Sylvio C. Leoni February 25, 1933 at Turin,
Italy, a native born citizen of the United States, July 19, 1888,
until his death October 1, 1951 at Milan, Italy) and daughter,
Patricia Agnes Leoni, and son, Carlo Alessandro Leoni, born of
an American father, and is for internment, loss of income, wrongful death of her husband, loss of support for herself and minor
children, as a result of the war in which Italy was engaged from
June 10, 1940 to September 15, 1947.

Section 304 of the aforesaid Act provides for the receipt
and determination by the Commission in accordance with the Memorandum of Understanding and applicable substantive law, including
international law, of the validity and amount of claims of nationals of the United States against the Government of Italy,
arising out of the war in which Italy was engaged, and with respect to which provision was not made in the Treaty of Peace with
Italy.

0258

The Commission has consistently held that claims for loss of income are speculative in character and are not compensable. Therefore, that portion of this claim relative to income must be and hereby is denied.

The facts as established by the evidence of record reveal that the claimant, Alessandra Borrione Leoni, has failed to furnish evidence which would support her contention that she is a national of the United States. Therefore, she is not eligible for compensation under Section 304 of the Act.

The record further reveals that Patricia Agnes Leoni and Carlo Alessandro Leoni are United States citizens and eligible claimants.

The record also appears to support the claimant's contention as to entitlement for personal injuries suffered by her late husband, wrongful death, and loss of support for herself and her two minor children, heretofore named.

A sovereign state may detain, intern, or even expel enemy subjects without violating international law, and the mere fact of internment itself is not a violation thereof in the absence of evidence showing that a rule of international law was violated during such internment or detention.

The records disclose that Sylvio C. Leoni (deceased) was arrested and during his imprisonment was, in fact, subjected to experiences which were not in conformity with the generally accepted precepts of international law, that he suffered personal injuries which were the proximate cause of his death, and that the result therefore was the denial of support of his wife and children.

0259

The record reveals that the loss and neglect occurred in a
series of events beginning in December 1943 as a consequence of
military operations in which Italy participated. While the
record fails to establish the definite date of loss and neglect,
it is deemed to have occurred on or about December 22, 1943 for
the purpose of this decision.

The Commission finds from the evidence and data before it
that the fair and reasonable extent of the loss suffered was
$7,500.00 and that the children of the decedent are each entitled
to one-third of said award.

### A W A R D

On the above evidence and grounds, this claim is allowed
and an award is hereby made to Patricia Agnes Leoni in the
amount of $2,500.00;

and an award is hereby made to Carlo Alessandro Leoni in
the amount of $2,500.00.

Dated at Washington, D. C.

DEC 30 1958

FOR THE COMMISSION:

J. Noble Richards, Director
Italian Claims Division

0260

[From the Dayton Daily News, Mar. 15, 1964]

*Why? Mother Asks*

## No Pay for Yank Captured in War

### (By Walter Bybeck)

WASHINGTON, February 29.—A 90-year-old Cincinnati woman can't understand why her son, captured by Italian Fascists, cannot get paid for injuries suffered during his imprisonment.

A $5 million fund to pay American citizens for personal injuries and property losses caused by the Italians still has over $1 million of unused money—but Carl L. Hauss has not been able to get a penny.

Hauss' mother lives in Cincinnati while he tries to support her from Italy, where he has resided since the end of World War I.

During World War II, Hauss fled to the hills and joined the underground. He was captured by Italians, put in solitary confinement for nearly 6 months and sent to other prison camps.

According to Hauss' letters, he was deprived of water for 2 months, rarely allowed to leave his cell, subjected to extreme cold, taken ill with chicken pox, and menaced by Fascist guards.

When he was liberated 2 years later by Americans, Hauss was 52 years old, suffering from complete loss of his teeth, rheumatic arthritis, nervous exhaustion, and other ailments.

The Foreign Claims Settlement Commission in Washington, however, denied Hauss' petition for reimbursement for his loss of health. Explained an official in the legal office:

"The Italian Government already capitulated on September 3, 1943, but Hauss was not arrested until November. The Germans, not the Italians, were in charge. It's just one of those things."

The fact that Hauss was captured by Italians, imprisoned by them, and charged in an Italian court for helping American and English soldiers escape makes no difference, ruled the claims officer.

"The Germans were in top control," he said.

The case is complicated because Italians in the north, where Hauss was, continued to fight the Allies after the Italians in the southern part of the country surrendered.

Yet the Claims Office, in case after case it approved, used the phrase "as a result of the war in which Italy was engaged from June 10, 1940, to September 15, 1947." So the treaty date, not the capitulation, would seem to be pertinent, especially in view of the continued Italian fighting in which Hauss was caught.

A similar case, uncovered by the Daily News, reveals that the "German responsibility," has not always prevailed:

The two children of Sylvio C. Leoni (now deceased) were awarded $2,500 each because of the inhuman treatment to their father. The decision notes:

"The loss and neglect occurred in a series of events beginning in December 1943 as a consequence of military operations in which Italy participated."

---

[From the Dayton Daily News, Mar. 15, 1964]

## Commission Baffled on POW Inequities—Bureau Agrees With Daily News But Doesn't Know What To Do About It

WASHINGTON, March 14.—The Foreign Claims Settlement Commission said it agrees with a recent Daily News story about an apparent inequity, but does not know what to do about it.

Carl L. Hauss, severely injured in Italian prison camps during World War II, was denied any money from the $5 million fund set up to repay American citizens for their losses.

At the time of this denial, the Claims Commission said it was because the injuries to Hauss (whose mother lives in Cincinnati) occured 2 months after the Italians capitulated to the Americans.

But the Daily News draws a parallel case where another man was injured by Fascists in northern Italy after southern Italy had capitulated.

0261

Ben Greer, staff attorney for the General Counsel of the Claims Commission, said detailed files would probably show some reason for the different treatment. After examining those files, however, Greer said:

"The facts appear substantially similar. There must have been some good reason. Sylvia Leon (the other man) was arrested before the capitulation, but his injuries also took place after the armistice, according to the records. I really can't say why both cases were not treated alike."

Greer further explained that, because of the statute of limitations, it is too late to do anything for Hauss, now 70 and still suffering disabilities.

Senator Stephen M. Young said he is interested in the *Hauss* case, especially since he was a a military governor in Italy after the American invasion.

The Ohio Democrat said he would discuss the *Hauss* case with Senator J. W. Fulbright, Democrat, of Arkansas. Fulbright, as chairman of the Foreign Relations Committee, is studying further legislation in connection with unmet war claims.

Hauss, who has lived in Italy since the First World War, fled to the hills to join the underground. He was captured by Italians and charged in an Italian court for aiding allied soldiers.

---

## AFFIDAVIT

I, Carl L. Hauss, being duly sworn, deposes and says as follows:

1. I am an American citizen, and have been so continuously since by my birth on January 30, 1894 at Norwich, Connecticut; I am presently residing at Milan, Italy, Via Plutarco 2, and I am in possession of American Passport No. 164349 issued at the American Consulate General at Milan, Italy, on July 28, 1958.

2. I was a business man in Italy when the United States declared war on Italy. I was unable to return to the United States, and was interned in Italy for five months, and then released. When the Allies landed in Italy in 1943, it was generally known that Americans were being inhumanly treated, both soldiers and civilians, and as a result the Americans in Italy fled to avoid capture. I escaped into the mountains, where I managed to survive only by living among the partisans, until I was captured by the Italian fascist forces in November 1943 and sent to San Vittore Prison in Milan, Italy, which was under joint Italian and German control, and held to await trial by an Italian Court for having assisted American and English soldiers in the mountains in avoiding capture.

3. I was held in San Vittore prison for 7 months, and during that time I was isolated for 6 months and only after the intervention of Dr. Gatti (as per Affidavit enclosed) the San Vittore prison doctor, who seeing my state of complete exhaustion (nervous breakdown) and physical condition managed to have me transferred to a normal cell where Mr. Aldo Carpi, well known painter and Brera Accademy professor made a sketch of me, of which I enclose a photocopy and also an affidavit from Professor Carpi.

During the six months of isolation, I was inable to leave my cell for any reason and although according to International Law I should have been allowed an hour's airing per day, this priveledge was practically never accorded me, except, on a few occasions. In this cell I could never obtain reading material of any kind and when I tried to talk with one of the guards, I was menaced by fascisti seargent to be beaten. I had absolutely no heating and with broken windows during an exceptionally cold winter. For the first two months I had no water, no towel, no soap, no tooth brush, no change of linnen, no sheets and only a light cover. Food consisted only in a would be soup once a day. My only contact with the world was the cries of fellow prisoners beeing beaten by fascisti and SS guards or beeing carried away to be shot. I also enclose a statement from Indro Montanelli, the newspaper correspondent of the Corriere della Sera, also well known after the war in the States, who was with me in San Vittore. From S. Vittore I was transferred to a prison camp in Bolzano where I was taken with chicken-pox and was cured by a fellow prisoner, an American, who I believe was taken prisoner in Florence, Italy, where he was studying. I do not remember his name.

4. As a result of my treatment by the Italians, my teeth were ruined, and I was obliged to have false teeth made after the war, as per statement by Doctor Dugnani. I contracted rheumatic arthritis, which has caused me continuing pain and incapacitation, as per the statement of Dr. Rohonci. Also my

0262

nervous system suffered from the condition of my imprisonment, and this condition has continued to the present day, as per the statement of Dr. Canale.

Owing to this continued nervous condition. I am obliged by Dr's advice not to drive my car during week days and have therefore a chauffeur, which subjects me naturally to an extra expense.

5. Finally I was liberated by the 70th Armored Infantry Battalion, and I worked with the Allied Military Government in Italy until January 23rd, 1946, when I had to start my business all over again, in my poor state of health, having lost everything as a result of the war, for which my only possibility of compensation is this claim.

CARL L. HAUSS.

REPUBLIC OF ITALY, *Province of Milan, City of Milan,*
*Consulate General of the United States of America, SS:*

Subscribed and sworn to before me, this 18th day of May 1959.
(To be used only by War Damages Office.)
Service No. 1474.
No fee prescribed.
Item 58A (copy).
[SEAL]

HARRY W. JACOBS,
*Vice Consul of the United States of America.*

---

### SATELLITE VESTING

The Congress of the United States, in Public Law 285 of the 84th Congress, established a program for the vesting of assets in the United States of Rumania, Hungary, and Bulgaria, to be used to pay war damages, and claims for nationalization after World War II by those countries of property of American citizens. The use of such property to pay nationalization claims was something unique, and for this reason, the Congress carefully limited the application of this seizure program to property belonging to the governments of these countries and to corporations organized in those countries, in light of the fact that all corporations had been nationalized under the Communist regimes. As stated in the staff memorandum of the Committee on Foreign Relations of the U.S. Senate in March 1963, on page 6:

"Accordingly, title II of the International Claims Settlement Act of 1949 (approved August 9, 1955) was enacted to authorize the vesting of assets in the United States owned by Bulgaria, Hungary, and Rumania and their nationals, other than natural persons. The exclusion of the latter category follows the principle of American law that the property of private individuals should not be used for the payment of debts out of acts of foreign governments. Therefore, title II provided that the assets of private persons would be retained in a blocked status 'subject to release when, as, and upon such terms as the President or his designee may prescribe.' The proceeds from the liquidation of the other vested assets, however, were transferred to special funds in the Treasury and used to pay compensation to qualified American claimants against the governments of the three countries referred to."

Senator Thruston B. Morton, then Assistant Secretary of State, testified in the hearings on this legislation in 1955 (hearings on H.R. 6382) before the Senate Foreign Relations Committee as follows, on page 13:

"The Department of State is of the opinion that the property of natural persons should be excluded from the vesting program. While the United States has the right to seize such property, it is considered undesirable to take this action; the assets of natural persons are relatively small in amount and we do not wish to alienate the support of friendly nationals of Bulgaria, Hungary, and Rumania or impair their faith in the United States. Thus, the legislation provides for keeping the assets of natural persons in a blocked status subject to release, when, and upon such terms as the President or his designee may prescribe."

The principal problem in connection with the program for divesting individually owned assets belonging to nationals of these three iron curtain countries was that of getting the information regarding the release provisions into their hands, isolated as they have been from news from the free world, and risky as it would have been for them to have taken any action regarding assets held in the free world, which would undoubtedly have been confiscated by their governments. The only possibility, for all practical purposes, lay in the possibility of escape.

**0263**

which was a very hazardous undertaking. The Office of Alien Property of the Department of Justice, the agency designated to administer the program, itself made an effort based on its records to make some divestments, but, of course, it did not have full information in many cases.

The funds of the three Communist satellite countries which were not divested were to be used for the payment of American claims, and for purposes of determining how much money was available to pay those claims, a 1-year statute of limitations was applied within which applications for divestment must have been presented. The claims program under the act has now been completed, and very substantial payments made to the American claimants in the case of Bulgaria and Rumania, both from the vested assets turned over to the Treasury Department by the Office of Alien Property, and through agreements made with the governments of those two countries for the payment of additional sums. Those agreements have been satisfied in full. There are still funds remaining with the Office of Alien Property which have not been turned over to the Treasury Department and are being held pending disposition of legislation before the Committee on Foreign Relations relating to the use of these funds. There have been cases where individuals have escaped from these Communist countries to the free world, and are now in a position to apply for the divesting of their property, although during the 1-year period provided for divesting applications, they were still behind the Iron Curtain, and without any knowledge of their divesting right or any possibility of making such application. In light of the earlier expressed policy of the Congress against the use of individually owned property for the purpose of paying war and nationalization reparations owing by the governments of these satellite countries, it would seem appropriate that legislation be enacted for the purpose of allowing the claims of these individuals who have succeeded in escaping from the Communist countries to apply for the divesting of their property, as long as there are moneys in the hands of the vesting agency available to compensate them.

It is for the purpose of remedying this inequity and for the purpose of carrying out the intention of Congress as expressed in the International Claims Settlement Act of 1949, as amended, that the following amendment is proposed:

AN ACT To amend the International Claims Settlement Act of 1949, as amended, and for other purposes

*Be it enacted by the Senate and House of Representatives of the United States of America in Congress assembled,* That the International Claims Settlement Act of 1949, as amended, is further amended by inserting at the end of section 202(a) the following sentence:

"At any time following one year from the date of vesting of any property under this subsection, and prior to the transfer of the net proceeds of any vested assets transferable but not yet transferred to the Bulgarian Claims Fund, Hungarian Claims Fund, and Rumanian Claims Fund, the President or his designee shall divest the portion thereof equivalent to the net proceeds of the interest vested under this subsection, upon application of the natural person determined by the President or his designee to be the beneficial owner of such vested interest, and return it to its blocked status prior to vesting, subject to release when, as, and upon such terms as the President or his designee shall prescribe."

## STATEMENT OF ABRAHAM S. HYMAN, ATTORNEY AT LAW, NEW YORK CITY

Senator SPARKMAN. Mr. Abraham S. Hyman, attorney at law, New York City.

Mr. Hyman, will you come around. We have your statement, and it will be printed in full in the record.

Mr. HYMAN. I want to thank this committee for the privilege of appearing before you to testify on S. 1935.

My name is Abraham S. Hyman. I live at 52 Riverside Drive, New York City, and am engaged in the practice of law in that city. From 1950 to 1953 I was the general counsel of the War Claims Commission, the predecessor of the present Foreign Claims Settlement Commission.

0264

## PROBLEM OF POLISH CLAIMS

I am here to voice my objections to that part of S. 1935 which calls for the Foreign Claims Settlement Commission to complete the Polish claims program "not later than March 31, 1966" (p. 2, lines 13–16).

Before I state the basis for my objections, I want to take this opportunity to make a few general remarks about the performance of the Commission in the adjudication of the claims filed under the Polish claims program. In my opinion the Commission has demonstrated a responsibility toward the claimants that shows that it is solidly committed to the principle that law was made to serve man and not man, law. Most of the people I represent are postwar citizens of the United States and their experience with their claims represents their first and only encounter with American jurisprudence. Because of the humanity which the Commission has breathed in the Polish claims program the faith of these people in American justice has been established.

But the Commission is neither omniscient nor omnipotent. In the last analysis, the Commission can decide the claims only on the basis of evidence, and that evidence—related to ownership, description, date of taking, et cetera—must be secured from Poland.

Under the agreement of July 16, 1960, between the United States and Poland the Polish Government agreed to furnish such evidence. I do not wish to appear critical of Polish authorities, for the fact is that in a very substantial number of cases they have replied to inquiries with dispatch and with answers generous in content, answers that have aided claimants immeasurably in establishing their claims. However, it is equally true that in many instances the Polish authorities have either failed to respond or have given inadequate information.

My own experience with these claims is instructive. I represent claimants in about 525 claims. To date I have received awards in about 210 claims and expect to receive awards, hopefully, in about 130 additional claims. In the rest—about 180 claims—there either have been or will be denials.

The denials are based upon the lack of proof and that, in turn, is due to three main factors: (1) the failure of the Polish authorities to reply to inquiries, (2) the destruction or the disappearance of the land records in Poland, accompanied by the failure of the local authorities to make a diligent inquiry from local residents as to what they know about the previous ownership of the property; and (3) the failure of the Polish authorities to give adequate information, such as the size of the land parcels, the nature of the improvements, and whether the improvements survived the war.

I do not believe that the performance of the Polish authorities shows a lack of good faith on their part. I believe that the chief difficulty stems from the fact that we were expecting the impossible from the understaffed Polish offices when we asked them to supply us with information on 10,000 claims within the limited period that has been allotted for this purpose. To this very day I continue to receive replies to letters of inquiry about property in Poland I wrote in 1963, and the Commission, which has undertaken to prod the Polish authorities for answers to our inquiries, continues to receive replies which establish claims that had been denied. Fortunately under the Commission's very liberal policy, they permit the reopening of claims even after the claims have been adjudicated—rather the claim has been

0265

denied—where evidence is presented to warrant an award even after the negative decision has been rendered, they reopen the claim and readjudicate it in the light of the new evidence, and that is, of course, to be commended.

Most of the claimants I represent are the survivors of the victims of nazism. I do not have to tell the members of your committee what unspeakable agonies these people have suffered and will continue to suffer as long as there is breath in their bodies. These people, you will surely agree, deserve to be spared the pain of being denied the right to salvage some of the possessions of their loved ones and the pain of being told that their loved ones had no property when they are certain beyond peradventure of doubt that they did.

There is one aspect of S. 1935 that has already had an unhappy effect. In anticipation that the Congress would enact the bill that is before you, the Foreign Claims Settlement Commission has taken steps that would enable it to complete its program within the stipulated period. One of these steps relates to joinder of claimants.

In all the claims programs which the Commission has administered it has permitted members of the family who have an interest in the property involved in the claims to join as parties claimant, on the theory that, having acquired jurisdiction of the res within the time fixed by law, it has the right to adjudicate the claims of all who assert an interest in that res. There was every reason to believe that in the light of the history of the Commission's handling of this issue, the Commission would continue to entertain petitions of joinder. However, in June of this year the Commission adopted the rule that it would not allow any petitions of joinder which had not been filed by January 31, 1965. What the Commission apparently hoped to achieve by this rule is to save the time required in securing reports from the Department of State on the citizenship status of petitioners. This acceleration step—a step taken, in effect, 15 months before the anticipated termination of the Polish program—has already worked a great hardship on many persons who are members of the family of the principal claimants.

### TERMINATION OF CLAIMS IS UNJUST

No counsel—certainly I did not—had reason to know prior to January 31, 1965, that the Commission would rule in June 1965, that all petitions for joinder filed after January 31, 1965, would be rejected. This situation would be remedied if the Commission did not feel rushed to terminate the Polish claims program. The situation must, in my judgment, be remedied because the failure to do so will result in generating jealousies and strife within families where one member secures compensation while others, equally entitled, through no fault of their own and through no fault of counsel, receive no compensation for their losses.

To sum up:

(1) I believe that confronted with many difficulties presented by the Polish claims, the Foreign Claims Settlement Commission has adjudicated them in a manner that reflects credit upon American justice and upon the fundamental humanity of the Commission itself.

(2) I believe that to the extent that the Polish Claims program falls short of its mark—to secure just compensation for American citizens whose property has been nationalized or otherwise taken by the Polish Government—it is due chiefly to the great burden imposed upon

0266

the Polish authorities in requiring them to respond to inquiries within too short a period of time.

(3) I believe that in a great percentage of the claims that have been denied the claimants could establish their claims if the Polish authorities were given additional time to answer the inquiries addressed to them and if this were coupled by a concerted effort on the part of the Commission to continue—I say "to continue," Mr. Chairman, because they certainly have done a great deal to try to get them to answer, but I ask them to continue to persuade the Polish authorities to answer these inquiries with dispatch.

I am in complete sympathy with the Commission in its zeal to bring the Polish claims program to an end. I would, in this context, suggest that the Commission be required to adjudicate all the Polish claims by March 31, 1966, but that it entertain petitions to reopen files any time before March 31, 1967, provided they are accompanied by full documentation on which the claimant relies for a favorable decision.

Inasmuch as the claimants will, in any event, have to wait another 15 years for compensation under the Polish claims program, there is no patent reason for unduly accelerating the termination of the claims program.

I recognize that speed in the adjudication of claims is a virtue to be pursued, but I submit that it is no virtue when the price for achieving it is justice itself.

### POLISH CLAIMS REQUIRE MORE TIME

If I may supplement this written statement of mine with some observations on the statement that has been presented by my very good friend and former colleague, Mr. McGuire, I would like to say this—that for the life of me I do not see the logic of a recommendation that suggests the termination of this claims program within 4 years when it is admitted by the Commission that Yugoslav program, which is one-sixth the size of the Polish program, and which is an entirely different program than Poland—you can go in and out of Yugoslavia and get the documentation, and you cannot do it in Poland.

Mr. Chairman, several years ago I knew what difficulties there would be, that I would have in securing evidence from Poland, and I asked for a visa from the Polish authorities to get into Poland so I could spend several months in securing documentation in support of my major claims. When I stated my purpose, it was denied, because they said, "You cannot get into Poland for this reason." That situation does not apply to the Yugoslav claims. And yet it is recommended by the Commission that the Polish claims program end the same time, or rather extend over the same period of time that it took to adjudicate the Yugoslav program, and it is admitted that the Polish program is six times the size of the Yugoslav program.

I do not see the logic when the bulk of the work is so much larger.

And then Mr. McGuire further stated that approximately 50 percent of the claims have fallen by the wayside. I know my claims, Mr. Chairman. I am confident that not 66⅔ percent but 90 percent of my claims are valid and I submit cannot proceed because of the impossibility of getting answers from Poland. I say that is where the effort ought to be directed. That, it seems to me, is the just course to take.

That is all I wish to say.

0267

Senator SPARKMAN. Thank you very much, Mr. Hyman. We will certainly consider your recommendations.

Next is Mr. Paul Neuberger, counselor at law, New York City.

## STATEMENT OF PAUL NEUBERGER, COUNSELOR AT LAW, NEW YORK CITY

Mr. NEUBERGER. My name is Paul Neuberger, and I am a member of the New York bar, with offices in New York, specializing in the field of international private law.

I am appearing before this honorable subcommittee to present the views of a group of my clients who assert claims against the Italian claims fund referred to in bill S. 1935 (par. 10, p. 6, lines 15–25, and p. 7, lines 1–3).

Senator SPARKMAN. Mr. Neuberger, would you hold up for a minute. I want to call a Congressman. He will be leaving soon for the House of Representatives.

Mr. NEUBERGER. To be sure. My whole statement, Mr. Chairman, is short.

Senator SPARKMAN. Excuse me for a minute.

(Whereupon, a short recess was taken, after which the hearing was continued.)

Senator SPARKMAN. All right, Mr. Neuberger, will you resume?

Mr. NEUBERGER. Yes, Mr. Chairman.

I wish to refer to paragraph 10 of the Italian claims fund to the bill S. 1935.

After 3 years, this bill finally contains a provision by which a great injustice done to claimants who claimed war damages from Italy has been corrected.

The bills submitted last year and 2 years ago contained a provision that the entire balance of the claims fund should be turned over to the Treasury Department, disregarding entirely the fact that a small group of claimants, who were entitled to claim on the basis of Public Law 604–85, were refused permission by the Foreign Claims Settlement Commission to file claims. On the other hand, those who filed claims in the original filing period prior to September 1956, although they were not entitled to file before the amendment of August 8, 1958 (Public Law 604–85) received a 100-percent recovery plus interest.

The above-cited section of bill S. 1935 corrects this injustice, but in section 10(e) (p. 7, line 25, and p. 8, lines 1–12) the policy again is followed that those who were not citizens at the time of the last amendment should be excluded, as, after payment in full of all awards pursuant to these subsections, the Secretary of the Treasury is authorized and directed to transfer the unobligated balance of the Italian claims fund into the war claims fund.

### CLAIMS FOR UNOBLIGATED BALANCE

I do not wish to object to the full payment of all those who were entitled to get their claims compensated on the basis of Public Law 604–85, but the same reasons which led the legislators to enact Public Law 604–85, these same intentions speak against the provision that the unobligated balance—I do not know how much it will be or whether there will be a balance—should be turned over to the war claims fund which amounts to about $260 million and will not become richer or more useful because of a few hundred thousand dollars to

0268

be turned over. I do not wish to object to the provision that first all the persons authorized by the amendment of August 8, 1958, should get full recovery, but I feel that if a balance again remains, it should not be turned over to the war claims fund, but should be used for compensation of the small number of remaining claimants who became American citizens before the date of enactment of the present bill. Such a provision would be the logical consequence of the policy which brought about the enactment of Public Law 604–85.

May I cite the argument given in the debate of the original amendment by Senator Russell B. Long, who presided at the hearings and was one of the proponents of that amendment. He expressly stated:

We find that we have funds over and above those necessary to take care of these claims (claims of those who were American citizens at the time of loss) which funds we shall proceed to devote to satisfy claims of those who became American citizens subsequent to the time the property was seized * * *.

Inasmuch as Italy has been more liberal than have most other nations, in making such funds available, we have provided that after those who have other claims have been satisfied, insofar as funds remain, they could be made available to American citizens who acquired American citizenship subsequent to the cutoff date * * *.

These statements clearly show that the surplus was to be used to satisfy claimants "left out" of the original section 304 of Public Law 285–84.

Today Mr. McGuire on page 10 said that the sum of $5 million had to be utilized in such manner as the Government of the United States might deem appropriate to be applied to claims of U.S. nationals arising out of the war with Italy.

If we consider this purpose of the Italian claims fund, then if there is any balance after paying in full all the other claimants for whom this amendment is proposed, this balance should be used for those claimants who were not citizens on August 9, 1955, but who became such up to the date of the enactment of the present bill.

I am aware that this suggestion will be opposed by the Department of State. Nevertheless, the Department of State supported the original amendment, and on the same principle should support the present proposal.

I present this proposal in the light of the recent decision of the U.S. Supreme Court which stated that "We start from the premise that the rights of citizenship of the native born and of the naturalized persons are of the same dignity and are coextensive." *Schneider* v. *Rusk,* 377 U.S. 163, 845 Ct., of May 18, 1964.

I am submitting the text of the amendment which I propose in this respect. Should I read it?

Senator SPARKMAN. Very well. I see it is attached to your statement.

Mr. NEUBERGER. It is attached.

Senator SPARKMAN. It is not necessary to read it.

(The attachment referred to follows:)

PROPOSED CHANGES TO BILL S. 1935, 89TH CONGRESS, AMENDING THE INTERNATIONAL CLAIMS SETTLEMENT ACT OF 1949, AS AMENDED

I. After subsection (10) (c) another subsection should be inserted as (d):

"(d) Upon full payment of the principal amounts with interest of all awards rendered under provisions (b) and (c) of this section and certified to the Secretary of the Treasury for claimants described in the aforecited subsections, with

0269

respect to the remaining balance in the Italian claims fund the Commission shall determine the validity and amounts of claims owned by persons who were nationals of the United States prior to the effective date of this amendment, under the same conditions and provisions described in subsections (b) and (c) hereof."

II. Subsection (f) is to be deleted and subsections (d) and (e) in the present Bill should be designated as subsections (e) and (f).

## RESTRICTION OF ATTORNEY'S FEES

Mr. NEUBERGER. Mr. Chairman, may I add a few comments regarding the amendment proposed concerning the restrictions of attorney's fees. You, yourself, during the testimony of the General Counsel of the Foreign Claims Settlement Commission, Mr. McGuire, raised some questions in this respect and, as I have been informed, the Bar Association of the District of Columbia, in 1962, submitted an amendment with regard to the restriction of fees.

As I learned today, this amendment was not resubmitted in this session, but I still wish to make some suggestions with regard to section 1(f) of the present bill.

The Chairman of the Foreign Claims Settlement Commission, the Honorable Edward Re, in a thoughtful and interesting speech held before the Consular Law Society, emphasized the great importance that able lawyers should present cases not only before courts but also before administrative agencies, and complained that there are many lawyers who do not wish to represent cases before the Foreign Claims Settlement Commission.

May I say that perhaps one of the reasons why competent and effective presentation of cases is made so difficult is the present statutory restriction on fees. I do not mean the 10 percent as such, but I mean the extension of this limited fee to services rendered outside of the representation of claims before the Foreign Claims Settlement Commission. I mention this because there are circumstances which make it impossible sometimes to give proper services, especially to claim matters which arose in foreign countries.

It sometimes takes 2 or 3 years to establish the basis for a claim in a foreign country, taking administration proceedings, the correct rendering and especially in countries which are behind the Iron Curtain, and you have to pay for this through the lawyers who are there.

Now, no client, especially the poor claimant, is able to pay a flat fee. If they would agree to a contingent fee with the lawyer, then this contingent fee has to be included by the text of the agreement in this 10 percent of the U.S. lawyer. This is one thing which should be corrected, because these foreign lawyers sometimes ask 10 percent if they have a lot of work to do and does not get anything on account.

If they agree on a contingent fee, then by the text of the provision of the International Claims Settlement Act, this fee of the foreign lawyer, if it is in a percentage of the award, must be included in the statutory 10-percent fee of the U.S. lawyer representing the claimant before the Commission, because, according to the text:

Whoever, in the United States or elsewhere, demands or receives, on account of services so rendered, any remuneration in excess of the maximum permitted by this section, shall be fined not more than $5,000 or imprisoned not more than twelve months, or both.

Consequently, many cases remain without necessary evidence or without proper representation, and, perhaps, a few well-to-do claimants who want to risk flat fees for the lawyers in the foreign

0270

country can obtain their proper awards, while the poor man remains unprotected.

I personally, in the Yugoslav claims program, have many cases where I am unable to procure evidence because there is no one who can pay, and I cannot enter into a contingent fee agreement with the Yugoslav lawyer.

There could be more examples given, but I wanted to call the attention of the honorable subcommittee to such cases in order to provide the necessary protection for claimants as well as for attorneys who would like to represent their claimants conscientiously and successfully before the Foreign Claims Settlement Commission.

This could be established by excluding from the statutory contingent fee of the lawyer in the United States any contingent fee which claimant contracted by him or by the client in the foreign country for work to be performed in connection with the procurement of evidence.

Thank you very much.

Senator SPARKMAN. Thank you very much, Mr. Neuberger.

Our next witness is Mr. D. J. Casarella, Bulgarian Claims Committee, Rego Park, N.Y.

We are glad to have you. We have your statement. Will you proceed as you see fit?

## STATEMENT OF D. J. CASARELLA, BULGARIAN CLAIMS COMMITTEE, REGO PARK, N.Y.

Mr. CASARELLA. Mr. Chairman and members of the committee, my name is Donny J. Casarella, and I am the vice chairman of the Bulgarian Claims Committee, a committee properly registered in accordance with the Lobbying Act in both Houses of Congress and which committee was organized in order to protect the interests of American claimants who lost their property through nationalizations and confiscatory measures of the Bulgarian Government.

The Bulgarian Claims Committee has authorized me to present its views before this committee in connection with S. 1935, 89th Congress, 1st session. This bill is an omnibus bill which contains, among other things, provisions with regard to the additional sum of $400,000—which has been accepted, pursuant to a claim settlement agreement, by the U.S. Government in full payment and settlement of claims of American citizens for losses suffered in Bulgaria.

### UNNECESSARY AMERICAN SACRIFICES

I respectfully submit that this executive agreement between the United States and Bulgaria represents a classic example of how the interests of American citizens are being sacrificed for alleged political reasons and in order to achieve friendly relations with countries behind the Iron Curtain.

By this agreement the United States accepted a lump sum of $3,543,398 as full and final settlement of its claim against Bulgaria, in which lump sum were included vested Bulgarian assets in the United States in the value of $3,143,398, so that the Bulgarian Government paid only an additional sum of $400,000, payable in installments of $200,000 each on July 1, 1964, and July 1, 1965.

In return the United States waived (1) all claims falling within article 23 of the Treaty of Peace with Bulgaria, and (2) all claims

52-255—65——7

0271

falling within the provisions of the settlement agreement without regard to whether the claimants are compensated pursuant to U.S. legislation. This means that the 217 awards which were previously allowed American claimants by the Foreign Claims Settlement Commission in a total amount of $6,571,825—including $4,684,187 in principal and $1,887,638 in interest—is fully settled by the additional payment of $400,000. But this $400,000 is not to be devoted solely to the satisfaction of these claimants, but, according to S. 1935, as may be seen in section 7, and section 9, it will also cover the claims of all new claimants whose property was taken between August 9, 1955, and the effective date of the United States-Bulgaria Claims Agreement of July 2, 1963.

According to the bill, these new claimants will receive the same quota as the previous claimants received, and the balance will be distributed equally among all claimants, whether earlier awardees or new claimants.

To this provision I wish to submit the objections of our committee, because we consider that because of the provisions of the Peace Treaty with Bulgaria and the International Claims Settlement Act of 1949, as amended, the new executive agreement cannot waive the claims of those who received less than the full amount of their award and had a right to claim the remaining balance from the Bulgarian Government. I desire to call the committee's attention to section 313 of Public Law 285, 84th Congress, in which the Congress stated as follows:

> Payment of any award made pursuant to section 303 or 305 shall not, unless such payment is for the full amount of the claim, as determined by the Commission to be valid, with respect to which the award is made, extinguish such claim, or be construed to have divested any claimant, or the United States on his behalf, of any rights against the appropriate foreign government or national for the unpaid balance of his claim or for restitution of his property. All awards or payments made pursuant to this title shall be without prejudice to the claims of the United States against any foreign government.

A procedure to the contrary simply means that the U.S. Government, by sacrificing the balance of the claims of its nationals, must itself assume an obligation to compensate its citizens for the property taken without due process of law.

### U.S. PROTECTION REQUIRED

If the United States refuses protection to a wronged citizen because the Department of State thinks that in so doing it is acting for the benefit of the entire country, the United States should, as a matter of justice and equity, compensate these citizens for the balance of their award sacrificed by the executive agreement.

Former Secretary of State Dulles, when the Japanese Peace Treaty was under deliberation, expressly stated that those U. S. nationals whose claims were sacrificed by the Japanese Peace Treaty "should look to the Congress for relief."

I respectfully submit this fact to the honorable committee in order that in our case a provision should be enacted giving us full compensation for the unpaid balance of our awards. We do not question the right of American citizens whose property was taken between 1955 and the effective date of the above-cited executive agreement with Bulgaria, but, first, the claims of those who receive awards based

0272

on a law enacted by Congress should receive payment and, the new claimants participate in the balance, if any.

I respectfully submit these remarks for your favorable consideration, and I wish to thank you for permitting me to present my views to your committee.

Mr. Chairman, may I ask permission from the honorable committee to submit, subsequently for the record, a proposed amendment?

Senator SPARKMAN. You wish to submit what?

Mr. CASARELLA. A proposed amendment.

Senator SPARKMAN. A proposed amendment?

Mr. CASARELLA. Yes. I would like to have your permission, Mr. Chairman, to submit this subsequently, because in this short time——

Senator SPARKMAN. Yes. When will you do that?

Mr. CASARELLA. In a couple of days.

Senator SPARKMAN. All right. You get it down to us so that we will have it ready by the time the record is closed.

(The following amendments were subsequently received for the record:)

PROPOSED AMENDMENTS TO S. 1935, 89TH CONGRESS, AMENDING THE INTERNATIONAL CLAIMS SETTLEMENT ACT OF 1949, AS AMENDED, WITH REFERENCE TO THE BULGARIAN CLAIMS FUND

I. On page 6, paragraph 9, in the newly added subsection (4) of section 303, title III, line 8, the word "Bulgaria" shall be omitted.

II. On page 9, paragraph 12, subsection (6) now reading as follows:

" '(6) Whenever the Commission is authorized to settle claims by the enactment of paragraph (4) of section 303 of this title with respect to Rumania and Bulgaria, no further payments shall be authorized by the Secretary of the Treasury on account of awards certified by the Commission pursuant to paragraphs (1), (2), or (3) of section 303 of the Bulgarian or Rumanian claims funds, as the case may be, until payments on account of awards certified pursuant to paragraph (4) of section 303 with respect to such fund have been authorized in equal proportion to payments previously authorized on existing awards certified pursuant to paragraphs (1), (2), and (3) of section 303.' "

shall read as follows:

" '(6) Whenever the Commission is authorized to settle claims by the enactment of paragraph (4) of section 303 of this title with respect to Rumania, no further payments shall be authorized by the Secretary of the Treasury on account of awards certified by the Commission pursuant to paragraphs (1), (2), or (3) of section 303 of the Rumanian claims fund until payments on account of awards certified pursuant to paragraph (4) of section 303 with respect to such fund have been authorized in equal proportion to payments previously authorized on existing awards certified pursuant to paragraphs (1), (2), and (3) of section 303.' "

---

PROPOSED AMENDMENT TO S. 1935, 89TH CONGRESS, AMENDING THE INTERNATIONAL CLAIMS SETTLEMENT ACT OF 1949, AS AMENDED, WITH REFERENCE TO THE BULGARIAN CLAIMS FUND

On page 9, paragraph 12, subsection (6) shall be deleted and replaced by the following:

"(6) (a) Whenever the Commission is authorized to settle claims by the enactment of paragraph (4) of section 303 of this title with respect to Rumania, no further payments shall be authorized by the Secretary of the Treasury on account of awards certified by the Commission pursuant to paragraphs (1), (2), or (3) of section 303 of the Rumanian claims fund until payments on account of awards certified pursuant to paragraph (4) of section 303 with respect to such fund have been authorized in equal proportion to payments previously authorized on existing awards certified pursuant to paragraphs (1), (2), and (3) of section 303.

"(b) Within thirty (30) days from the enactment of this subsection, legislation shall be enacted to provide for appropriations covering the full amount of the awards to be granted on claims for compensation for the nationalization,

0273

compulsory liquidation, or other taking of property of nationals of the United States in Bulgaria between August 9, 1955 and the effective date of the Claims Agreement between Bulgaria and the United States, entered into on July 2, 1963, such awards being made to persons who became United States citizens after August 9, 1955, and whose claims arose after that date."

Mr. CASARELLA. I wish to finally mention our people, the members of our committee, are people over 70. Some are 85. This is the last resort for money which they expect. We believe that once having the final decision of the Senate and the Congress, which is the highest institution of the land, that this decision will be respected by the other branches of the administrative government and will not be deprived of this last $400,000. How much can everyone get from this? This is the last resort for these poor people. They have lost everything.

Senator SPARKMAN. Yes. We shall be very glad to receive your proposed amendments.

Mr. CASARELLA. Thank you.

Senator SPARKMAN. And they will be given consideration.

Mr. CASARELLA. Thank you.

Senator SPARKMAN. I thank you very much.

I thank all of the witnesses for the very thoughtful and helpful statements that have been given to us.

The committee stands adjourned.

(Whereupon, at 11:55 a.m., the committee was adjourned.)

(The following material was subsequently received for the record:)

MEMORANDUM TO THE FOREIGN RELATIONS COMMITTEE OF THE U.S. SENATE

Re denial of Foreign Assets Control License applications of M. Golodetz & Co., New York, N.Y. (C. 2728) ; and Monten Corp., Philadelphia, Pa. (C. 2729).

My name is Joseph B. Friedman. I am a practicing attorney in Washington, D.C., associated with attorney and former U.S. Senator Scott W. Lucas.

On behalf of M. Golodetz & Co., a New York partnership whose partners are citizens and residents of the United States, and Monten Corp., a Pennsylvania corporation doing business solely in the United States, I filed with the Foreign Assets Control of the Treasury applications to unblock the following property situated in the United States which has been blocked as "Cuban" assets:

1. Certain entries on the books of a New York partnership (all of the partners being U.S. citizens and residents) reflecting indebtedness to three corporations organized under the laws of Cuba many years ago. These corporations have been completely out of business and in a state of de facto liquidation since 1960 as a result of the Castro takeover. The stock of one of the corporations is owned 100 percent by citizens and residents of the United States and the stock of the other two is owned 91.3 percent by citizens and residents of the United States and 8.7 percent by citizens and residents of the United Kingdom. None of the stockholders has ever been a blocked national.

2. Four hundred shares of stock in a U.S. corporation which is engaged in the real estate business in the United States and which has never done business in Cuba. These 400 shares are nominally held in the name of a corporation organized under the laws of Cuba many years ago but which has been completely out of business and in a state of de facto liquidation since 1960 as a result of the Castro takeover. The share certificates are physically situated in the United States. The stock of the defunct Cuban corporation is and always has been owned 100 percent by U.S. citizens and residents who have never been blocked nationals. The remaining 500 shares of the U.S. corporation have always been owned directly by U.S. citizens and residents.

0274

After Castro came into power in 1960, the above-mentioned Cuban corporations were put out of business and the small amount of property which they had in Cuba was taken by the Castro government. It should be noted that these corporations above described are now defunct having been wiped out by the confiscatory action of the Castro regime.

I filed two applications with the Treasury to unblock such property situated in the United States in order to permit the American owners to receive what is in fact their own property. The applications were denied by an assistant to the Secretary of the Treasury in a letter of March 25, 1965, in which, among other things, it was stated:

"It is the Department's view that these funds should remain blocked until such time as an overall decision is reached by appropriate congressional or executive action as to the disposition of all blocked Cuban assets in the United States."

This opinion was given by the Treasury notwithstanding the fact that in testimony presented to the House committee when the first Cuban claims bill was introduced in 1964, the General Counsel of the Treasury at that time, Mr. G. d'Andelot Belin, in reporting the results of the Treasury census pointed out the existence of a third category of assets affected by the reporting requirement in addition to assets owned by the Cuban Government and those owned by private Cuban citizens. This class of assets was described by Mr. Belin as follows:

"The third point is that some of the amounts reported as owed to Cuban firms by American corporations are actually owed to subsidiary firms which, although incorporated in Cuba, are wholly or substantially owned by the American debtor. Thus, a large portion of the blocked Cuban assets may not be available for distribution to other claimants." (Hearings, p. 162.)

As a result of the hearings, a new bill was introduced which completely eliminated any vesting authority. The bill was favorably reported by the House Foreign Affairs Committee and passed by the House of Representatives.

By its action, the House of Representatives made it perfectly clear that there was no intention ever to touch the assets of American-owned Cuban corporations. The assets involved in the present case are precisely the kind described by the General Counsel of the Treasury.

At the present session, H.R. 9336 to amend title V of the International Claims Settlement Act relating to claims against Cuba has been considered by the House Committee on Foreign Affairs and, in view of the Treasury's opinion that it needed guidance with respect to blocked assets of the kind here in question, the committee has recommended as follows in House Report No. 706:

"It has been called to the committee's attention that assets totaling millions of dollars belonging to U.S. nationals who directly and indirectly own 50 percent or more of the outstanding capital stock or other beneficial interest in Cuban corporations are being blocked under the Cuban Assets Control Regulations, July 8, 1963 (31 C.F.R., pt. 515, et seq.). The same regulations provide for release of blocked assets in the United States belonging to Cuban nationals when such nationals arrive from Cuba. Under such circumstances, it appears that U.S. nationals should be afforded the same treatment as Cuban nationals.

"The State Department is on record as opposing the vesting of private Cuban assets as being confiscatory, but it is opposed, also, to the unblocking of U.S.-national-owned assets. The Treasury Department has stated that Congress should provide the guidelines as to the disposition of blocked U.S.-owned assets.

"Blocked U.S. privately owned and Cuban privately owned assets should be given the same treatment. Facts of a recent case disclosed the urgency for relief for U.S. privately owned blocked funds. A sum of money was due and owing to a U.S. national from a Cuban debtor. With the assistance of the Department of the Treasury, a license was given to the U.S. national to allow the sum of money due on the debt to be brought to the United States. Upon arrival in the United States the sum of money was immediately blocked by the Treasury Department. This action is unreasonable and inequitable, and the funds should be released.

"While the committee does not recommend wholesale unblocking of all U.S.-owned assets, it does recommend that a thorough examination be made by the Department of the Treasury on a case-by-case basis to determine from the evidence and equities involved in each case the proper disposition of U.S.-national-owned blocked assets and that, where proper, it unblock U.S. privately owned assets. The Department of the Treasury now has this authority and therefore is

0275

able under existing law and administrative regulations to determine and act upon the merits of each case."

It is my understanding that some claimants do not want their funds unblocked while others do. We are in the latter category, and we contend that we definitely fall within what the House committee had to say about the unblocking of privately owned assets beneficially owned by Americans as stated in the third paragraph quoted above. In short, it is our view that under the directive in the committee report our application for unblocking should now be granted.

It is indeed ironic that these funds should remain blocked in view of the fact that under the Cuban Assets Control Regulations a "subject or citizen of Cuba" or any person "who has been within" Cuba on or since July 8, 1963, is a "national" of Cuba to exactly the same degree "as a corporation * * * organized under the laws" of Cuba (31 C.F.R. 515.302). Yet any such person who has come or may still come to the United States (except Cuban agents) after July 8, 1963, has been completely unblocked by the Treasury, as have corporations, partnerships, etc., which were originally blocked because of such person's interest therein (31 C.F.R. 515.505). Thus, suppose a Cuban citizen who came to the United States from Cuba 1 day, 1 month, or 1 year ago who owns 100 percent of the stock of a corporation organized under the laws of Venezuela. Suppose also that the Venezuelan corporation had substantial funds on deposit in New York. Are such funds blocked by the Treasury? No; they are not. In contrast, the funds in New York held in the name of a defunct Cuban corporation beneficially owned by U.S. citizens are denied to their true owners. No possible justification exists for this discriminatory action. And continued blocking in my opinion, represents an arbitrary and capricious deprivation of property in violation of the fifth amendment.

It is our sincere hope that the Senate Foreign Relations Committee will see fit to recognize the merits of our claim and be able to give proper directions to the Treasury to unblock the same.

---

EXCERPTS FROM MINUTES OF THE BOARD OF DIRECTORS, THE BAR ASSOCIATION OF THE DISTRICT OF COLUMBIA, HELD ON FRIDAY, JANUARY 5, 1962

"Mr. Walter A. Slowinski appeared on behalf of the international law committee of which he is the chairman in support of the committee's recommendations that the association support proposed amendments to the International Claims Settlement Act of 1949 which would, in effect, limit attorney fees to 10 percent of the first $1,000 actually received by the claimant, plus 30 percent of any amount actually received in excess of $1,000 provided that the total of such remuneration may never exceed 10 percent of the face amount awarded by the Commission. He noted that S. 1987 was introduced in the Senate at the request of the Foreign Claims Settlement Commission of the United States and that his committee was unanimously in favor of the proposed amendments. On motion duly made and seconded the board approved the recommendations of the international law committee with the proviso that if the Foreign Claims Settlement Commission of the United States should agree to fix fees, this alternative would also be acceptable."

---

REPORT OF THE COMMITTEE ON INTERNATIONAL LAW ON LEGAL FEES IN FOREIGN CLAIMS SETTLEMENT COMMISSION CASES

A subcommittee, consisting of Milo G. Coerper, chairman, Samuel Herman, Sidney B. Jacoby, and George B. Searls, was established to review the provisions of the International Claims Settlement Act of 1949, as amended (22 U.S.C.A. 1622–1642) (hereinafter referred to as "the act") regarding limitations on fees for services rendered with the view of making recommendations for the just liberalization of such provisions taking into account any views, formal or informal, of the Foreign Claims Settlement Commission of the United States (hereinafter referred to as "the Commission") regarding such provisions. This subcommittee reported to the full committee on December 5, 1961, and the full committee adopted the subcommittee report with some modifications as follows:

The act, as it presently stands, consists of four titles. Title I was enacted to provide implementing legislation for the Yugoslav Claims Agreement of 1948 (62 Stat. (3)2658). Titles II and III were enacted to provide for the settle-

0276

ment of certain Bulgarian, Hungarian, Rumanian, Soviet, and Italian claims. Title IV was enacted to provide for the settlement of certain Czechoslovakian claims. On May 29, 1961, Senator Fulbright introduced S. 1987, an omnibus bill, which contains proposed implementing legislation for the Polish Claims Agreement (55 A.J.I.L. 540) and provides to this end for the amendment of title I of the act.

The relevant provisions regarding fees for these various programs are contained in title I, section 4(f) [22 U.S.C.A. 1623(f)], title III, section 317 [22 U.S.C.A. 1641(P)] and title IV, section 414 [22 U.S.C.A. 1642(m)], respectively. The omnibus bill, S. 1987, would amend title I, section 4(f), for purposes of the Polish agreement, to read the same as title IV, section 414. These relevant provisions are set forth in appendix I, attached hereto. A review of these provisions will reveal that in each program the limitation on attorney's fees was keyed to the amount paid pursuant to an award and not to the amount of the award itself.

Under each program rough estimates were made in advance as to the percentage of the award which could be paid out of the funds available in each case. These estimates were fairly accurate and the percentages actually paid (estimated in the case of the Czechoslovakian program) were as follows:

| Program: | Amount paid |
|---|---|
| Yugoslav | 89 percent, exclusive of interest. |
| Bulgarian | 60 percent, exclusive of interest. |
| Hungarian | 3 percent, exclusive of interest. |
| Rumanian [1] | 30 percent, exclusive of interest. |
| Soviet | 9.7 percent, exclusive of interest. |
| Italian | 100 percent, including interest. |
| Czechoslovakian | 5-10 percent, exclusive of interest. |

[1] Under the Rumanian agreement recently negotiated, small additional payments will be made. (54 A.J.I.L. 742.)

In the Yugoslav program the Congress was informed that the amount of the payments would approach the amount of the awards and, accordingly, there was no injustice in limiting attorney's fees to 10 percent of the total amount paid. Accordingly, such a limitation was placed in title I at section 4(f). In the title III claims, it was clear that the payments would be far less than the awards under some of the programs, and it was clearly recognized that a 10 percent limitation on fees could cause an injustice. Accordingly, title III, section 317(b) provided a procedure whereby the Commission could order the payment of remuneration in excess of 10 percent if it found the existence of "special circumstances of unusual hardship." Pursuant to this provision the Commission did allow remuneration in excess of 10 percent, and it is known that in certain cases the Commission allowed attorney's fees of 33⅓ percent of payments made under an award.

The title III provision would have been appropriate for the Czechoslovakian program (title IV) because it was estimated that the payments under that program would be between 5 and 10 percent of the award. However, the Commission decided it no longer wanted the additional job of adjudicating fees. Accordingly, the Commission recommended a simplified version of title I, section 4(f) placing a flat limitation on fees of 10 percent on any payments made under an award. This provision, if maintained, would work a substantial hardship on attorneys representing claimants before the Commission. Assuming, optimistically, that the payments under this program will amount to 10 percent of the award, the attorney will be limited to a fee of 1 percent. Often an attorney will have to put in many hours in the preparation and presentation of the claim. The burden of proof is on the claimant. Among other things the claimant must establish nationality, ownership, confiscation, and value. In most of these cases the collection of evidence is most difficult. Often, even though the claim is allowed, there may be detailed questions of valuation which the attorney will have to resolve through a hearing before the Commission.

Because there is a priority payment for all claims of $1,000, an attorney, if he is successful, will never receive a fee of less than $100 (providing the award is for at least $1,000), but assume that he procures an award of the magnitude of as much as $100,000—then his fee would be limited to $1,000. Most of the claims are of a smaller magnitude so that in such cases the fee limitation of something less than $1,000 discourages most attorneys from taking these cases. This results in claimants not being properly represented before the Commission.

0277

It is realized that the intention of Congress in placing this limitation on the fees was to protect the claimant against an unscrupulous attorney. However, in this connection, it should be noted that the statutory language places no limitation on the fees an attorney may charge if he is unsuccessful. Accordingly, you have the inconguous situation wherein an unsuccessful attorney may charge more than one who is successful. The best protection for the claimant is an agreement in advance as to fees aside from any statutory limitation. Accordingly, this committee would recommend no limitation on fees. However, it realizes that the Congress will probably insist on some limitation. Thus, it would recommend the language of title III, section 317(b), but it has been informed that the Commission would recommend against such a provision because the Commission does not want to be involved in the adjudication of fees.

Accordingly, it has felt that a recommendation which would increase the limitation on fees but would not require adjudicatory action on the part of the Commission is in order, not only for the new Polish program which is presently the subject of legislation, but also for the Czechoslovakian program which is presently being administered by the Commission.

This committee recommends that any remuneration on account of services rendered be limited to 10 percent of the award (not of any payments under the award) provided that such remuneration be limited to 10 percent of any priority payment and to 30 percent of any subsequent payments under the award. Thus, the priority payment would be diminished by attorneys fees to no greater degree than is allowed under present legislation, but as to any subsequent payments an attorney would be allowed up to 30 percent. Thus, using the example given earlier of an award of $100,000, wherein $10,000 is paid, an attorney might receive $2,800 ($100 on the $1,000 priority payment and $2,700 on the subsequent payment, i.e., 30 percent of $9,000). If at some future time further payments are made on the award up to the full amount of $100,000, in no case could the attorney receive more than a total of $10,000 in fees. (In those few cases where there is a possibility of both a very high award and a very high payment, the claimant may always limit the attorney fees by agreement with his attorney. As these claimants will in every case be substantial corporations or well-to-do individuals, the Congress need not fear that they will be in a weak bargaining position vis-a-vis the attorney.) It is, of course, most unlikely, under most programs, that the full amount of any award will ever be paid. This could be done only if the United States received more funds from certain foreign countries or if the U.S. Congress decided to appropriate funds to make additional payments on these awards.

Under the Polish program, payments are to be made by Poland to the United States over a 20-year period. Apparently, under this program, payments on any award will also be made over a 20-year period. Assuming that all of the payments will equal about 10 percent of the award, under the present proposed legislation (S. 1987) an attorney would be limited to a fee of one-twentieth of 1 percent each year of the total award. Thus, for example, if a claimant received an award of $10,000 resulting in 20 annual payments of $500 each, an attorney would receive $50 per year for the 20-year period. (This excludes consideration of the priority payment.) This is certainly an unsatisfactory situation and will result in most attorneys refusing to take these cases. Using our suggested legislation in the above hypothetical case (again excluding consideration of the priority payment), an attorney could receive a fee of $3,000 over the 20-year period or $150 per year and would receive the $1,000 fee, allowed under the present proposed legislation, in about 7 years. (The suggested legislation is still, quite obviously, unsatisfactory where payments are made over a 20-year period, but is apparently the best that can be expected if attorneys fees must be keyed to payments made.)

Accordingly, this committee recommends that the omnibus bill, S. 1987, of the 87th Congress, 1st session, be amended as follows:

As regards title IV (the Czechoslovakian program), that following paragraph (12) the following be added:

"(13) Section 414 of title IV is hereby amended to read as follows:

" 'SEC. 414. No remuneration on account of services rendered on behalf of any claimant in connection with any claim filed with the Commission under this title shall exceed ten per centum of the first $1,000 or less actually received by the claimant pursuant to an award of the Commission certified under this title, plus thirty per centum of any amount actually received by the claimant in excess of $1,000 pursuant to such award; provided however that the total of such re-

0278

muneration may never exceed ten per centum of the face amount of such award of the Commission. Any agreement to the contrary shall be unlawful and void. Whoever, in the United States or elsewhere, demands or receives, on account of services so rendered, any remuneration in excess of the maximum permitted by this section, shall be guilty of a misdemeanor, and, upon conviction thereof, shall be fined not more than $5,000 or imprisoned not more than twelve months, or both.'"

As regards title I (for the Polish program) that paragraph (1) of S. 1987 be amended to read as follows:

"(1) Subsection (f) of section 4, title I, is hereby amended to read as follows: "'(f) No remuneration on account of services rendered on behalf of any claimant in connection with any claim filed with the Commission under this title shall exceed ten percentum of the first $1,000 or less actually received by the claimant pursuant to an award of the Commission certified under this title, plus thirty per centum of any amount actually received by the claimant in excess of $1,000 pursuant to such award; provided however that the total of such remuneration may never exceed ten per centum of the face amount of such award of the Commission. Any agreement to the contrary shall be unlawful and void. Whoever, in the United States or elsewhere, demands or receives, on account of services so rendered, any remuneration in excess of the maximum permitted by this section, shall be guilty of a misdemeanor, and, upon conviction thereof, shall be fined not more than $5,000 or imprisoned not more than twelve months, or both.'"

It is further suggested that similar amendments might be appropriate for the following bills relating to the War Claims Act of 1948, presently before the Committee on Interstate and Foreign Commerce of the House of Representatives, H.R. 7479, H.R. 7283, and H.R. 1117. Copies of these bills and of S. 1987 are attached to this report.

---

WALTHAM, MASS., *August 4, 1965.*

Senator JOHN SPARKMAN,
*Senate Office Building,*
*Washington, D.C.:*

Request following be made part of record of proceedings of ad hoc committee discussing settlement of Rumanian claims under Foreign Claims Settlement Act. Brandeis University, as beneficiary of a claim under Rumanian Claims Act urgently requests early and affirmative action on S. 1935 since no substantive issue is involved in this legislation and funds are in hand to distribute proceeds under previously adjudicated claims. Hopeful your committee will take steps to expedite claims payments. Many thanks for your assistance in freeing these urgently needed funds.

A. L. SACHAR,
*President, Brandeis University.*

---

NEW YORK, N.Y., *August 11, 1965.*

Hon. JOHN J. SPARKMAN,
*Chairman, Subcommittee of the Committee on Foreign Relations,*
*U.S. Senate, Washington, D.C.*

DEAR SENATOR SPARKMAN: My conscience urges me to submit the following additional facts concerning bill S. 1935, termination of the Polish program. Ask you respectfully to make this wire part of the record public hearing of August 5, 1965. I am afraid that the most important facts are not yet known to your committee.

Abraham S. Hyman, Esq., and the writer represent 525 and approximately 750 claims or several thousand claimants representing a fair sampling of a total of 10,239 claims filed. Awards have been handed down in about 40 percent of our 12 percent, approximately 510.

For good and valid reasons as late citizenship of claimants or location of property in Russia, 10 percent or approximately 125 have been denied. The frightening amount of 50 percent of all cases filed by us which have not yet been decided positively can under no circumstances be overlooked.

The Foreign Claims Settlement Commission for the past several months denied a very substantial amount of this 50 percent because claimants were unable to obtain evidence from Poland. Under the circumstances claimants must appeal to the U.S. Government for help. Help accorded so far through the Commission's field office in Warsaw has not been sufficient. I ask your committee respectfully, but urgently to demand a written report from the Foreign Claims Settlement Commission: How many cases have been denied so far for lack of evidence?

How many more cases must by necessity be denied for lack of evidence within the next few months should the program be terminated March 31, 1966? Although those cases appear to be valid claims?

How many inquiries have been sent altogether to the Commission's field office in Warsaw?

How many inquiries have been sent by the Commission to the Bank Handlowy in Warsaw?

How many satisfactory answers have been received from Poland by the Commission?

How many years must claimants and the Foreign Claims Settlement Commission wait for answer from Poland?

Are answers to inquiries sent to Poland in 1962, 1963, 1964 still open, and how many? And how many for each individual year? The public records of the Foreign Claims Settlement Commission show that substantially more than 1,000 cases have been denied for lack of evidence because the Polish authorities responded too slowly, and many of those inquiries sent to Poland in 1963, 1964 by the Foreign Claims Settlement Commission itself were still unanswered. Would welcome opportunity to submit to your committee several dozen denials due to insufficient time, and to give me another opportunity to appear before your committee.

Thanking you on behalf of several thousand claimants.

Yours very truly,

FREDERIO M. ALBERTI, *Attorney at Law.*

WASHINGTON, D.C., *August 4, 1965.*

HON. JOHN J. SPARKMAN,
*U.S. Senate, Senate Office Building,*
*Washington, D.C.*

DEAR SENATOR: It is my understanding that an ad hoc committee of which you are the chairman will hold hearings on August 5 on S. 1935, a so-called omnibus claims bill.

I write to express my interest, on behalf of a number of clients, in this proposed legislation.

The clients on whose behalf I write are American citizens whose claims have been presented to, and adjudicated by, the Foreign Claims Settlement Commission, mainly in connection with claims against the Government of Rumania, arising out of war damage to and/or expropriation of their property in Rumania. These claims have all been adjudicated, and partial payment has already been made on all of them. Pursuant to arrangements between the United States and Rumania, additional payments have been made by the Government of Rumania into the Rumanian claims fund. It is my understanding that these payments were completed approximately a year ago. Despite the fact that the claims have been adjudicated and that funds have been available for the payment on them for this substantial period of time, until now, the additional funds made available by the Government of Rumania have not been distributed to the claimants. The reason for this delay has been the position of the administration·that additional legislation was necessary in order that what might seem to be the routine step of distribution of these additional funds could be taken.

It is my hope, on behalf of these claimants, that the Congress will act during the present session so as to enable the Foreign Claims Settlement Commission promptly to make these funds available. No substantive issues are involved. Many of the claimants are aged and in need. The funds are in the hands of the U.S. Government and should be distributed promptly.

If you feel it appropriate, it would be desirable to insert this expression of interest in the record of the hearings.

Sincerely yours,

SEYMOUR J. RUBIN.

0280

LETTERS FROM THE EXECUTIVE BRANCH COMMENTING ON PROPOSED AMENDMENTS

DEPARTMENT OF STATE,
Washington, August 9, 1965.

Hon. JOHN J. SPARKMAN,
Chairman, Subcommittee on Claims Legislation, Committee on Foreign Relations,
U.S. Senate.

DEAR MR. CHAIRMAN: This is in response to your request for the views of the Department of State on certain proposals made by public witnesses at a hearing held on August 5, 1965, before the Subcommittee on Claims Legislation on S. 1935. a bill to amend the International Claims Settlement Act of 1949, as amended, to provide for the timely determination of certain claims of American nationals settled by the United States-Polish Claims Agreement of July 16, 1960, and for other purposes.

Mr. D. J. Casarella at the hearing suggested that the additional payment of $400,000 made by Bulgaria to the United States pursuant to the claims agreement of July 2, 1963, between the two Governments be utilized to pay in full the unpaid balance of awards granted by the Foreign Claims Settlement Commission of the United States on claims against Bulgaria pursuant to section 303 of the International Claims Settlement Act of 1949, as amended. That section authorized the Commission to receive and determine claims of American nationals for the nationalization or other taking of property by Bulgarian authorities prior to August 9, 1955, for war damage to property and for certain debts owed to U.S. citizens. S. 1935, if enacted, would provide for the determination of a small number of claims against Bulgaria for the taking of property between August 9, 1955, and July 2, 1963, the date of the agreement with Bulgaria, and for the payment of such claims to the same extent as claims already determined by the Commission under section 303 of the International Claims Settlement Act of 1949, as amended.

The agreement of July 2, 1963, between the United States and Bulgaria, was in full payment of all claims of nationals of the United States against Bulgaria which arose prior to the date of the agreement. If Mr. Casarella's suggestion were to be adopted, claims of persons against Bulgaria for the taking of their property during the period August 9, 1955, and the date of the agreement would not be paid. In the circumstances, the Department of State is opposed to Mr. Casarella's proposed amendment.

Mr. Abraham S. Hyman in his statement before the subcommittee proposed an extension of the windup date of the Polish claims program of the Foreign Claims Settlement Commission to permit the reopening of claims up to March 31, 1967. S. 1935, if enacted, would require the Commission to complete the Polish claims program by March 31, 1966, that is, 4 years from the last day for filing such claims. The Department of State has consulted with the Commission concerning this matter and is in accord with its views on Mr. Hyman's proposal as communicated to you in its letter of August 9, 1965.

Mr. Paul Neuberger proposed an amendment to section 304 of the International Claims Settlement Act of 1949, as amended, to include claims of persons who were not citizens of the United States at the time of loss or damage but who were citizens of the United States on the date of the enactment of his proposed amendment.

S. 1935, if enacted, would reopen and extend the Italian claims program under section 304 to cover claims not previously compensable because of late filing, and claims of persons who had become nationals of the United States on or before August 9, 1955, and who had not filed under section 304 of the act, as amended by Public Law 85-604, approved August 8, 1958. S. 1935 would also include claims arising in territory ceded by Italy pursuant to the treaty of peace with Italy, including the Dodecanese Islands, which were heretofore excluded under the provisions of the act. Any balance remaining in the Italian claims fund after payment of claims as proposed under these amendments would be transferred into the war claims fund created under section 13 of the War Claims Act of 1948, as amended.

The Department of State is opposed to the amendment proposed by Mr. Neuberger.

It has generally been the policy of the U.S. Government not to permit citizens of the United States who did not have that status at the time of loss or damage to share in lump sums paid by foreign governments in settlement of nationalization claims or war damage claims. This policy rests upon the universally accepted principle of international law that a state does not have the right to ask another

0281

state to pay compensation to it for losses or damages sustained by persons who were not its citizens at the time of loss or damage. This policy seems never to have been questioned before the enactment of the International Claims Settlement Act of 1949. Ever since the passage of that act, however, bills have been introduced in the Congress to permit persons who were not citizens at the time of loss or damage to receive compensation out of vested Bulgarian, Hungarian, and Rumanian assets for nationalization and war damage in those countries. Bills have also been introduced to permit such persons with nationalization claims against Czechoslovakia to share in the proceeds of the sale of a steel mill of the Czechoslovak Government. Neither the executive branch nor the Congress favored any of such bills and none were enacted with the exception of a bill which permitted a small number of persons who were not citizens at the time of damage to share in the lump sum paid by Italy for war damages outside of Italy. That bill was not opposed because the lump sum paid by Italy exceeded the amount needed to satisfy claims of persons who were citizens at the time of damage.

The Department of State is not aware of a single instance in which persons who were not citizens of the United States at the time of loss, with the exception of the small number who shared or will share under S. 1935, if enatced, in the above-mentioned Italian fund and certain religious organizations in the Philippines which were affiliated with religious organizations in the United States, have been permitted to share in funds paid by foreign governments or funds derived from vested assets either for the taking of property or for war damage.

In view of the foregoing, payment of World War II war damage claims of persons who were not citizens of the United States at the time of loss or damage would establish an undesirable precedent. Should such a precedent be established, it is believed that those citizens who have not received compensation from any of the funds paid by foreign governments because they were not citizens at the time of loss or damage, would have grounds for insisting upon compensation from some source. In the Department's view it would be undesirable to provide this opportunity.

It may also be pointed out that the executive branch after careful study had concluded that with the exception of the categories of claims comprehended by S. 1935 no other claimants should participate in the Italian claims fund and that any remaining balance should be transferred to the war claims fund. It is understood that the war claims fund will not be sufficient to pay war damage claims of persons who were citizens of the United States at the time they sustained war damage which are provided for in the War Claims Act of 1948, as amended, October 22, 1962. It is believed that such persons should be favored over persons who were not citizens at the time they sutained damage.

Mr. Robert H. Reiter at the hearing proposed an amendment to section 304 of the the International Claims Settlement Act of 1949, as amended, to include claims of American nationals for personal injury and suffering arising out of the war in which Italy was involved from June 10, 1940, to September 15, 1947. While the proposal is not entirely clear, we understand that it is intended to authorize the payment of claims of civilian American citizens who were captured in the Italian theater of war and suffered personal injuries.

Section 5 of the War Claims Act of 1948, as amended, authorized payment of detention, injury, disability, and death benefits to civilian American citizens who were captured by Japanese authorities on or after December 7, 1941, at Midway, Guam, Wake Island, the Philippine Islands, or on any territory or possession of the United States, or while in transit to or from any such place or went into hiding at any such place in order to avoid capture or internment by the Japanese. It is understood that these benefits were made available to civilian American citizens in recognition of the fact that when the situation in the Far East became critical and war was imminent, they were encouraged to remain where they were. On the other hand, it is understood that the benefits were not granted to civilian American citizens who were in other theaters of war because they were given ample warning of the danger of war and advised to return to the United States.

While not unmindful of the sufferings and hardships endured by U.S. citizens who were captured in areas other than the territories and possessions of the United States, it is the view of the Department of State that an undesirable precedent would be established by payment of detention, injury, disability, and death benefits to persons who were warned of the dangers and hardships they might endure and were urged to return to the United States. It is also the view

0282

of the Department of State that it would be undesirable to single out for special treatment persons who were captured in Italy. Although several bills were introduced in previous sessions of Congress to provide such benefits to persons imprisoned in Europe, no favorable action has been taken on the bills.

I hope that the foregoing comments will be helpful. If I can furnish any additional information, please do not hesitate to call on me.

The Bureau of the Budget advises that from the standpoint of the administration's program, there is no objection to the submission of this report.

Sincerely yours,

DOUGLAS MACARTHUR, II,
*Assistant Secretary for Congressional Relations.*

---

DEPARTMENT OF STATE,
*Washington, D.C., August 11, 1965.*

Hon. JOHN J. SPARKMAN,
*Chairman, Subcommittee on Claims Legislation,*
*Committee on Foreign Relations,*
*U.S. Senate.*

DEAR MR. CHAIRMAN: I understand that at the hearing Thursday, August 5, before the Subcommittee on Claims Legislation, Mr. Robert H. Reiter, a private attorney, proposed certain new legislation. This legislation would amend section 202(a) of the International Claims Settlement Act of 1949, as amended, so as to permit natural persons, despite the passage of a year since their property was vested, to apply for the release of the net proceeds of their vested property as long as there are funds transferable but not yet transferred to the Bulgarian, Hungarian, or Rumanian claims funds. Mr. Reiter, in his statement at the hearing, urged the consideration of the proposed legislation as designed to take care of individuals formerly resident behind the Iron Curtain who have not been able until now to apply for the divesting of their property.

I understand, further, that the comments of the Department on the proposed legislation are desired.

The Department has been in informal communication with representatives of the Office of Alien Property on the proposed legislation. We are not aware of the specific cases which fall in the category to be protected, nor the amounts involved, nor the merits of the individual cases. Further, from a technical standpoint, it is not seen why a similar amendment of section 202(b) is not also required; and both section 202(a) and section 202(b) may need further amendment to provide for proration if the claims exceed the amounts available.

Although the Department would defer to the views of the Department of Justice which has more knowledge on this subject, the Department does not consider that in the circumstances a sufficient showing has been made to justify the proposed legislation or its technical adequacy.

The Bureau of the Budget advises that from the standpoint of the administration's program there is no objection to the submission of this report.

Sincerely yours,

DOUGLAS MACARTHUR II,
*Assistant Secretary for Congressional Relations.*

---

DEPARTMENT OF STATE,
*Washington, August 9, 1965.*

Hon. JOHN J. SPARKMAN,
*Chairman, Subcommittee on Claims Legislation, Committee on Foreign Relations,*
*U.S. Senate.*

DEAR MR. CHAIRMAN: I have been informed that in connection with the consideration of S. 1826, a bill to amend title V of the International Claims Settlement Act of 1949 relating to claims of U.S. nationals against the Government of Cuba, an amendment has been proposed regarding claims based upon obligations owed by certain American corporations, associations, or other entities. The amendment would amend section 505(a) of the act as follows:

"A claim under section 503(a) of this title based upon a debt or other obligation owing by any corporation, association, or other entity which is a national of the United States shall not be considered if such corporation, association, or other entity files a claim under section 503(a) of this title for losses resulting from the nationalization, expropriation, intervention or other taking of, or special measures directed against, its property."

0283

I understand that your subcommittee has asked for the Department's view on this proposal.

The Department of State is opposed to the amendment in its present form. We believe, however, that with a slight change the amendment is desirable.

The amendment as drafted would exclude from the act claims of U.S. nationals based upon debts owed by American corporations, associations, or other legal entities who qualify as claimants under the act. By implication, however, it could be construed as including all claims based upon debts owed by American corporations, associations, or other legal entities which do not qualify as claimants. The Department is of the view that the Congress did not intend to include creditor claims based upon obligations owed by American corporations, associations, or other legal entities except those based upon a charge on property taken by the Castro government.

In the circumstances and to prevent any ambiguity as to the kinds of creditor claims covered by the act, the Department suggests that the proposed amendment be changed and section 505(a) of the act be amended to add at the end thereof the following:

"A claim under section 503(a) of this title based upon a debt or other obligation owing by any corporation, association, or other entity organized under the laws of the United States, or of any State, the District of Columbia, or the Commonwealth of Puerto Rico shall be considered, only when such debt or other obligation is a charge on property which has been nationalized, expropriated, intervened or taken by the Government of Cuba."

I hope that the foregoing information will be of assistance to your subcommittee. If I can furnish any additional information regarding the matter, please do not hesitate to let me know.

The Bureau of the Budget advises that from the standpoint of the administration's program there is no objection to the submission of this report.

Sincerely yours,

DOUGLAS MACARTHUR II,
*Assistant Secretary for Congressional Relations.*

---

FOREIGN CLAIMS SETTLEMENT COMMISSION OF THE UNITED STATES,
*Washington, D.C., August 9, 1965.*

Hon. JOHN SPARKMAN,
*Chairman, Subcommittee on Claims Legislation, Committee on Foreign Relations,
U.S. Senate, Washington, D.C.*

DEAR SENATOR SPARKMAN: Reference is made to your informal request for the view of the Commission relative to the various proposals made by the public witnesses during the hearing conducted on international claims on August 5, 1965.

Mr. Kenneth Sprague first proposed the elimination of claims based on debts owed by corporations, associations, or other entities which qualify as U.S. nationals. This appears to be a proper proposal inasmuch as (*a*) U.S. corporations, as such, were not taken by Cuba but merely the property of such entity located in Cuba, and (*b*) appropriate recourse is afforded such creditors in the courts of the United States. However, the Commission understands that the Department of State is this date suggesting certain modifications of Mr. Sprague's proposals. The Commission concurs in the Department's views on this subject.

Mr. Sprague makes reference to tax benefits. The Commission's report and statement address themselves to this point and indicate that it does not consider a tax benefit to be an offset within the meaning of section 506 which calls for deduction of "all amounts the claimant has received from any source on account of the same loss or losses."

The Internal Revenue Code requires the reporting of any recoupment of any loss on which a tax benefit has been taken. The purpose of the offset provisions is to preclude double recovery by a claimant.

Finally, Mr. Sprague suggests the inclusion of similar confiscatory claims which arose on China mainland. It is true that these claims are more remote in point of time and, of course, would be more difficult to establish. Nevertheless, from a practical standpoint the Commission is confronted with the task of researching the matter and the extent and cost of such a program. Until this

0284

can be accomplished the Commission feels that inclusion of a China program is premature. It is doubtful that the research could be accomplished during this session of the 89th Congress.

Abraham S. Hyman, Esq., proposes an extension of the Polish claims program permitting the reopening of claims up to March 31, 1967. This counters the Commission proposal to complete its affairs in the program by March 31, 1966.

Among other things, Mr. Hyman states that the Commission in June 1965, ruled that no otherwise qualified persons could join in claims after January 31, 1965. No new claims have been accepted after the latter date. On the other hand, the Commission is accepting joinders in claims over which it has jurisdiction on a day-to-day basis.

Moreover, the Commission has committed itself over the years both to the Bureau of the Budget and to the Congress through the Appropriations Committees of both Houses, and through the Foreign Relations and Foreign Affairs Committee in the form of legislative proposals to close out this program by March 31, 1966. Accordingly, appropriations, staffing and scheduling have been geared to that date. To accommodate Mr. Hyman's proposal would entail seeking additional appropriations and maintaining staff to handle an unknown quantity of claims.

Because of the vastly extensive property damage in Poland during World War II, the obliteration of 60 percent of the land records, and the removal of large segments of former residents from given areas, it is impossible for Polish authorities to furnish some of the information which Mr. Hyman seeks for his clients. It would thus appear that this program could be drawn out interminably. Therefore, the Commission adheres to its proposal of a March 31, 1966, terminal date.

Robert Reiter, Esq., proposes extending the Italian claims program to include death and disability claims. The only programs including similar claims were those concerning U.S. citizens who were interned in the Philippines during World War II. The Congress included this group because they were encouraged to remain in the Philippines at the onset of hostilities for morale purposes because the islands were the U.S. territory. All other U.S. citizens in zones of danger were warned to return to the United States.

The only other known category of such claims are those of U.S. citizens who were in the process of returning home at the outbreak of hostilities who suffered death or injury as the result of sinking of passenger vessels at the hands of Axis submarines.

The only exception was one case under the Italian program wherein the Commission determined that there was a violation of international law on the part of Italy. The Commission feels that the present statute is sufficient to accommodate comparable instances.

The Commission adheres to its proposals in this respect and is opposed to broadening the amendments as suggested by Mr. Reiter.

Paul Neuberger, Esq., suggests that the eligible date for late national claimants under the proposed extension of the Italian claims program be established as of the date of enactment of the amendment. It was only after lengthy deliberation that the various interesed agencies of the executive branch agreed on the proposed extension of the program on the proviso that the eligibility date be fixed at August 9, 1955. The Commission is opposed to this proposal.

Mr. D. J. Cassarella suggests that the en bloc settlement in the amount of $400,000, made by the Bulgarian Government under the agreement of July 2, 1963, be reserved for additional payments to present awardees. However, the agreement settled all claims of U.S. nationals which arose prior to July 2, 1963. To adopt this suggestion would be to deny the claims of U.S. nationals against Bulgaria, which may have arisen between August 9, 1955, and the date of the agreement. The Commission understands that few, if any, such claims exist. The terms of the agreement should stand.

In conclusion, I should like to take this opportunity to thank you and your committee for all of the courtesies extended to the Commission.

The Commission has received informal advice from the Bureau of the Budget that there is no objection to the submission of this report.

Sincerely yours,

EDWARD D. RE,
*Chairman.*

0285

NEW YORK, N.Y., *August 10, 1965.*

Hon. JOHN J. SPARKMAN,
*Chairman, Subcommittee of the Committee on Foreign Relations,*
*U.S. Senate, Washington, D.C.*

DEAR MR. SPARKMAN: This is to supplement the statement I made before your committee on August 5, 1965, in testifying on S. 1935.

The General Counsel of the Foreign Claims Settlement Commission, in response to a question propounded by you, estimated that approximately 50 percent of the claims that the Commission had adjudicated were denied.

Actually, there have been denials in about 60 percent of the claims that have thus far been adjudicated.

This, in my opinion, is a very high percentage of rejections and can be explained only by the lack of ample opportunity extended to the claimants to secure documentary proof in support of their claims. And, I would submit, this lack of opportunity is due to the impossible burden imposed on the Polish authorities to provide within a 4-year period the documentation for the nearly 10,500 claims that have been filed with the Commission under the Polish Claims Agreement.

I would reemphasize that the ultimate success of the Polish claims program will be judged not by the speed in which the program is wound up but rather by the number of the valid claims that are approved. It is submitted that the number of favorable awards will increase substantially if the claimants are given an additional year beyond the date of March 31, 1966, suggested in the bill before you, in which to present their evidence.

Finally, I submit that the Foreign Claims Settlement Commission should not be expected to complete the Polish claims program, admittedly six times the size of the Yugoslavian program and more than twice the size of the Czechoslovakian program, in the same period of time—4 years—that it took to wind up the latter two programs.

The Congress will surely be furthering the cause of justice by extending to claimants who have filed claims under the Polish claims program an additional year beyond March 31, 1966, in which to present their evidence in support of their claims.

Respectfully yours,

ABRAHAM S. HYMAN,
*Attorney at Law.*

0286

CLAIMS ARTICLES OF OTHER SOFA's

0287

# Claims Article

~~U.S. General Rights in~~ Ethiopia

( 5.3 위치(H/) )
( US가 제1 )

## Art. XIX

1. Subject to the provisions of subparagraph of Article
IV, each Government waives all its claims against the other
for damage to any property in Ethiopian territory owned or
controlled by ~~it~~ if such damage (1) was caused by a member
of the United States forces or by a member of the armed
forces or an employee of the Imperial Ethiopian Government
while engaged in the performance of his official duties, or
(2) arose from the use of any vehicle, vessel or aircraft
owned or controlled by the other Government. Each Government
waives claims for maritime or aircraft salvage against the
other provided that the vessel or aircraft or cargo salvaged
was owned by the other Government or being used by the United
States forces or by the armed forces or an employee of the
Imperial Ethiopian Government at the time the incident occurred.

2. Each Government waives all its claims against the
other for injury or death suffered by any member of the
United States forces or by any member of the armed forces or any
employee of the Imperial Ethiopian Government, while such
member or employee was engaged in the performance of his official
duties.

3. The Government of the United States agrees to pay
just and reasonable compensation in settlement of all claims
cognizable under United States foreign claims laws of
inhabitants of Ethiopia for damage to, loss or destruction of
property, or for injury or death, caused by members of the
United States forces. All such claims will be processed and
paid in accordance with the applicable provisions of the
laws of the United States.

0288

<u>Iceland</u>

<u>Art. 12</u>

1. (a) The United States waives all claims against the
Government of Iceland for damage to any property owned by it
and used by the United States forces and for injury to or death
of members of the United States forces caused by an employee
of the Government of Iceland.

(b) The Government of Iceland waives all claims
against the United States for damage to property owned by
it in any of the agreed areas and will make compensation and
waive all claims against the United States for injury or death
of an employee of the Government of Iceland occurring in such
area while such employee is therein by reason of his duties, as
determined by representatives of the United States and Iceland
to be appointed by each, when such damage, injury or death is
caused by a member of the United States forces.  The Government
of Iceland also waives all claims for damage to any property
owned by it and for injury to or death of an employee of
the Government of Iceland occurring outside any of the agreed
areas caused by a member of the United States forces when it is
determined by representatives of the United States and
Iceland, to be appointed by each, that such property or
employee was, at the time of said damage, injury or death, being
utilized or employed in any respect with carrying out
the provisions of this Agreement.

(c) The United States and Iceland waive all their
claims against each other for damage to a vessel owned by
the United States or Iceland while such vessel is being used in
connection with the operation of this Agreement, wherever such
damage shall occur, and whether it is caused by a member of the
United States forces or by an employee of the Government of
Iceland.  Claims for maritime salvage by the United States

0289

or Iceland shall be waived, provided that the vessel or cargo salved was ¢¢/¢ owned by the United States or Icelnad as the case may be, in connection with the operation of this Agreement.

(d) For the purpose of this paragraph the expressions "owned by the United States," "owned by Iceland" or "owned by the United States or Iceland" include a vessel on bare boat charter to the United States or Iceland, as the case may be or requisitioned by either government on bare boat terms or otherwise in the possession of the United States or Iceland (except to the extent that the risk of loss or liability is borne by some person other than the United States or Iceland or its insurer).

2. Claims (other than contractual claims) arising out of acts done by members of the United States forces and causing damage to, or loss or destruction of, the property of persons or bodies in Iceland or the injury or death of individuals therin (except as provided in the preceding paragraph,) shall be settled by Iceland in accordance with the following provisions:

(a) Claims shall be filed, considered and settled or xxjxudxx adjudicated in accordance with the laws and regulations of Iceland with respect to claims arising from acts of its own employees.

(b) Iceland may settle any such claims, and payment of the amount agreed upon or determined by adjudication shall be made by Iceland in its currency.

(c) Such payment, or the final adjudication of the competent tribunals of Iceland denying payment, shall be binding and consulsive upon the United States and Iceland.

(d) Every claim paid by Iceland shall be communicated to the United States military authorities together with full particulars.

0290

上記 補償金의 經費는 아리의 다음과 같이 分十.
日 이 責任時
Iceland 15%
美 12 85%

② 美軍構成員가 Iceland 12民이 共同責任時
= 이 50%
美 12 50%

④ 6個月마다 決算 (Iceland이 貨幣로 支拂하되 不遲히).

⑥ 本項의 範圍에 屬하는 □事件에 관하여는 美軍構成員은 어떠한 訴訟의 對象도 안된다.

請求 不同한 處理
① 美 12가 戰爭하 또는 12국에 12民
② 上記 12국가의 同盟關係에 또는 12국에 12民
③ 敵의 行動으로 因한 損害.
④ 戰鬪行爲로 因한 損害.

協調事項

訴訟 收拾에 相互協助에 관하

(e) The cost incurred in satisfying claims pursuant to the preceding sub-paragraph shall be distributed between the United States and Iceland as follows:

(1) Where the United States alone is responsible, the amount awarded or adjudged shall be distributed in the proportion of 15% charteable to Iceland and 85% chargeable to the United States.

(2) Where members of the United States forces and nationals of Iceland contrioute to the damage, the amount awarded or adjudged shall be distributed equally betwenn the United States and Iceland.

(3) Every half-year, a statement of the sums paid by Iceland in the course of the half-yearly period in respect of every case shall be sent to the United States together with a request for reimbursement. Such reimbursement shall be made within the shortest possible time, in the currency of Iceland.

(f) A member of the United States forces shall not be subject to any suit with respect to claims arising by reasonn of an act done which is within the purview of this paragraph.

3. Claimsp presented by a national of any ɛɴᴍʀᴛᴉʀʏxᴀᴛxwᴀᴇ country at war with the United States or by an ally of such enemy country and claims resulting from action by the enemy or resulting directly or indirectly from any act by the United States forces engaged in combat are npt considered to be within the provisions of this Article.

4. The military authorities of the United States and the appropriate officials of Iceland shall cooperate in the procurement of evidence for a fair hearing and disposal of claims in regard to which the United States and Icdland are concerned.

0291

本條의義務를
遂行하기爲해서
를 一必要한
立法措置를한다

5. The United States undertakes to procure the legislation necessary to implement its responsibilities as set forth in this Article.

## Japan-Administrative Agreement (1952)

### Art. XVIII

公二人의公務同中
軍人및政府工員은
에對한 請求를
相互抛棄.

1. Each party waives all its claims against the other party for injury or death suffered in Japan by a member of its armed forces, or a civilian governmental employee, while such member or employee was engaged in the performance of his official duties in cases where such injury or death was caused by a member of the armed forces, or a civilian employee of the other party acting in the performance of his official duties.

公務公務同中
政府財産에對한
抛棄.

2. Each party waives all its claims against the other party for damage to any property in Japan owned by it, if such damage was caused by a member of the armed forces or a civilian governmental employee of the other party in the performance of his official duties.

公務中第三者에
對한 損害
↓

3. Claims, other than contractual, arising out of acts or omissions of members of, or employees of the United States armed forces in the performance of official duty or out of any other act, omission or occurrence for which the United States armed forces is legally responsible, arising incident to non-combat activities and causing injury, death, or property damage in Japan to third parties shall be dealt with by Japan in accordance with the following provisions:

① 日本法에依據
處理
② 1年以內에
請求提起

(a) Claims shall be filed within one year from the date on which they arise and shall be considered and settled or adjudicated in accordance with the laws and regulations of Japan with respect to claims arising from the activities of its own employees.

0292

(b) Japan may settle any such claims, and payment of the amount agreed upon or determined by adjudication shall be made by Japan in yen.

(c) Such payment, whether made pursuant to a settlement or to adjudication or the case by a competent tribunal of Japan, or the final adjudication by such a tribunal denying payment, shall be binding and conclusive.

(d) The cost incurred in satisfying claims pursuant to t the preceding subparagraphs shall be shard on terms to be agreed by the two Govermnłts.

(d) In accordance with procedures to be established, a statement of all claims approved or disapproved by Japan pursuant to this paragraph, together with the findings in each case, and a statement of the sums paid by Japan, shall be sent to the United States perdiodically, with a request for reimbursement of the share to be paid by the United States. Such reimbursement shall be made within the shortest possible time in yen.

4. Each party shall have the primary right, in the execution of the foregoing paragraphs, to determine whether its personnel were engaged in the performance of official duty. Such determination shall be made as soon as possible after the arising of the claims concerned. When the other party disagrees with the results of such determination, that party may bring the matter before the Joint Committee for consultation under the provisions of Article XXVI of this Agreement.

5. Claims against members of or employees of the United States armed forces arising out of tortious acts or omissions in Japan not done in the performance of official duty shall be dealt with in the following manner:

(a) The Japanese authorities shall consider the claim and assess compensation to the claimant in a fair and just manner, taking into account all the circumstances of the case,

0293

including the conduct of the injured person, and shall

prepare a report on the matter.

(b) The report shall be delivered to the United States
authorities, who shall then decide without delay whether they will
offer an _ex gratia_ payment, and if so, of what amount.

(c) If an offer of ex gratia payment is made, and
accepted by the claimant in full satisfaction of his claim, the
United States authorities shall make the payment themselves and
inform the Japanese authorities of their decision and of the sum
paid.

(d) Nothing in this paragraph shall affect the jurisdiction of the Japanese courts to entertain an action against a
member or employee of the United States armed forces, unless
and until there has been payment in full satisfaction of the claim.

6. (a) Members of and civilian employees of the United
States armed forces, excluding those employees who have onky
Japanese nationality shall not be subject to suit in Japan with
respect to claims specified in paragraph 3, but shall be subject
to the civil jurisdiction of Japanese courts with respect to all
other types of cases.

(b) In case any private movable property, excluding that
in use by the United States armed forces, which is subject
to compulsory execution under Japanese law, is within the
facilities and areas in use by the United States armed
forces, the United States authorities shall upon the request
of Japanese courts, possess and turn over such property to the
Japanese authorities.

(c) The United States authorities shall cooperate with
the Japanese authorities in making available witnesses and
evidence for civil proceedings in Japanese tribunals.

7. Disputes arising out of contracts concerning the procurement of materials, supplies, equipment, services, and labor by or

for the United States armed forces, which are not resolved by
the parties to the contract concerned, may be submitted to the
Joint Committee for conciliation, provided that the provisions
of this paragraph shall not prejudice any right which the parties
to the contract may have to file a civil suit.

## Japan-Status of UN Forces (1954)

① 反共卒明亨
② Contractual dispute 明亮.

### Art. XVIII

1. Each Party to this Agreement waives all its claims
against any other Party to this Agreement for injury or
death suffered in Japan by a member of the forces of, or a
civilian governmental employee of the former Party, while such
member or employee was engaged in the performance of his official
duties, in cases where such injury or death was caused by a
member of the forces of, or a civilian governmental employee
of the other Party in the performance of his official duties.

2. Each Party to this Agreement waives all its claims against
any other Party to this Agreement for damage to any property in
Japan owned by it, if such damage was caused by a member of the
forces of, or a civilian governmental employee of the other
Party in the performance of his official duties.

3. Claims, other than contractual, arising out of acts or
omissions of members of employees of the United Six Nations
forces doen in the performance of their dx official duties, or
out of any other act, omission or occurrence for which the
United Nations forces are legally responsible, arising incident
tox non-combat activities and causing injury, death or property
damage in Japan to third parties shall be dealt with by
Japan in accordance with the following provisions:

(a) Claims shall be filed within one year from the
date on which they arise, and shall be considered and settled or
adjudicated in accordance with the laws and regulations of
Japan with respect to claims arising from the activities of is
own employees.

0295

(b) Japan may settle any such claims, and payment of the amount agreed upon or determined by adjudication shall be made by Japan in yen.

(c) Such payment, whether made pursuant to a settlement or to adjudication of the case by a competent tribunals of Japan, or the final adjudication by such a tribunal denying payment, shall be binding and conclusive.

(d) The cost incurred in satisfying claims pursuant to the preceding subparagraphs shall be shared by the Parties to this Agreement as follows:

(i) Where one sending State alone is responsible, the amount agreed upon or adjudged shall be shared in the proportion of 75% chargeable to the sending State and 25% chargeable to Japan.

(ii) Where more than one sending State is jointly responsible, the amount agreed upon or adjudged shall be shared in such proportion that the shares of the sending States concerned shall be equal among themselves and the share of Japan shall be one half of thix that of one of such sending States.

(iii) Where the injury, death or property damage was caused by the United Nations forces of more than one sending State and it is not possible to atribute it specifically to any of the United Nations forces, all of the sending States concerned shall be regarded as respohsible for the cause of such injury, death or property damage and the provisins of item (ii) above shall apply thereto.

(c) In acoordance with procedures to be established, a statement of all claims xprn approved or disapproved by Japan pursuant to this paragraph, the findings in each case, and a statement of the sums paid by Japan, shall be sent periodically to the sending State concerned, together with a request for reimbursement of the share to be paid by such sending State.

0296

Such reimbursement shall be made in yen within the shortest possible period of time.

4. Each Party to this Agreement shall have the primary right, in the execution of the foregoing paragraphs, to determine whether its personnel were engaged in the performance of official duty. Such determination shall be made as soon as possible after the arising of the claim concerned. When any other Party concerned disagrees with the results of such determination, that Party may bring the matter before the Joint Board for consultation.

5. Claims against members or employees of the United Nations forces arising out of torious acts or omissions in Japan not done in the performance of their official duties shall be dealt with in the following manner:

(a) The Japanese authorities shall consider the claims and assess compensation to the claimant in a fair and just manner, taking into account all the circumstances of the case, including the conduct of the injured person, and shall prepare a report on the matter.

(b) The report shall be delivered to the authorities of the sending State concerned, who shall then decide without delay whether they will offer an ex gratia payment, and if so, of what amount.

(c) If an offer of ex gratia payment is made, and accepted by the claimant in full satisfaction of his claim, the authorities of sending State shall make the payment themselves and inform the Japanese authorities of their decision and of the sum paid.

(d) Nothing in this paragraph shall affect the jurisdiction of the courts of Japan to entertain an action against a member or employee of the United Nations forces unless and until there has been payment in full satisfaction of the claims.

0297

6. (a) Members and employees of the United Stitinnx
Nations forces, excluding those employees who have only Japanese
nationality, shall not be subject to suit in Japan with
respect to claims specified in paragraph 3, but shall be subject
to the civil jurisdiction of Japanese courts with respect
to all other types of cases.

(b) In case any private movable property, excluding that
in use by the United Nations forces, which is subjct to
compulsory execution under Japanese law, is within the
facilities in use by the United Nations forces, the authorities
of the sending State concerned shall, upon the request of Japanese
courts, possess and turn over such property to the Japanese
authorities. In the case of a sending State the forces of which
have ho legal authority to take such action, the authorities
of that State shall allow the appropriate Japanese authorities
to take possession of such property in accordance with Japanese
law.

(c) The authorities of every sending State shall
cooperate with the Japanese authorities in making available
witnesses and evidence for a fair hearing and disposal of
claims under the provisions of this Article.

Libya

Art. XIX

CLAIMS AND JURISDICTION IN CIVIL MATTERS

(1) The Government of the United States of America
agrees to pay just and reasonable compensation for valid claims
of the Government of the United Kingdom of Libya for damage,
loss or destruction of its property caused by military members of
the United States forces who are in Libya under the terms of the
oresebt Agreement, or by civilian kxxxpkxx employees of the
United States armed services, including those who are

0298

natopm

nationals of or ordinarily resident in Libya, in connection with
operations under the present Agreement.

(2) The Government of the United States pf America,
(reasonable compensation for valid claims of persons)
agrees to pay just and persons who are nationals of
Libya, or inhabitants of that xxxxixxx xxxxixx country,
for damage, loss or destruction of property, or for injury
or death, caused by military members of United States
forces who are in Libya under the terms of the present Agreement
or by civilian employees of the United States armed
services, including those who are nationals of or ordinarily
resident in Libya, in connection with operations under the
present Agreement.

(3) All such claims will be processed and paid in
accordance with the applicable provisions of United States
law, and the courts of Libya will not entertain any such
claims against members of the United States forces.

(4) In all other civil cases involving members of the
United States forces the Libyan courts will have jurisdiction.


NATO

Art. VIII

1. Each Contracting Parties waives all its claims against
any other Contracting Party for damage to any property
owned by it and used by its land, sea or air armed fxxxx
services, if such damage -

(i) was caused by a member or an employee of the
a med services of the other Contracting party in the execution of his duties in connexion with the operation of the
North Atlantic Treaty: or

(ii) arose from the use of any vehicle, vessel or

0299

aircraft owned by the other Contracting party and used
by its armed services, provided either that the vehicle, v
vessel or aircraft causing the damage was being used in
connexion with the operation of the North Atlantic Treaty,
or that the damage was caused to property being so used.
Claims for maritime salvage by one Contracting Party against any
other Contracting Party shall be waived, provided that the
vessel or cargo salved was owned by a Contracting Party and
being used by its armed services in connexion with the
operation of the North Atlantic Treaty.

2. (a) In the case of damage caused or arising as stated
in paragraph 1 to other property owned by a Contracting Party
and located in its territory, the issue of the liability of
any Contracting Party shall be determined and the amount of damage shall be assessed, unless the Contracting Parties concerned
agree otherwise, by a sale arbitrator selected in
accordance with subparagraph (b) of this paragraph. The
arbitrator shall also decide any counter-claims arising
out of the same incident.

(b) The arbitrator referred to in sub-paragraph
(a) above shall be selected by agreement between the
Contracting Parties concerned from amongst the nationals
of the receiving State who hold or have held high judicial
office. If the Contracting Parties concerned are unable,
within two months, to agree upon the arbitrator, either may
request the Chairman of the North Atlantic Council Deputies to s
select a person with the foresaid qualifications.

(c) Any decision taken by the arbitrator shall be
binding and conclusive upon the Contracting Parties.

(b) The amount of any compensation awarded by the
arbitrator shall be distributed in accordance with the
provisions of paragraph 5(c) (i), (ii) and (iii) of this
Article.

0300

(e) The compensation of the arbitrator shall
be fixed by agreement between the Contracting Parties
concerned and shall, together with the necessary expenses
incidental to the performance of his duties, be defrayed in
equal proportions by them.

(f) Nevertheless, each Contracting Party waives its
claim in any such case where the damage is loss than:-

Belgium: B. fr. 70,000

Canada: $1,460.

Denmark: Kr. 9,870

France: F. fr. 490,000

Iceland: Kr. 22,800

Italy: Li. 850,000

Luxembourg: L. fr. 70,000

Netherland: Fl. 5,320

Norway: Kr. 10,000

Portugal: Es. 40,250

United Kingdom: L 500

United States: $1,400.

Any other Contracting Party whose property has been damage
in the same incident shall also waive its claim up to
the above amount. In the case of considerable variation
in the rates of exchange between these currendies the
Contracting Parties shall agree on the appropriate adjust-
ment of these amounts.

3. For the purpose of paragraphs 1 and 2 of this
Article the expression "owned by a Contracting Party" in
the case of a vessek includes a vessel on bare boat charter
to that Contracting Party or requisioned by it on bare
baat terms or seized by it in prize (except to the extent that

0301

the risk of loss or liability is borne by some person other such
Contracting Party).

4. Each Contracting Party waives all its claims against any
other Contracting Party for injury or death suffered by any member of its armed services while such member was engaged in the
performance of his official duties.

5. Claims (other than contractual claims and those to which
paragraphs 6 of 7 of this Article apply) arising out of
acts or omissions of members of a force or civilian component done
in the performance of official duty or out of any other act,
omission or occurrence for which a force or civilian component is
legally responsible, and causing damage in the territory
of the receiving State to their third parties, other than
any of the Contracting Parties, shall be dealt with by the receiving State in accordance with the following provisions:

(a) Claims shall be filed, considered and settled
or adjudicated in accordance with the laws and regulations of
the receiving State with respect to claims arising from
the activities of its owned armed forces.

(b) The receiving State may settle any such claims,
and payment of the amount agreed upon or determined by
adjudication shall be made by the receiving State in its
currency.

(c) Such payment, whether made pursuant to a settlement or to adjudication of the case by a competent tribunal
of the receiving State, or the final adjudication by such
a tribunal denying payment, shall be binding and conclusive
upon the Contracting Parties.

(d) Every claim paid by the receiving State shall
ber communicated to the sending States concerned
together with full particulars and a proposed distribution
in conformity with subparagraphs (e) (i), (ii) and (iii)
below. In default of a reply within two months, the
proposed distribution shall be regarded as accepted.

0302

(e) The cost incurred in satisfying claims pursuant to the preceding sub-paragraph 2 of this Article shall be distributed between the Contracting Parties, as follows:-

(i) Where one sending State alone is responsible, the amount awarded or adjudged shall be distributed in the proportion of 25 per cent. chargeable to the xxxxx receiving State and 75 per cent. chargeable to the sending State.

(ii) Where more one State is responsible for the damage, the amount awarded or adjudged shall be distributed equally among them: however, if the receiving State is not one of the States responsible, its contribution shall be half that of each of the sending States.

(iii) Where the damage was caused by the armed services of the Contracting Parties and it is not possible to attribute it specially to one or more of those armed services, the amount awarded or adjudged shall be distributed equally among the Contracting Parties concerned: however, if the receiving State is not one of the States by whose armed services the damage was caused, its contribution shall be half that of each of the sending States concerned.

(iv) Every half-year, a statement of the sums paid by the receiving State in the course of the half-yearly period in respect of every case regarding which the proposed distribution on a percentage basis has been accepted, shall be sent to the sending States conce ned, together with a request for reimbursement shall be made within the shortest possible time, in the currency of the receiving State.

(f) In cases where the application of the provisions of sub-paragraph (b) and (e) of this paragraph would cause a Contracting Party serious hardship, it may request the North Atlantic Council to arrange a settlement of a different nature.

0303

(g) A member of force or civilian component shall
not be subject to any proceeding for the enforcement of any
judgment given against him in the receiving State in a
matter arising from the performance of his official duties.

(h) Exeept in so far as sub-paragraph (e) of this
paragraph applies to claims covered by paragraph 2 of
this Article, the provisions of this paragraph shall not
apply to any claim arising out of or in connexion with
the navigation or operation of a ship or the leading,
carriage, or discharge of a cargo, other than claims for
death or personal injury to which paragraph 4 of this Article
does not apply.

6. Claims against members of a force or civilian
component arising out of totious acts or omissions in the
receiving State not done in the performance of official duty shall
be dealt with the following manner:

(a) The authorities of the receiving State shall
considered the claim and assess compensation to the
claimant in a fair and just manner, taking into acoount
all the circumstances of the case, including the
conduct of the injured person, and shall prepare a report on the
matter.

(b) The report shall be delivered to the authorities
of the sending State, who shall then decide without delay whether
will offer an ex gratia payment, and if so, of what amount.

(c) If an offer ex gratia payment is made, and
accepted by the claimant in full satisfaction of his claim, te
the authorities of the sending State shall make the payment themselves and inform the authorities of the receiving State of their
decision and of the sum paid.

(d) Nothing in this paragraph shall affect the

jurisdiction of the courts of the receiving State to
entertain an action against a member of a force or of a
civilian component unless and until there has been payment
in full satisfaction of the claim.

7. Claims arising out pf the unauthorized use of any
vehicle of the armed services of a sending State shall be dealt
with in accordance with paragraph 6 of this Article in so
far as the force or civilian component is legally responsible.

8. If a dispute arises as to whether a totious act or
omission of a member of a force or civilian component
was done in the performance of official duty or as to whether
the use of any vehicle of the armed services of a
sending State was unauthorised, the question shall be
submitted to an arbitrator appointed in accordance
with paragraph 2(b) of this Article, whose decision on
this point shall be final and conclusive.

9. The sending State shall not claim immunity from
the jurisdiction of the courts of the receiving State
for members of a force or civilian component in respect
of the civil jurisdiction of the courts of the receiving State
except to the extent provided in paragraph 5(g) of this Article.

10. The authorities of the sending State and of the
receiving State shall cooperate in the procurement of
evidence for a fair hearing and disposal of claims in
regard to which the Contracting Parties are concerned.


The Philippines

Art. XXIII

Civil Liability

For the purpose of promoting and maintaining friendly
relations by the prompt settlemant of meritorious claims,

0305

the United States shall pay just and reasonable compensation, when
accepted by claimants in full satisfaction and in
final settlement, for claims, including claims of insured but
excluding claims of subrogees, on account of damage to or loss
or desruction of private property, both real and personal, or per-
sonnal injury or death of inhabitants of the Philippines,
when such damage, loss, destruction or injury is caused by
the armed forced of the Unitdd States, or individual members
thereof, including military or civilian employees thereof, or
otherwise incident to non-combat activities of such forces;
provided that no claim shall be considered unless presented
within one year after the occurance of the accident or incident out of which such claim arise.

Germany

### Art. 41

1. The settlement of claims in respect of damage caused
by acts or omissions of a force, a civilian component or their
members, or by other occurences for which a force or a civilian
component is legally responsible, shall be governed
by the provisions of Article VIII of the NATO Status of
Forces Agreement and the provisions of this Article supplementary thereto.

2. No compensation shall be payable in respect of

(a) damage to public roads, highways, bridges, navigable
waterways and other public traffic facilities resulting from their
use by a force or a civilian component for normal traffic purposes;

(b) loss of or damage to property which has been constructed
or procured far from occupation costs, mandatory expenditures
or support costs funds, to the extent that such loss or damage
was caused while the property was at the disposal
of a force or a civilian component for its use.

0306

3. (a) The Federal Republic shall waive all its claims against a sending State in respect of loss of, or damage to, property owned by the Federal Republic and made available for the exclusive use of the force or of the civilian component. This shall apply equally if such property is made available for use by the forces of several sending States or is used by the force of one or more sending States jointly with the German Armed Forces. This waiver shall not apply to damage caused willfully or by gross negligence, nor to damage damage to the property of the German Federal Republic Railways or German Federal Post.

(b) The provisions of subparagraph (f) of paragraph 2 of Article VIII of the NATO Status of Forces Agreement shall not apply to loss of or damage to property owned by the German Federal Railways or the German Federal Post nor to damage to Federal roads.

4. The Federal Republic shall relieve the sending States of Liability for claims arising from loss of or damage to property owned by a Land, if the loss or damage was caused prior to the entry into force of the present Agreement.

5. Each sending State shall waive all its claims against the Federal Republic in respect of loss of or damage to property owned by such sending State caused by members or employees of the German Armed Forces in the performance of official duties or by the use of vehicles, ships, or aircraft of the German Armed Forces, provided that it is property used by the force or the civilian component of that State and that it is located in the Federal territory. This waiver shall not apply to damage caused wilfully or by gross negligence.

0307

✓ 6. The provisions of paragraph 5 of Article VIII of the NATO Status of Forces Agreement and of this Articles shall not apply to damage suffered by members of a force or of a civilian component and caused by acts or omissions of other members of the same force or the same civilian component, or by other occurrences for which such force or such civilian component is legally responsible.

✗ 7. The organizations referrdd to in paragraph 2 of Article 71 shall for the purpose of the settlement of damage claims in accordance with Article VIII of the NATO Status of Forces Agreement in conjunction with this Article be considered to be, and treated as, integral parts of the force concerned unless it is agreed that any such organization shall not enjoy in that respect exemption from German jurisdiction.

✗ 8. The liability of a force or of a civilian component shall not be affected by the fact that such force or civilian component enjoys exemption from German regulations. Where the German Armed Forces enjoy the same exemptions, compensations shall be payable only if and to the extent that compensation is payable for damage caused by the latter.

✗ 9. (a) In case where an occurrence causing damage to a third party and compensable under paragraph 5 of Article VIII of the NATO Status of Forces Agreement has also given rise to damage to the sending State concerned, and where the third party is liable to compensate for such damage, the claim of the sending State is to be set off against the claim of the third party.

(b) The Federal Republic shall, in accordance with administrative agreements, and at the request of a sending State, assert for that State claims against persons resident in the Federal territory and arising out of damage caused there to such State; this shall not apply to contractual claims. Such expenses which 0308

Federal Republic incurs in asserting claims over and above the general costs of administration shall be reimbursed by the sending State .

10. In the respect of claims concerning damage to accommodation or loss of, or damage to, movables, other than accommodation or movables owned by the Federation or by a Land, which were made available for exclusive use by a force or a civilian component before 5 May 1955, and which are released by the force or the civilian component after the entry into force of the present Agreement, compensation shall be borne by the Federal Republic and the sending State concerned in equal parts.

11. (a) Except in cases where after inquiry of the forces concerned it is not possible to establish to which of them the loss or damage is attributable, the force shall furnish a certificate concerning questions dealt with in paragraph 8 of Article VIII of the NATO Status of Forces Agreement; it shall, at the request of the German authorities, review such certificate if, during investigation of a claims, a German authority or a German German court considers that circumstances exist which would lead to an inference diffe-rence from that contained therein.

(b) If a difference of opinion remains that cannot be resolved in further discussions between the two parties at higher level, the procedure provided in paragraph 8 of Article VIII of the NATO Status of Forces Agreement shall be followed.

(c) The German authorities or courts shall make their decisions in conformity with the certificate or the decision of the arbitrator respectively.

0309

12. (a) The provisions of Article VIII of the NATO Status of Forces Agreement and of this Article shall apply to those damages which are caused or which are deemed to be caused after the entry into force of the present Agreement.

(b) Damages which were caused before the entry into force of the present Agreement, or which are deemed to have been caused before that date, shall be dealt with the regulations which were until then applicable.

13. Administrative agreements shall be concluded to regulate procedures as between the authorities of a force and the German authorities for the settlement of damage claims.

0310

Re Article 41

    1.   Article 41 shall not be applicable to claims concerning damage arising under contracts or quasi-contractual relationships.

    2.   (a) (i) In the case of damage to public roads and of damage to property of the Federal Republic, except property of the German Federal Railways and of the German Federal Post, caused by manoeuvres and other training exercises for which compensation would have been payable under Article 41, a force may, in lieu of paying such compensation, itself repair the damage.

    (ii) If a force wishes itself to repair damage to public roads, it will consult the competent German authorities and will refrain from itself carrying out the repair if the German authorities object for <u>cogent technical building</u> or traffic police control reasons. In these cases and in other cases of damages referred to in item (i) of this sub-paragraph contact shall not be necessary in individual cases if previously there has been an understanding on carrying out of repairs by the force on a general basis.

    (b) Nothing shall preclude a force itself making good the damage, in agreement with the person having suffered it, in cases other than those referred to in sub-paragraph (a) of this paragraph.

    (c) In the cases referred to in sub-paragraphs (a) and (b) of this paragraph, nothing shall preclude the person suffering the damage asserting any

0311

possible claim to which he may be entitled if in his opinion the damage has not been repaired either fully or properly.

3. In order to permit speedy settlement of compensation proceedings, a reasonable period of time should be provided within which to file compensation claims under Article VIII of the NATO Status of Forces Agreement in conjunction with Article 41. To this end, the Federal Republic shall enact suitable legislation.

4. The waiver given by the Federal Republic in sub-paragraph (a) of paragraph 3 of Article 41 shall not apply to damage arising from non-fulfilment of the accepted responsibility for repair and maintenance. To the extent that the agreements (Uberlassungs-vereinbarungen) do not contain provisions for the settlement of such damage claims, the procedure for settling them shall be laid down in administrative agreements.

5. Insofar as property of juristic persons whose shares are in the hands of the Federation is made available free of charge to a force or a civilian component for exclusive use, the Federal Republic shall relieve the sending State of liability in respect of damages to this property to the same extent as the Federal Republic has waived, in accordance with sub-paragraph (a) of paragraph 3 of Article 41, compensation for damage to property which it owns.

6. (a) If in the cases referred to in the last sentence of sub-paragraph (a) of paragraph 3 and the last sentence of paragraph 5 of Article 41, there is a difference of opinion between the competent German authorities and the authorities of a force as to whether or not damage was caused wilfully or by gross negligence, the authorities on both sides shall enter into negotiations.

0312

(b) If a difference of opinion remains that cannot
be resolved in further discussions between the
parties at higher level, the arbitrator referred
to in sub-paragraph (a) of paragraph 2 of Article
VIII of the NATO Status of Forces Agreement shall
decide.

7.   In respect of property owned by a Land and made
available for use by a force (paragraph 4 of Article 41),
the authorities of the force and the German authorities shall
determine jointly the condition of such property as at the date
of the entry into force of the Supplementary Agreement.  A
similar determination shall be made at the time of the
release of such property. Claims for damages or loss, if any,
shall be settled on the basis of the condition of the property
on these dates.

8. The American Red Cross and the University of Maryland
shall not be deemed to be, nor be treated as, integral
parts of the force for the purpose of paragraph 7 of Article
41 and in respect of the settlement of damage claims shall
not be exempt from German jurisdiction.

9.   The administrative agreements referred to in paragraph
13 of Article 41 may also contain arrangements which differ
from the procedural arrangements contained in Artifle VIII
of the NATO Status of Forces Agreement.

한·미국 간의 상호방위조약 제4조에 의한 시설과 구역 및 한국에서의 미국군대의 지위에 관한 협정(SOFA)
전59권. 1966.7.9 서울에서 서명 : 1967.2.9 발효(조약 232호) (V.53 민사청구권 관계자료, 1964-66) 319

## Settlement of Disputes

### Article 44

1. In the settlement of disputes arising from contracts concluded by the German authorities for the account of the authorities of a force or of a civilian component there shall at all times be close co-operation between those authorities, whether or not court proceedings are involved. This shall apply mutatis mutandis to disputes arising out of work, personnel representation, or social insurance of civilian labour with a force or a civilian component, as well as to disputes which arise from procedures referred to in sub-paragraph (c) of paragraph 1 of Article 62 of the present Agreement. Details of such cooperation shall be laid down in administrative agreements.

2. So far as they relate to court proceedings instituted against the Federal Republic, the agreements referred to in paragraph 1 of this Article shall be based on the following principles:

(a) The authorities of the force or of the civilian component shall be notified without delay of the lodging of a plaint and shall be consulted at all material stages of the proceedings.

(b) The decision as to whether or not an appeal should be lodged shall be taken only in agreement with the authorities of the force or of the civilian component. Failing agreement, the German authorities shall lodge an appeal if an authority of the force or, where applicable, an authority of the civilian component, at highest level, confirms its essential interest in that action being taken.

To the extent that the reasons underlying the confirmation of the interest referred to in the second and third sentences of this paragraph have not become known

0314

to the other party in the course of negotiations on the lodging of an appeal, such reasons shall be given on request.

3. Paragraph 2 of this Article shall apply mutatis mutandis to court proceedings instituted by the Federal Republic, it being understood that the principles set out in subparagraph (b) of paragraph 2 shall also be applied to the lodging of plaints.

4. Whether or not court proceedings are involved in the disputes referred to in paragraph 1 of this Article, the German authorities shall terminate such disputes only in agreement with the authorities of the force or of the civilian component.

5. (a) The sending State concerned shall meet all the obligations laid upon, and shall enjoy any benefits accruing to the Federal Republic as a result of judgments, decisions, orders and settlements (vollstreckbare Titel) in the court proceedings arising from disputes referred to in paragraph 1 of this Article.

(b) Where, solely as a result of a Federal authority at the highest level having confirmed its essential interest in the lodging of a plaint or an appeal, the force or the civilian component has raised no objection to that action being taken, and if the plaint or appeal gives rise to additional costs in the court proceedings, agreement shall be reached on a case to case basis as to whether and to what extent the obligations arising from such court proceedings are chargeable to the sending State or to the Federal Republic.

한·미국 간의 상호방위조약 제4조에 의한 시설과 구역 및 한국에서의 미국군대의 지위에 관한 협정(SOFA) 전59권. 1966.7.9 서울에서 서명 : 1967.2.9 발효(조약 232호) (V.53 민사청구권 관계자료, 1964-66) 321

(b) Costs arising in connection with court proceedings which are not included in the costs awarded by the court shall be paid by the sending State if the force or the civilian component has given its agreement before the costs were incurred.

6. (a) Disputes arising from direct procurement by the authorities of a force or of a civilian component of goods and services in the Federal territory shall be settled by German courts or by an independent arbitration tribunal. Where the German courts are to decide the dispute, the plaint shall be lodged against the Federal Republic, which shall conduct the case in its own name in the interest of the sending State. Paragraphs 2, 4 and 5 of this Article shall apply mutatis mutandis as regards relations between the Federal Republic and the sending State.

(b) Agreements between the Federal Republic and a sending State shall, however, take precedence over the provisions of sub-paragraph (a) of this paragraph.

0316

## Article 47

### Procurement of Goods and Services

1. The Federal Republic shall accord to a force or a civilian component treatment in the matter of procurement of goods and services not less favourable than is accorded to the German Armed Forces.

2. Having regard to any measures which may become necessary under the second sentence of paragraph 2 of Article IX of the NATO Status of Forces Agreement, the authorities of a force or of a civilian component shall, on request, inform the German authorities of their requirements for defined categories of supplies.

3. A force or a civilian component may procure goods and services which they need either direct, or, after prior agreement, through the appropriate German authorities.

4. Where the authorities of a force or of a civilian component procure goods and services direct.

(a) they may apply their normal procedure, provided, however, that they respect the principles applying in the Federal Republic regarding public procurement which are reflected in the regulations concerning competition, preferred tenderers, and prices applicable to public contracts;

(b) they shall inform the German authorities of the subject and size of the order, the name of the supplier and the agreed price, except in the case of minor orders.

5. Where the authorities of a force or of a civilian component procure goods and services through the German authorities.

한·미국 간의 상호방위조약 제4조에 의한 시설과 구역 및 한국에서의 미국군대의 지위에 관한 협정(SOFA) 전59권. 1966.7.9 서울에서 서명 : 1967.2.9 발효(조약 232호) (V.53 민사청구권 관계자료, 1964-66) 323

(a) the authorities of the force or of the civilian component shall inform the German authorities in good time of their requirements in detail, giving, in particular, technical specifications and special conditions of delivery and payment;

(b) contracts in respect of goods and services shall be concluded between the German authorities and the suppliers; the German legal and administrative provisions governing public contracts shall apply thereto;

(b) the German authorities, without prejudice to their exclusive competence vis-a-vis the supplier, shall allow the authorities of the force or of the civilian component to participate in the placing and carrying out of contracts to the extent necessary for taking their interests duly into account; in particular, no contract will be placed or modified without the written consent of the authorities of the force or of the civilian component; unless otherwise agreed, acceptance of goods and services shall be made jointly;

(d) the sending State shall reimburse the Federal Republic in respect of:

(i) any expenditure incumbent upon the Federal Republic under German law relating to public contracts, provided that expenditure arising from settlements out of court shall be reimbursed only if the force has consented to the settlement;

(ii) ex gratia payments made with the consent of the force;

0318

(iii) expenditure, which cannot be charged to the
contractor, arising from measures taken
by the German authorities in cases of emergency
in order to safeguard the interests of the
force or of the civilian component;

(e) the necessary funds shall be made available by the
authorities of the force and of the civilian component
in time to permit payment to be made on due dates;

(f) the authorities of the force or of the civilian
component shall be entitled, in a manner to be agreed,
to audit documents relative to payments made by the
competent German payment agencies;

(g) details of the procedures under sub-paragraphs (a),
(c), (d), (e) and (f) of this paragraph shall be
established in administrative agreements between the
German authorities and the authorities of the force or
of the civilian component, with the particular object
of ensuring the carrying out of the procurement procedure
within the time limits laid down.

0319

## Art. 62

### Requisitioning Procedures

1. Where requisitioning procedures (Anforderungsverfahren) are carried out on behalf of a force or a civilian component under German procurement legislation, the following provisions shall apply:

(a) The proceedings shall be instituted by the German authorities to be determined in consultation with the authorities of the force or of the civilian component.

(b) In accordance with administrative agreements, the competent German authorities shall undertake the exercise of the rights and the fulfilment of the obligations arising out of the position of the force or the civilian component as recipients of goods, services and facilities (Leistungsempfanger). However, the force or the civilian component shall itself fulfil such obligations as by their nature cannot be fulfilled by the German authorities. The German authorities representing the interests of the force or of the civilian component in matters concerning the amount of compensation payable shall consent to proposals in that regard made by the person liable to supply goods, services and facilities (Leistungspflichtiger) or by the assessment authority only after consultation with the authorities of the force or of the civilian component; similarly, they shall themselves make proposals regarding the amount of compensation payable only after such consultation. The provisions of Article 63 of the present Agreement shall remain unaffected.

(c) Lawsuits on behalf of, or against, the force or the civilian component arising out of their position as recipients of goods, services and facilities shall be instituted or defended by the Federal Republic in its own name.

0320

2.   The provisions of paragraph 1 of this Article shall
not apply in respect of the Restricted Areas Law and the
Land Procurement Law.

0321

Art. 12

(1) Each Government waives all its claims against the other Government for damage to any property owned by it and used by its land, sea or air armed forces where such property is in Australia or is being used outside Australia in connection with mutual defence activities, such as mutual participation in operations or exercises, provided that such damage:

(a) was caused by a member or an employee of the armed forces of the other Government in the performance of his official duties; or

(b) arose from the use of any vehicle, vessels or aircraft owned by the other Government and used by its armed forces provided either that the vehicle, vessel or aircraft causing the damage was being used for official purposes, or that the damage was caused to property being so used.

Claims for maritime salvage by one Government against the other shall be waived, provided that the vessel or cargo salved was owned by a Government and used by its armed forces for official purposes.

(2) (a) In the case of damage caused or arising as stated in paragraph (1) of this Article to other property owned by either Government and located in Australia, the issue of the liability of the other Government shall be determined and the amount of damage shall be assessed. unless the two Governments agree otherwise, by a sole arbitrator selected in accordance with subparagraph (b) of this paragraph. The arbitrator shall also decide any counter-claims arising out of the same incident.

(b) The arbitrator referred to in subparagraph (a) of this paragraph shall be selected by agreement between

0322

the two Governments from amongst the nationals of Australia who hold or have held high judicial office.

(c) Any decision taken by the arbitrator shall be binding and conclusive.

(d) The amount of any compensation awarded by the arbitrator shall be distributed as follows:

(i) where the armed forces of one Government alone are responsible for the damage, the amount awarded shall be distributed in the proportion of 75 per cent chargeable to that Government and 25 per cent chargeable to the other Government;

(ii) where the two Governments are responsible for the damage, the amount ~~mxdmx~~ awarded shall be distributed equally between them;

(iii) where the damage was caused by the armed forces of the United States or Australia and it is not possible to attribute responsibility for the damage specifically to one or both of those armed forces, the amount awarded shall be distributed equally between the United States and Australia.

(e) The remuneration of the arbitrator shall be fixed by agreement between the two Governments and shall together with the necessary expenses ~~xmxixmkx~~ incidental to the performance of his duties be defrayed in equal proportions by them.

(f) Nevertheless, each Government waives its claim in any such case up to the amount of 1,400 United States dollars or 625 Australian ppunds. In the case of considerable variation in the rate of exchange between these currencies the two Governments shall agree on the appropriate adjustments of these amounts.

0323

(3) For the purposes of paragraphs (1) and (2) of this Article the expression "owned by a Government" in the case of a vessel includes a vessel on bare boat charter to that Government or requisitioned by it on bare boat terms or seized by it in prize (except to the extent that the risk of loss or liability is borne by some person other than such Government).

(4) Each Government waives all its claims against the other Government for injury or death suffered by any member of its armed forces while such member was engaged in the performance of his official duties.

(5) In accordance with the requirements of Australian law, the United States Government shall insure official vehicles of the United States Forces against third party risks.

(6) United States contractors and sub-contractors shall be required to effect public risk insurance.

(7) Except in the case of claims arising out of the use of official vehicles of the United States Forces insured in accordance with the requirements of Australian law, claims (other than contractual claims and those to which paragraph (9) of this Article apply) arising out of acts or omissions of members or employees of the United States Forces done in the performance of official duty, or out of any other act, omission or occurrence for which the United States Forces are legally responsible, and causing damage in Australia, other than damage suffered by one of the two Governments, shall, unless the interested parties otherwise agree, be dealt with by the Australian Government in accordance with the following provisions:

(a) Claims shall be filed, considered and settled or adjudicated in accordance with the laws and regulations of Australia with respect to claims arising from the activities of Australia's own armed forces.

0324

(b) The Australian Government may settle any such claims, and payment of the amount agreed upon or determined by adjudication shall be made by the Australian Government.

(c) Such payment, whether made pursuant to a settlement or to adjudication of the case by a competent Australian tribunal or the final adjudication by such a tribunal denying payment, shall be a binding and conclusive discharge of the claim.

(d) Every claim paid by the Australian Government shall be communicated to the appropriate United States authorities together with full particulars and a proposed distribution in conformity with sub-paragraph (e) of this paragraph.  In default of a reply within two months the proposed distribution shall be regarded as accepted.

(e) The cost incurred in satisfying claims pursuant to the preceding sub-paragraphs of this paragraph shall be distributed between the Governments as follows:

(i) where the United States alone is responsible for the damage, the amount awarded or adjudged shall be distributed in the proportion of 25 per cent chargeable to Australia and 75 per cent chargeable to the United States;

(ii) where the two Governments are responsible for the damage, the amount awarded or adjudged shall be distributed equally betwenn them;

(iii) where the damage was caused by the armed forces of the United States or Australia and it is not possible to attribute responsibility for the damage specifically to one or both of those armed forces, the amount awarded or adjudged shall be distributed equally betwenn the United States and Australia.

0325

(f) The provisions of this paragraph shall not
apply to any claim arising out of or in connection with the
navigation or operation of a ship or the loading, carriage
or discharge of a cargo other than claims for death or
personal injury to which paragraph (4) of this Article does
not apply.

(8) Every three months a statement of the sums paid
by each Government in the course of the quarterly period
in respect of every claim dealth with under paragraph (2)
or (7) of this Article regarding which the proposed distribution on a percentage basis has been accepted shall be
sent to the appropriate authorities of the other Government
together with a request for prompt reimbursement.

(9) Except in the case of claims arising out of the
use of official vehicles of the United States Forces insured
in accordance with the requirements of Australian nx law,
claims against members of the United States Forces and of
the civilian component and dependents arising out of
tortious acts or omissions in Australia not done in the
pxfmx performance of official duty shall be dealt with in the
following manner.

(a) The Australian Government shall consider
the claim and assess compensation to the claimant
in a fair and just manner, taking into account all the
circumstances of the case, including the conduct of
the injured person, and shall prepare a report on the
matter.

(b) The report shall be delivered to the United
States Government which shall then decide without delay
whether it will offer an ex gratia payment and if so, of what
amount.

0326

(c) If an offer of ex gratia payment is made and accepted by the claimant in full satisfaction of his claim, the United States Government shall make the payment itself and inform the authorities of Australia of its decision and of the sum paid.

(d) Nothing in this paragraph shall affect the jurisdiction of the courts of Australia to entertain an action against a member of the United States Forces or of the civilian component or a dependant unless and until there has been payment in full satisfaction of the claim.

(10) If a dispute arises as to whether a tortious act or omission was done in the pxfxxfxx performance of official duty, the question shall be submitted to an arbitrator appointed in accorance with subparagraph (b) of paragraph (2) of this Article, whose decision on this point shall be final and conclusive.

(11) (a) The United States shall not claim immunity from the jurisdiction of the courts of Australia for members of the United States Forces or of the civilian component or dependants in respect of the civil jurisdiction of the courts of Australia.

(b) In case any private movable property, excluding that in use by the United States Forces, which is subject to compulsory execution under Australlian law, is within areas in use by the United States Forces, the United States authorities shall, upon request, assist the appropriate Australian authorities to take possession of such property.

(c) The authorities of the United States and Australia shall cooperate in the procurement of evidence for a fair hearing and disposal of claims under this Article.

(12) Paragraphs (2) and (7) of this Article shall apply only to claims arising incident to non combatant activities.

Dominican Rep.

Art. VI

The contracting Government shall take all precautions against dangers and damages resulting from developing and operation of the said LORAN Transmitting Stations. The Government of the United States of America agrees to make reasonable indemnification for valid claims presented by the Government of the Dominican Rep. on account of injuries to Dominican nationals or loss or damages to property belonging to Dominican nationals resulting from operation of the LORAN Transmitting Stations.

Greece

Art. IV

1. In civil matters, including damages arixxng arising from automobile accidents, Grekk courts will exercise juzisdxx jurisdiction as provided in Article VIII of NATO Status of Forces Agreement.

Nicaragua

Art. IV

Claims

(1) The Government of the United States of America agrees to pay, in Nicaraguan currency, in accordance with and to the extent possible under the applicable laws of the United States of America, all meritorious claims for damage to, or loss or destruction of, property, or injury or death, arising out of acts or omissions in the perform-ance of official duties of members of the United States

0328

Coast Guard in connection with the establishment,
maintenance, and operation of the Loran Station.

(2) It is understood that in the determining of
compensation with regard to claims described in paragraph
(1), due consideration shall be given to any provisions of
Nicaraguan law which would determine the liability of
the Government of Nicaragua in similar circumstances.

(3) Settlement of any claims by the Government of
the United States of America shall operate as a
complete satisfaction of such claims and as a release
of the Government of the United States of America and
the individuals on whose acts or omissions the claim is based
from all liability arising out of such acts or omissions.

(4) Members of the United States Coast Guard shall
be immune from the civil jurisdiction of Nicaragua in
matters arising from acts or omission in the performance
of their official duties in connection with the establishment, maintenance, and operation of the Loran Station.


Spain-Procedural Agreement

10. a. Members of the United States Forces shall
not be subject to the civil jurisdiction of Spanish courts
or authorities    for/acts or omissions arising out of the
performance of their official duties.  A certificate from
the United States military authorities attesting the
status in this regard of a member of the United States
Forces shall be considered conclusive by Spanish
authority.

b. None of the foregoing procedures shall
prejudice the rights of the injured party to indemnification
either by following the ordinary Spanish civil prodedures
or by making an administrative claim for the damages incurred
under the applicable laws of the United States.

0329

The United States authorities shall adjudicate all claims presented expeditiously. Persons who elect to undertake a suit in the Spanish civil courts shall thereafter be barred from seeking administrative relief xf form the United States government for claims arising out of the same act.

*Agreement Between the U.S.A and the Republic of Turkey Relative to the Implementation of the "NATO SOFA"*

Turkey

*personnel subject to US military law 인 경우*

~~Art.~~ 7. It is understood that in the case of any damages in Turkey, caused by persons xfxfxx referred to in paragraph 2 above who are not paid from appropriations made to the United Stated Department of Defense, which require, under the provisinns of Article VIII of the aforesaid NATO Agreement, the payment of an amount in order to satisfy the claimant with repect to such damages, the Turkish Government shall pay such amount, Procedures with repect to the reimbursement to the Turkish Government of such amounts shall be the subject of special arrangements agreed between the two Governments.

*amended, april 22, 1956 PX, Commissaries, Off Clubs.*

MINUTE OF UNDERSTANDING REGARDING PARAGRAPH 7 OF THE AGREEMENT BETWEEN THE REPUBLIC OF TURKEY AND THE UNITED STATES OF AMERICA RELATIOE TO THE IMPLEMENTATION OF THE "AGREEMENT BETWEEN THE PARTIES TO THE NORTH ATLANTIC TREATY REGARDING THE STATUS OF THEIR FORCES"

It is understood that the United States Government is able to accept responsibility for repayment only with respect to claims arising from the acts of employees paid from appropriated funds of the Department of Defense. With respect to claims arising from the acts of all other members of the civilian component it xx is understood that the United States will exercise its good offices to make

satisfactory arrangements with responsible entities for
reimbursing the Turkish Government.  However, the United
States Government under existing laws can accept no financial
liability with respect to the latter category of claims.

United Kingdom (the Oceanographic Research Stations)

Art. XXII

Claims for Compensation

(1) The Government of the United States of America
undertakes (to) pay adequate and effective compensation, which
shall not be less than the sumpx payable under the law
of the Bahama Islands and (to) indemnity the Government
of the United Kingdom and/Government of the
Bahama Islands and all other authorities, corporations
and persons in respect of valid claims arising out of:

(a) the death or injury of any person exept persons
employed by the Government of the United Kingdom in
connection with an Oceanographic Research Station, resulting
from the establishment, maintenance or use by the
Government of the United States of America of an Oceanographic Research Station;

(b) damage to property resulting from any action
of the Government of the United States of America in connection with the establishment, maintenance or use of an
Oceanographic Research Station;

(c) The acquisition of private property or rights
affecting private property (other than such property
or rights acquired under Article III or Article IV)
to enable any rights of the Government of the United
States of America under this Agreement to be exercised.

(2) Compensation payable under subparagraph (1)
(c) of this Article shall be assessed in accordance with
the law of the Bahama Islands.

0331

(3) For the purpose of this Article the law of the
Bahama Islands shall be the law in force at the time
of the signature of this Agreement, provided that
any subsequent alteration of the said law shall have
effect if the Contracting Government so agree.

West Indies

### Art. X

Civil Claims

(1) The Unitxx United States Government agrees to pay
just and reasonable compensation in settlement of civil
claims (other than contractual claims) arising out of acts
or omissions of members of the United States Forces
done in the performance of official duty or out of any
other act, omission or occurrence for which the United
States Forces are legally responsible.

(2) All such claims shall be processed and settled
in accordance with the applicable provisions of United
States law.

No tortious acts?

Continued

0332

AGREED MINUTE WITH RESPECT TO ARTICLE X OF THE AGREEMENT OF
FEBRUARY, 10, 1961 CONCERNING UNITED STATES DEFENCE AREAS
IN THE FEDERATION OF THE WEST INDIES

1.    With respect to paragraph (2) of Article X, the United
States delegation explained that in handling claims under
this provision United States authorities would exercise the
broad authority provided under United States laws relating
to Foreign Claims and regulations issued thereunder.  These
laws provide for simple, administrative procedures for the
settlement of claims against the United States overseas.
Under these procedures any inhabitant of the Federation
who believes he has a valid claim would, upon application
to any United States authority, be referred to the appropriate
United States Foreign Claims Commission which is authorised
by law to settle foreign claims.

2.    A Claims Commission's procedures in considering claims
referred to it are expeditious and very informal, although
a full record is developed in each case.  A Claims Commission
is not bound by judicial rules of evidence and may consider
any material which is relevant to the claim.  Claims must be
presented to a Commission within two years from the time
of the loss or injury.

3.    Except where settlement is accepted in full satisfaction,
a claimant is not precluded from pursuing such remedies as
local law provides.

4.    The United States delegation explained that in settling
claims which are described in paragraph (1) of Article X
as arising ".... out of any other act, omission or occurrence
for which the United States Forces are legally responsible",
United States authorities would take into consideration

0333

local law and practice.  An example would be a claim based

upon an injury caused by a falling structure that was

under the full control of the United States Forces.

(5.)  It was understood that should the ~~procedures~~ <ins>waiver formula</ins> provided

for under Article X prove to be unsatisfactory, upon the <ins>in the light of</ins>

<ins>implementation at an early period after ent-</ins>

request of the Government of the Federation of The West

<ins>waiver provisions should be negotiated and</ins>

Indies a new claims articles would be adopted which would

be equivalent in substance to paragraph (5) of Article VIII

of the NATO Status of Forces Agreement.[1]

| | |
|---|---|
| John Hay Whitney | Grantley Adams. |
| George L P Weaver | V. C. Bird |
| Hector Perez Garcia | H. Gordon Cummins. |
| Ivan B. White | N. W. Manley. |
| William E. Lang | G. F Charles |
| | Eric Williams |

Port of Spain,

    10 February, 1961

---

[1] TIAS 2846; 4 UST 1806.

0334

NETHERLANDS

NORTH ATLANTIC TREATY

Stationing of United States Armed Forces in the
Netherlands

Agreement, with annex,

Effected by exchange of notes

Signed at The Hague August 13, 1954;

Entered into force November 16, 1954.

———————

The American Ambassador to the Netherlands Minister for
Foreign Affairs and the Netherlands Minister without
Portfolio

No. 73

EXCELLENCIES:

I have the honor to refer to our recent discussions
regarding the manner in which our two Governments, as
parties to the North Atlantic Treaty, may further the
objectives of Article III of that Treaty to strengthen
their individual and collective capacity to resist armed
attack through the stationing of United States armed
forces in The Netherlands.  I have the honor to inform
Your Excellencies that the Government of the United States
is willing to conclude with the Government of The Netherlands an agreement on the following terms.

1. The Governments of the United States and the
Netherlands agree that the United States Government may
station its force in The Netherlands, as may be mutually
determined, in furtherance of the objectives of the
North Atlantic Treaty.      - 1 -

2. The Netherlands Government will, without cost to
the United States, provide land areas and utilities
connections, including access roads, agreed to be
necessary for the purposes of this agreement. The other
expenses involved in carrying out this agreement shall
be borne by the United States and the Netherlands
Governments in proportions to be determined between them.
Use of the utilities and services required by United
States forces will be facilitated by the Netherlands
Government.  When at the expense of the United States
Government, charges for the use of such utilities and
charges for services requested and rendered will be
no higher than those paid by the Netherlands armed
services.

3. Title to removable equipment, materials and
supplies brought into, or acquired in, The Netherlands by
or on behalf of the United States in connection with this
agreement will remain in the United States Government,
This property will be free from all duties, inspections
and other restrictions, whether on import or export, and
from all taxes.  At the termination of any operation
under this agreement, the United States will be compensated
by the Netherlands Government for the residual value, if
any, of installations developed at the expense of the
United States under this agreement.  The amount and manner
of compensation shall be determined between the appropriate
authorities of the two Governments.

4. The provisions of the Agreement signed at London on
June 19, 1951, Between the Parties to the North Atlantic

- 2 -

0336

Treaty Regarding the Status of Their Forces, together
with such understandings as the two Governments may reach
concerning the implementation of these provisions, shall
govern the status of United States forces in The Netherlands.

5. It is recognized that the provisions of the exchange
of notes on relief from taxes signed at The Hague on
March 7, 1952, as supplemented, are applicable to expenditures
made by or on behalf of the United States for the purposes of
this agreement.

6. The arrangements referred to in this note will remain
in effect for the duration of the North Atlantic Treaty, or
until such time as the two Governments mutually agree upon
their termination.

7. After the approval constitutionally required in The
Netherlands has been obtained, the present agreement shall
enter into force on the date of receipt by the United States
Government of a relevant notification from the Netherlands
Government. (1)

If the foregoing provisions and the Annex attached hereto
are acceptable to your Government, this note and Your
Excellencies' reply thereto indicating such acceptance shall
be honored as constituting the agreement of our two Governments
concerning this matter.

---

[1]Notification received Nov. 16, 1954
- 3 -

한·미국 간의 상호방위조약 제4조에 의한 시설과 구역 및 한국에서의 미국군대의 지위에 관한 협정(SOFA)
전59권. 1966.7.9 서울에서 서명 : 1967.2.9 발효(조약 232호) (V.53 민사청구권 관계자료, 1964-66)

Please accept, Excellencies, the renewed assurances of my highest consideration.

H. FREEMAN MATTHEWS

AMERICAN EMBASSY,

The Hague, August 13, 1954.

Their Excellencies

    J. W. BEYEN, Minister for Foreign Affairs,

       and

         J. M. A. H. LUNS, Minister without Portfolio,

            Royal Netherlands Ministry

              for Foreign Affairs,

                The Hague.

- 4 -

0338

ANNEX

With respect to paragraph 4 of the exchange of notes
dated August 13, 1954, the United States Government and
The Netherlands Government have reached the following
understandings between them concerning the implementation
in The Netherlands of the Agreement signed at London on
June 19, 1951, Between the Parties to the North Atlantic
Treaty Regarding the Status of Their Forces.

1. The expression "dependent" in paragraph 1 (c) of
Article I also includes relatives who habitually reside
with and are actually dependent on a member of a United
States force or civilian component.

2. The Netherlands authorities do not require the counter-
signature of movement orders referred to in paragraph 2 (b)
of Article III.

3. The Netherlands authorities, recognizing that it is the
primary responsibility of the United States authorities to
maintain good order and discipline where persons subject to
United States military law are concerned, will, upon the
request of the United States authorities, waive their
primary right to exercise jurisdiction under Article VII,
except where they determine that it is of particular
importance that jurisdiction be exercised by the Netherlands
authorities. The United States assumes the responsibility
for custody pending trial. The United States authorities
will make these people immediately available to Netherlands
authorities upon their request for purposes of investigation
and trial and will give full attention to any other special
wishes of the appropriate Netherlands authorities as to the

- 5 -

0339

way in which custody should be carried out.

4. The Netherlands Government confirms that persons
subject to United States military law, prosecuted under
Netherlands jurisdiction, will be entitled to have a
representative of the United States Government present
during their trial, which will be public except when the
court decrees otherwise in accordance with Netherlands law.

5. In applying paragraph 10 (a) of Article VII to areas
jointly used by the forces of the United States and The
Netherlands, internal secutity measures will be a matter
of joint consultation between the authorities of these
forces.

6. With respect to paragraph 2 of Article IX, United
States forces may procure supplies, facilities and services
directly from local sources in The Netherlands. In order
to avoid such procurement having an adverse economic effect
locally, the Netherlands authorities may indicate, when
necessary, purchases which should be restricted or controlled.

7. United States forces may, at the installations put at
their disposal, establish and operate United States military
post offices for the handling of official mail and that of
authrorized individuals between these and other United States
post offices. The Netherlands authorities will not inspect
offical mail in United States military postal channels.
Any inspection of non-official mail in such channels which
may be required by regulations of The Netherlands will be
conducted by Netherlands authorities in accordance with
mutually determined procedures.

8. In connection with paragraph 4 of Article IX, the
manner in which local civilian labor requirements of United
States forces in The Netherlands will be satisfied shall be

- 6 -

0340

mutually determined.

9. With respect to paragraph 4 of Article IX, United States forces may import free of duty reasonable quantities of supplies and other goods for the use of members of United States forces and civilian components, and their dependents and distribute them through official activities. In this connection, military sales exchanges, commissaries, officers' clubs and similar activities may be established and operated without being subject to taxes, including those on sales by these activities, licenses or other charges. United . States authorities will cooperate closely with Netherlands authorities to prevent unauthorized resales of duty-free items on the local market or other abuses of these privileges.

10. With respect to paragraph 5 of Article XI, members of United States forces and civilian components, and their dependents may import free of duty their new and used personal effects and furniture during a period of six months from the date of their first arrival.

11. Sales of duty-free items taking place between members of United States forces and civilian components, and their dependents are not subject to duties or taxes in The Netherlands.

12. In connection with Article XIV, the following arrangements will apply.

a. (i) United States forces may use Netherlands currency available in any United States Government accounts for transactions in The Netherlands.

(ii) United States forces, members of these forces and civilian components, and their dependents may acquire Netherlands currency needed for their operations

- 7 -

0341

in The Netherlands, and for personal expenditures, from
the central bank of the Netherlands or other agencies
designated by the Netherlands authorities, as well as
that Netherlands currency available under a (i) above.

(iii) The authorities of the two Governments will
determine from time to time the appropriate exchange
rate to be used under this agreement.

(iv) At the request of the United States authorities, a
at any time, the Netherlands Government through the
central bank of The Netherlands will purchase any
unutilized balances of guilders which are held as official
funds of the United States Government or any instrumentality
thereof and which were acquired by United States forces in
accordance with the arrangements referred to in a. (ii)
above. Such purchases will be made in United States dollars
at the rate of exchange at which such balances were acquired.

b. United States forces shall have the right to:

(i) import into, export from and possess in The
Netherlands for official purposes United States dollars
and dollar instruments, other non-Netherlands currency and
instruments, and military payment certificates denominated
in United States dollars; and

(ii) make payments to members of United States forces
and civilian components, and their dependents freely in
United States dollar currency, instruments, and military
payment certificates, in Netherlands currency and
instruments, and, to the extent of the requirements of
such persons for travel outside of The Nehtelands, in
other non-Netherlands currency and instruments.

c. Subject to the regulations of United States forces,
members of these forces and civilian components, and

- 8 -

0342

their dependents shall have the right freely to import into
The Netherlands United States currency, instruments and
military payment certificates, and to export from The
Netherlands non-Netherlands currency and instruments and
United States military payment certificates which they
have imported or received from the authorities of the
United States.

d. The United States authorities will take appropriate
measures to assure that the use of United States military
payment certificates is restricted to transactions within
areas in use by United States forces and with mutually
authorized financial institutions.  The Netherlands authorities
will take the necessary steps to prevent persons under its
jurisdiction not authorized to use United States military
payment certificates from engaging in unauthorized traffic
in such military payment certificates.  Neither the United
States Government nor any of its agencies will have any
obligation to the Netherlands Government nor to any other instrumentality or person as a result of any unauthorized use
of such military payment certificates.

e. United States authorities, in cooperation with Netherlands
authorities, will take measures to safeguard the Netherlands
foreign exchange regulations insofar as they may be applicable
to the members of United States forces and civilian components,
and their dependents.

- 9 -

0343

The Netherlands Minister for Foreign Affairs and the

Netherlands Minister without Portfolio to the

American Ambassador


MINISTRY OF FOREIGN AFFAIRS THE HAGUE

General Affairs Department

No 98123.                          THE HAGUE, August 13, 1954.

EXCELLENCY,

We have the honour to acknowledge receipt of your note
no 73 of August 13, 1954, reading as follows:

"I have the honor to refer to our recent discussions
regarding the manner in which our two Governments, as
parties to the North Atlantic Treaty, may further the
objectives of Article III of that Treaty to strengthen their
individual and collective capacity to resist armed attack
through the stationing of United States armed forces in
The Netherlands.  I have the honor to inform Your Excellencies
that the Government of the United States is willing to
conclude with the Government of The Netherlands an agreement
on the following terms.

1. The Governments of the United States and the Netherlands agree that the United States Government may station
its forces in The Netherlands, as may be mutually determined,
in furtherance of the objectives of the North Atlantic
Treaty.

2. The Netherlands Government will, without cost to the
United States, provide land areas and utilities connections,
including access roads, agreed to be necessary for the purposes
of this agreement.  The other expenses involved in carrying
out this agreement shall be borne by the United States and the
Netherlands Governments in proportions to be determined

- 10 -

0344

between them.  Use of the utilities and services required by
United States forces will be facilitated by the Netherlands
Government.  When at the expense of the United States
Government, charges for the use of such utilities and charges
for services requested and rendered will be no higher than
those paid by the Netherlands armed services.

3. Title to removable equipment, materials and supplies
brought into, or acquired in, The Netherlands by or on
behalf of the United States in connection with this agreement
will remain in the United States Government.  This property
will be free from all duties, inspections and other
restrictions, whether on import or export, and from all
taxes.  At the termination of any operation under this
agreement, the United States will be compensated by the
Netherlands Government for the residual value, if any, of
installations developed at the expense of the United States
under this agreement.  The amount and manner of compensation
shall be determined between the appropriate authorities of
the two Governments.

4. The provisions of the Agreement signed at London on
June 19, 1951, Between the Parties to the North Atlantic
Treaty Regarding the Status of Their Forces, together with
such understandings as the two Governments may reach concerning the implementation of these provisions, shall govern
the status of United States forces in the Netherlands.

5. It is recognized that the provisions of the exchange of
notes on relief from taxes signed at The Hague on March 7,
1952, as supplemented, are applicable to expenditures made by
or on behalf of the United States for the purpose of this
agreement.                    - 11 -

0345

6. The arrangements referred to in this note will remain in effect for the duration of the North Atlantic Treaty, or until such time as the two Governments mutually agree upon their termination.

7. After the approval constitutionally required in The Netherlands has been obtained, the present agreement shall enter into force on the date of receipt by the United States Government of a relevant notification from the Netherlands Government.

If the foregoing provisions and the Annex attached hereto are acceptable to your Government, this note and Your Excellencies' reply thereto indicating such acceptance shall be honored as constituting the agreement of our two Governments concerning this matter."

The provisions set forth above and the Annex attached to your note are acceptable to Her Majesty's Government and we therefore have the honour to state that your note and the present reply, including the Annex attached hereto, constitute the agreement of our two Governments on this matter, which will come into force on the date of receipt by the United States Government of a notification of the Netherlands Government that the approval constitutionally required in the Netherlands has been obtained.

Please accept, Excellency, the renewed assurances of our highest consideration.

J LUNS                                    J W BEYEN

His Excellency

H. FREEMAN MATTHEWS,

Ambassador extraordinary and plenipotentiary of the United States of America.

- 12 -

0346

**외교문서 비밀해제: 주한미군지위협정(SOFA) 22**
**주한미군지위협정(SOFA) 서명 및 발효 22**

초판인쇄 2024년 03월 15일
초판발행 2024년 03월 15일

지은이  한국학술정보(주)
펴낸이  채종준
펴낸곳  한국학술정보(주)
주  소  경기도 파주시 회동길 230(문발동)
전  화  031-908-3181(대표)
팩  스  031-908-3189
홈페이지  http://ebook.kstudy.com
E-mail  출판사업부 publish@kstudy.com
등  록  제일산-115호(2000. 6. 19)

ISBN  979-11-7217-033-2  94340
      979-11-7217-011-0  94340 (set)